More
MEXICAN
EVERYDAY

Also by Rick Bayless

Frontera: Margaritas, Guacamoles and Snacks
(with Deann Groen Bayless)

Fiesta at Rick's
(with Deann Groen Bayless)

Mexican Everyday
(with Deann Groen Bayless)

Rick and Lanie's Excellent Kitchen Adventures
(with Lanie Bayless and Deann Groen Bayless)

Mexico—One Plate at a Time
(with JeanMarie Brownson and Deann Groen Bayless)

Salsas That Cook
(with JeanMarie Brownson and Deann Groen Bayless)

Rick Bayless's Mexican Kitchen
(with Deann Groen Bayless and JeanMarie Brownson)

Authentic Mexican
(with Deann Groen Bayless)

More
MEXICAN
EVERYDAY

Simple, Seasonal, Celebratory

Rick Bayless

WITH DEANN GROEN BAYLESS

Photographs by Hirsheimer and Hamilton

W. W. Norton & Company

NEW YORK • LONDON

Manufacturing by Courier Kendallville
Book design by Chalkley Calderwood
Production manager: Anna Oler

ISBN 978-0-393-08114-5

W. W. Norton & Company, Inc.
500 Fifth Avenue, New York, N.Y. 10110
www.wwnorton.com

W. W. Norton & Company Ltd.
Castle House, 75/76 Wells Street, London W1T 3QT

1 2 3 4 5 6 7 8 9 0

This book is dedicated to all home cooks. It is because of your simple acts of nourishing creativity that folks are drawn together with delight and open hearts.

Contents

Acknowledgments **15**

Introduction **18**

PART ONE: Simple Ways to Create Dynamic Flavor

HOW TO WIN A TOP CHEF QUICKFIRE CHALLENGE 22

My Most Relied-on Equipment for Creating Great Flavor **23**

Balance Is the Key to Any Great Dish **26**

My Most Relied-on Pantry Items for Creating Great Flavor **28**

Four Secret Weapons I Always Have in My Refrigerator **33**

- Green Chile *Adobo* **33**
- Quick Red Chile *Adobo* **37**
- Roasted Garlic *Mojo* **39**
- Sweet-Sour Dark Chipotle Seasoning **40**

GO-TO MEALS TO KNOW BY HEART 44

- Creamy Roasted Poblano *Rajas* and Two Delicious
  Dishes to Make from Them **47**
    - Creamy Zucchini, Corn and Roasted Poblanos **52**
    - Roasted Poblano Cream Soup **53**
- Roasted Tomato Salsa and Three Delicious Dishes to Make from It **57**
    - *Huevos Rancheros* **60**
    - Salsa-Braised Fish (or Tofu or Eggplant) **64**
    - Tomato–Green Chile Seafood Rice **67**
- Roasted Tomatillo Sauce Base and Three Delicious Dishes to Make
  from It **69**
    - Roasted Tomatillo Enchiladas **73**
    - Tomatillo-Sauced *Chilaquiles* **77**
    - Pork (or Chicken) with Roasted Tomatillos, Poblanos and Potatoes **79**

- *Carne Asada* Dinner 86
- Skillet Tacos 93
- Pork and Black Bean Dinner 100
- Weekend Dish: Red Peanut *Mole* with Chicken 105
- Red Chile Roast Chicken 112
- Chipotle Meatballs 117

PART TWO: Vegetables at the Heart of the Mexican Kitchen

COOKING GREENS 124
- Greens and Beans with Red Chile and Fresh Cheese 126
- Mustard Greens Soup with Poblanos and Almonds 129
- Crispy Cakes of Greens, Potato and Green Chile 132
- Eggs Poached with Ancho Chile, Kale, Potatoes and Fresh Cheese 134
- "Sturdy Greens" Salad with Mango and Habanero 138

TRADITIONAL MEXICAN VEGETABLES, NEW IDEAS 140
- Roasted Chayote with Herbs and Tofu (or Goat Cheese) 142
- Fresh Corn in Spicy-Herby Broth 144
- Herby, Spicy Fried Corn 146
- Steamed Roots with Roasted Poblano and Tomatillo 147
- Grilled Tostadas with Bacon, Avocado Mayo and Heirloom Tomatoes 150
- Pickled Tomatillo Salad with Little Gem Lettuce and Pumpkin Seeds 152
- Roasted Knob Onions with *Crema* and Aged Mexican Cheese 154
- Four Seasons Grilled Salad with Smoky Knob (or Green) Onions and Sesame 156
- Jícama-Beet Salad with Radicchio, Peanuts and Lime 160

- *Nopal* Cactus and Poached Egg in Roasted Tomato–Chipotle Broth 163
- Fresh Fava Bean *Enfrijoladas* 166

WINTER SQUASH, SUMMER SQUASH, BLOSSOMS AND A RELATIVE 170

- Butternut with Bacon, Tomatillo and Chipotle 174
- Weekend Dish: Fettuccine with Butternut Squash and Red Poblano *Crema* 177
- Kuri (or Butternut or Pumpkin) Soup with Ancho and Apple 180
- Pan-Roasted Summer Squash with Garlic *Mojo* and Güero Chile 182
- Spaghetti Squash *Fideos* with Chipotle, Chorizo, *Crema* and Avocado 185
- Charred Cucumber Salad with Red Chile and Lime 188
- Squash Blossom Soup 190
- Ribbon Salad with Creamy Two-Chile *Vinagreta* 192

UNEXPECTED VEGETABLES IN THE MEXICAN KITCHEN 194

- Roasted Sunchoke Salad with Creamy Garlic *Mojo* and Herbs 196
- Grilled Asparagus with Creamy Pasilla Chile 198
- Weekend Dish: Shell Beans and Artichokes with Roasted Tomatillos, Cilantro and *Añejo* Cheese 201
- Yellow *Mole* with Grilled Fennel and Portobello Mushrooms 204
- Celery Root Pancakes with Chipotle *Crema* and Cilantro 208
- Tangy Sorrel *Salsa Verde* with Stir-Fried Shrimp 210
- Banana Pepper–Leek Soup with White Beans and Crispy Chorizo 212
- Spicy Chipotle Eggplant with Black Beans 215
- Braised Artichokes with Tomatoes, Jalapeños, Olives and Capers 218

PART THREE: Daily Inspirations for Busy Cooks

BREAKFAST ANYTIME 222

- Spring Green *Licuado* 224
- Stone Fruit (or Mango) *Licuado* 226
- Carrot, Beet and Orange *Licuado* 227
- Xoco's Granola 228
- Open-Face Red Chile–Chard Omelet 230
- Open-Face Squash Blossom Omelet with Charred Tomato, Chile and Goat Cheese 232
- Open-Face Egg-Chorizo Tortas 234
- Cornmeal Pancakes 237
- Butternut-Pecan Muffins with Brown Sugar Crumble 240
- *Horchata* French Toast 243

RICE-COOKER SIMPLICITY 246

- Creamy Rice and Beans in Three Classic Flavors 250
- Black Bean Rice with Plantains and Smoky Pork 254
- Chorizo Rice with Lentils 256
- Herb Green Chicken and Rice 258
- Chipotle Rice with Shrimp 260
- Mexican Red Rice and Three Delicious Dishes to Make from It 262
  - Creamy Rice Soup with Poblano and Spinach 264
  - Crispy Rice Cakes with White Beans, Roasted Garlic, Aged Cheese and Smoky Chile 265
  - Spicy Bacon-and-Egg Fried Rice with Pickled Jalapeños and Cilantro 266

SLOW-COOKER SATISFACTION 268

- Mexican Chicken Soup 270
- Red Chile Short Rib Soup 272
- Weekend Dish: Red Chile Pozole with Pork 276
- Weekend Dish: Pork Carnitas Dinner 280
- Five Simple Meals from a Pot of Beans 284
  - Silky Tortilla Soup 285
  - Scrambled Eggs with Beans, Green Onions and Avocado 286
  - Plantain-Bacon *Enfrijoladas* 287
  - Beans and Greens with Clams and Chorizo 289
  - Cheesy Open-Face *Mollete* 289
- Green Chile–Braised Beef with Potatoes and Caramelized Onions 291
- Lamb or Beef *Barbacoa* 294
- Roasted Garlic Chicken with Mushrooms, Potatoes and Spinach 296

THE GRILL, STOVE AND OVEN 300

- Weekend Dish: Slow-Grilled Pork Shoulder with Ancho Barbecue Sauce 302
- Green Chile Chicken Thighs 305
- Weekend Dish: Grilled Red Chile Ribs 308
- Grilled Lamb Chops with Charred Eggplant Salsa 311
- Weekend Dish: *Queso Fundido* Burger 314
- Grilled Salmon in Toasty Peanut Salsa 316
- Spicy, Garlicky Grilled Cauliflower Steaks with Browned Butter, Toasted Nuts and Tequila Raisins 319
- Grilled Fish with Creamy Cool Cucumber *Pipián* 322
- Chicken *Barbacoa* 324

- Beer-Glazed Beer-Can Chicken **327**
- Cilantro-Poached Halibut **330**
- Mussels (or Clams) with *Salsa Macha,* Mexican Beer and Ham **333**

A DOZEN DESSERTS: MEXICAN CHOCOLATE AND FARMERS' MARKET FRUIT 336

- Mexican Chocolate–Pumpkin Seed Cake **338**
- Unbaked Mexican Chocolate Flan **341**
- Nutty Triple-Chocolate Pudding **344**
- Warm Rice Pudding with Mexican Chocolate and Toasted Almonds **346**
- Mexican Chocolate Truffles **348**
- Mexican Chocolate Sorbet **350**
- Coconut Bread Pudding **351**
- Farmers' Market Fruit with Warm Tequila-Lime *Espuma* **354**
- Mango Ricotta Cheesecake **356**
- Plantains (or Fresh Fruit) with 24-Hour *Cajeta* and Bitter Chocolate **358**
- Raspberry Soft-Serve Ice Cream **361**
- Coconut-Lime Ice Pops **363**

Index **365**

ACKNOWLEDGMENTS ◇◇◇◇◇◇◇◇◇◇◇◇◇◇◇◇◇◇◇◇◇◇◇◇

I am a very lucky guy, surrounded as I am by inventive, tireless and enthusiastic cooks for whom the flavors of the Mexican kitchen are the flavors of life. From the crack of dawn until our restaurants serve their last guests, someone on our team is exploring, creating and sharing something beautiful and delicious. Perhaps it's the development staff for the Frontera retail line, JeanMarie Brownson and Kelsey Coday, working on the best flavors for *barbacoa* done slow-cooker style. Maybe it's the Xoco staff—Wil Bravo, José Ramírez, Alonso Sotelo, Isaac Magaña, Adrian Black—working through a new take on pozole or a delicious new muffin or *mollete*. Though Tortas Frontera, our quick-service airport locations, seem simple, Andrew Gietzen and Renee Ragin invest endless amounts of creative energy in figuring out how to get local farmers' market ingredients into the terminals and onto full-flavored Mexican tortas. And the Frontera Grill and Topolo chefs—Andrés Padilla, Richard James, Jennifer Jones, Joel Ramírez, Lisa Despres, Jennifer Melendrez, Brian Pirronen, Hector Cotorra, Jim Ortiz—innovate continuously, and so much of the endless stream of wonderful food they've shepherded into existence has made its way into these pages. Maybe not in the elegant way those dishes are offered to the guests in their respective dining rooms, but created with the same spirit.

And then there are the cooks of Mexico, who have inspired, perfected and so generously shared the seminal flavors without which there would be no *More Mexican Everyday*. They are the true heroes here, because they responded brilliantly to what was right in front of them—the geography, the history, the quirkiness of culture—and turned it into something memorable.

A book doesn't just leap into existence, though. It takes an incredible amount of dogged determination to progress from the opening sentence to the final word. Deann Bayless is the one who provides the energy, intelligence and wisdom that makes it all happen. She was backed up by David Tamarkin, who edited, organized and played pinch-hit writer as we moved from the inception to completion. Katy Lawrence cooked—and recooked and recooked—every recipe, shopping in groceries all over town, trying out all kinds of equipment, talking to all types of cooks, just to make sure these recipes will become your go-to favorites.

Turning a book from uninspiring black-and-white manuscript pages to a thing of beauty requires skill I can only admire from a distance. Maria Guarnaschelli, my lifelong editor, is one of the few truly great culinary editors, and I thank her for another inspired collaboration. I also thank the team at Norton, including Sophie Duvernoy, Anna Oler, Joe Lops, Nancy Palmquist, and Susan Sanfrey. Doe Coover—my agent, my friend—gets the grand prize for allowing me to carve out creative space while balancing the demands of publishing timelines. Liz Duvall beautifully polished my occasionally coarse prose. And, of course, without the brilliant photographer Christopher Hirsheimer and stylist Melissa Hamilton, you'd never be fully inspired by the vast beauty and satisfaction that simple, everyday food can offer.

Writing a book is a consuming, long-term project. Though for some it can threaten familial stability, I can say that I have never felt anything but support from my wife, Deann, and my daughter, Lanie. Again, I say: I am a lucky man.

INTRODUCTION ◇◇

I want you to cook more. It's good for you. You know exactly what you're nourishing yourself with (which for me almost always includes a healthy dose of fresh vegetables). It allows you to feel the natural rhythms of life in a way that microwaved frozen dinners never can. And cooking often draws people to the table, encouraging dialogue and providing a moment to appreciate the good (and truly tasty) things in life.

I know: if I want you to cook more, I need to make it easy for you. And to my way of thinking, that means I need to help you with three things: First, I need to help wean you from a slavish dependency on recipes—I need to hand you a few go-to recipes that are easily varied depending on what you have on hand, and teach you to look at other recipes with an eye to how they can be varied to suit your own tastes and kitchen. Second, I need to help you know what ingredients and basic preparations to have on hand so that a good meal is never more than a few minutes away. And third, I need to help you know which kitchen equipment will enable you to create delicious food fast (and, of course, I need to guide you in how to use it to its best advantage).

I can do all that.

And if you like the vibrant flavors of the Mexican kitchen (which, I believe, is why you're holding this book in your hand right now) and want to enjoy them more frequently, I can help with that, too.

If you cooked through the first volume of *Mexican Everyday*, you know that each recipe was created to utilize a small number of easily available fresh ingredients, to be completed in a half hour or so, and to be what I call "weekday lean"—the kind of simple, flavor-packed, healthy food I like to eat Monday through Friday. These dishes make a beautiful complement to the kinds of weekend celebration dishes I like to make for family and friends.

More Mexican Everyday follows pretty much the same guidelines, though it's a little less restrictive, for two reasons. One, more and more Mexican ingredients are available every week all across America. And two, since many of you told me that you were using my "everyday" recipes for your weekend "invite the friends over" cooking, I felt comfortable including a new special category of weekend-friendly recipes—simple dishes that may take a little longer in the kitchen, use less-common ingredients, or are a little richer than those I typically think of as "everyday."

My wish for *More Mexican Everyday* is that it will be more than just a cookbook you turn to regularly for great-tasting dishes. I want it to be your guide to becoming a more confident and less recipe-dependent cook. That confidence will enable you to approach the stove with greater ease, more creativity and playfulness, and, yes, more frequency. That'll be your tastiest reward of all.

PART 1

SIMPLE WAYS TO CREATE DYNAMIC FLAVOR

HOW TO WIN A TOP CHEF QUICKFIRE CHALLENGE

When I was competing on *Top Chef Masters*, especially during the Quickfire challenges, I began to see a pattern in the dishes that won. Chefs who seemed to have a knack for making something delicious, beautiful and quick nearly always relied on the same three things to create their winning dishes. And it's those things—those principles—that guided me when I put together all the recipes for this book. First, the chefs who won always seemed to have a laser focus. They kept their dish simple and clear, meaning that they could describe their dish in a short phrase, and when you looked at the finished plate, it was precisely that description come to life. Second, those winning chefs seemed to know instinctively just the right pots and pans, blenders, whisks and knives to use to create amazing flavor in no time flat. Third—and most important—they understood flavor (how to concentrate and balance it) and texture (how to utilize it to enhance deliciousness). The first two principles—honing simplicity and mastering equipment—are building blocks that anyone can master with a little practice. The third one—wrestling with flavor and texture—is every cook's lifelong pursuit.

Those who cook enough to journey a long way down that path become the great cooks whose food we all crave. Plus, they tend to be the cooks who are most successful at introducing innovation into tried-and-true tradition.

Cooks who've mastered that flavor-and-texture thing usually understand (intuitively or in a learned way) how to capitalize on umami, the "fifth flavor," which blossoms beyond sweet, sour, bitter and salty. It is a concentration of what the scientists tell us are glutamates that creates an aura of deliciousness in a dish. If this is new to you, think about it this way: umami is what makes us smile (or swoon) when we taste cured meats or aged cheese or slow-cooked mushrooms or tomatoes. Another thing those cooks have figured out is how to weave together contrasting tastes (the tanginess of lime-marinated fish ceviche with bits of sweet-ripe tomato, the salty sweetness of cured pork with the bitterness of greens) and textures (the crispy crumbs on baked macaroni and cheese, the dollop of creamy guacamole on the perfect steak taco). These things are what keep all the senses engaged, bite after bite.

My Most Relied-on Equipment for Creating Great Flavor

I know most people imagine that my home kitchen is filled with pretty much all the gadgets and appliances ever thought up by kitchen inventors. It's not. In fact, I find most of those inventions kind of annoying, space hogs designed for single tasks I only rarely perform. To illustrate how basic things can get for me, consider my "travel kitchen." If I have an idea that I may be asked to cook something when I travel (it'll come as no surprise that people ask me to whip up a little something pretty much everywhere I go), there are just two things I pack: a large, heavy nonstick skillet and my chef's knife. Those are my two can't-do-without pieces of kitchen equipment. If I find a basic heat source, I can turn out some pretty wonderful meals.

At home, however, I want a really good heat source, so I have invested in a good stove, one with powerful burners that can be adjusted really low, too. I like to cook on gas or induction burners (I find electric burners a little hard to control), though I must say that electric *ovens* typically provide quite even heating, the heat being drier than that of a gas oven (good for pastries). Convection is a plus for

ovens, and once I really learned how to use mine, I found it comes in very handy for quick and even browning.

Besides a good stove, a refrigerator, a sink and a small workspace (all of which I like to be only a step or two apart), the equipment I most rely on is:

▣ **SHARP KNIVES:** For everyday cooking, I use an 8-inch chef's knife, either the traditional curved-blade one or the straight-blade Japanese-style Santoku. Divoted blades are said to release the food effortlessly from the blade, though my experience says they're not much more effective than flat blades. There are many websites that rate different knives, but I've found myself agreeing regularly with the ratings at cooksillustrated.com. Besides my all-purpose chef's knife, I frequently reach for my pointy paring knife, my serrated bread knife and, because I like to bone meat, my boning knife. On special occasions I use a thin-bladed slicing knife for big cuts of meat, but I could slice almost as effectively with my chef's knife. Of course, if my knives aren't sharp, they're either useless or dangerous (more people cut themselves with dull knives than sharp ones). I sharpen my knives with a steel nearly every time I use them—just a few licks on a steel from the same manufacturer as the knife. About once a year, when I notice that my steel is no longer getting them sharp enough, I get out my whetstone and bring them back to full-on sharpness. The Internet offers many tutorials on how to sharpen your knives with steels and stones.

⊡ **A HEAVY 12-INCH SKILLET:** The reason many cooks have trouble creating restaurant-quality flavor is that they don't have a large, heavy pan. A small, lightweight skillet won't provide you with the room or even heating to brown meat or fish or vegetables properly, at least without working in frustratingly small batches. I have an inexpensive 12-inch cast-iron skillet that I bought nearly forty years ago, and it's so well seasoned that nothing sticks to it. Yes, it's heavy and requires me to clean it carefully (no soap, no harsh abrasives), dry it over a burner and oil it before putting it away. But it's an amazing pan to cook in. Much easier to work with (lighter, a breeze to wash and store) is my 12-inch heavy nonstick skillet. That's the one I take when I travel.

⊡ **A BLENDER:** Many folks, unless they're into smoothies or blended cocktails, put their blenders away a long time ago. That is, unless they make the *moles*, *pipianes* and red chile sauces of real

Mexican food. Honestly, a blender is the most used appliance in my kitchen. It reduces the tomatoes, tomatillos, nuts and seeds, dried chiles and so forth to as smooth a texture as I want—smoother than a food processor will give me, especially when nuts, seeds or most dried chiles are involved. The reason is simple: the design of a blender causes food to be pulled into close contact with blades that whir at a much faster speed than those of food processors. An immersion blender isn't nearly as effective, though I like to use one for some simple salsas, tomato or tomatillo sauce and certain soups. I know they're expensive, but my life changed when I got my first high-speed blender (it was a Vitamix). A high-speed blender can create stunning textures in a flash.

⊡ **A GRILL AND A GRILL PAN:** I really can't cook without a grill. We have wood-burning grills or ovens in every restaurant I own. I have so many grills at home that my wife made me build a lean-to on the back of the house so I could get them out of the garage. The fireplace in my living room is big enough for me to set up a little "Tuscan grill" in it. And I have a cast-iron grill pan to use on the stove when I'm in a hurry. Why? Because grilled food is just about the most elementally attractive and thrillingly delicious food in the world—smoky char, I'm assuming, connects us to our ancient roots in an undeniably satisfying way. And that grill pan? Yes, there's no flame, no charcoal, no wood, but I've used it to convincing effect when no grill was in sight.

◉ **A MORTAR:** I know, I know. Who needs a mortar in this day and age? Unless, of course, you've adopted the back-to-basics, hipstery DIY thing (I'm old enough to have participated in the first iteration in the late '60s). Or unless you've tasted a dish that has fresh-ground spices or a salsa that's made from mortar-crushed roasted garlic and serrano chiles. Once is enough to convince you that you need a mortar. Most of the Mexican basalt (lava rock) mortars (*molcajetes*) that have been available in the United States (except in a few Mexican grocery stores) have been what I call "tourist models"—the ones that look great on your mantel but are made of such soft, pitted and porous basalt that they are useless in the kitchen, unless, of course, you're into grinding the soft stone into food. Lately, though, I've seen real kitchen-worthy *molcajetes* showing up in the United States. The best are a uniform gray, heavy and solid-feeling, smooth on the outside and a little rough on the inside, and hold about 3 cups.

◉ **A FOOD PROCESSOR:** What can I say? I really like my food processor and I use it a lot. Sure, my blender can breeze through all the hard pureeing tasks, and I *could* do all the remaining chopping and shredding by hand, but when I'm cooking quickly, I turn to my processor for ease and speed. It also makes awesome pie dough.

◉ **A MICROWAVE:** Not too many chefs admit that they use a microwave, but I do, especially at home (we don't have one in our restaurants' kitchens). I use my microwave at home extensively for quick steaming of vegetables (as a quick, no-fuss steamer, my microwave is unparalleled), for heating corn tortillas, for melting chocolate, for occasional dehydrating in the more modernist tradition, for warming plates and, just like everyone else, for reheating food. If you are microwave averse, feel free to steam-blanch vegetables I've microwave-blanched. Because of its ease and speed, the microwave is called for frequently in these pages.

◉ **A SLOW COOKER:** My slow cooker is a favorite piece of kitchen equipment for three reasons. First, whatever's slowly cooking away in it fills the house with such a wonderful aroma that it puts me in a great mood for hours. Second, the temperature is so even and low that practically everything you put in it turns out juicy and tender. And third, beans cooked in a slow cooker have a creamy texture that I never get using a pot on the stovetop. As long as you don't try to use your slow cooker for foods that should be cooked quickly, like chicken breasts, fish fillets and most green vegetables, what's not to like? Simple, delicious, satisfying.

▣ **A RICE COOKER AND A PRESSURE COOKER:** Okay, now I'm sounding like a geek, especially for someone who said he doesn't fill his kitchen with a lot of gadgets and appliances. And I could easily do without either of these. But I wouldn't be honest if I failed to tell you that I use them both in my everyday cooking. A rice cooker keeps the rice or rice dish at the ideal temperature even when I'm not serving for some time. Plus, I never have to worry about whether I've adjusted the heat under the rice to the ideal low temperature to ensure a perfect outcome. Now, about the pressure cooker: that's less of a necessity. I asked for one for Christmas, and I'm here to report that when I don't have all day to turn out beans or lamb stew or beef tongue, I reach for the pressure cooker. Truthfully, though, I use it more to make the most beautiful chicken stock ever and a stunning "cheater" risotto in about 6 minutes.

Balance Is the Key to Any Great Dish

You can have the best-equipped kitchen in the world, but if you don't know how to cook—if you don't have a sense of how to choose, develop and balance flavors—the dishes you turn out won't be delicious. Sure, you can follow recipes from cooks who understand both how to cook really well and how to write good recipes (two very different skills, neither of which is easy to master). But better still, you can learn what makes a good dish and bring that to any preparation (written as a recipe or dreamed up in your head) and turn out something folks will talk about for a long time. Here are what I consider to be the basic principles.

▣ **BALANCE FUNDAMENTAL FLAVORS.** What I mean by fundamental flavors are those your tongue can perceive: salty, sweet, bitter, sour and umami. The first four are easy for us to think about; I tackle umami in the section below. When I'm developing a dish, I quickly scan the ingredients to determine if all the fundamental flavors are present. And if they're not, I figure out how to weave in the missing flavors. Take tomatillo sauce, for instance: It's all about the sourness of tomatillo, so I need to balance that with sweetness, which I do in two ways—roasting the tomatillos (which develops natural sweetness) and adding additional sweetness from roasted garlic and onion. Char on the roasted tomatillos, garlic and onion adds just the right amount of bitterness. Now, I know many of us think of bitterness as something to stay away from, but we shouldn't. A little bitterness always adds depth and complexity; too much can throw a dish out of whack. There's very little naturally occurring sodium in tomatillos, so I need to add salt to get the balance right—a task that takes experience and one that I find beginning cooks have trouble with, especially in dishes that celebrate tanginess. I've also come across cooks who praise dishes with low sodium as ones that are morally superior, but I don't buy it.

▣ **UNDERSTAND HOW TO PACK A DISH WITH UMAMI.** When you take a bite of something and find yourself completely captivated by it, it's usually because the dish is packed with umami. Umami, a concentration of glutamates, is found in fish and shellfish, cured meats, aged cheeses, mushrooms, seaweed, stuff that's fermented and—this is really important for the cuisine I work in—a lot of *ripe* vegetables, especially tomatoes.

Think about where you find great flavors in your life. Off-season, store-bought tomatoes have nothing to offer compared with ripe farmers' market tomatoes. Steamed green beans aren't nearly as appealing as ones cooked with cured bacon and caramelized onions. A simple lettuce salad dressed with white vinegar and vegetable oil won't be nearly as memorable as one dressed with aged balsamic vinegar, olive oil and aged Parmesan cheese. The reason Caesar salad has been such a staple is that it relies on both aged Parmesan and anchovy, an umami bomb.

▣ **BALANCE TASTE AND TEXTURE.** The scientists tell us that taste is 10% fundamental flavors and 90% aroma. So as cooks, we always have to be attuned to the complexity we're working with. In our restaurant kitchens, we're always putting words to the aroma side of tastes: "It tastes like a forest floor smells," "Wow, there's a hint of fresh-cut grass here," "There's something in the taste that reminds me of a rose garden." The more we can articulate those earthy, complex, herbal, floral, citrusy, meaty, smoky, whatever tastes, the more we can think of combining them in balanced ways to create the most complex and appealing dishes. Typically, I like to balance textures as well as flavors. That's pretty easy: most of us lump textures into general categories such as soft, crisp, crunchy, juicy, meaty/chewy, brothy/saucy, bready/starchy. With a few exceptions, I've noticed that the more of these categories I incorporate in a single dish, the more engaged people stay.

◻ **WHY WE LOVE *ENCHILADAS VERDES*: A CASE STUDY IN BALANCE.** We've already gone over the fundamental flavors of a great tomatillo sauce, one that balances the natural sourness of tomatillos with sweetness (from roasted onion and garlic), bitterness (from that hint of roasting char) and saltiness. When we ladle that saucy, spicy, citrusy-tasting *salsa verde* over the satisfying starchiness and whole-grain goodness of corn tortillas that have been rolled around meaty chicken and strewn with bright-tasting, crunchy raw onion and herby-fresh cilantro—well, we've got a symphony of flavors and textures. If we've brined the chicken, it'll be juicier and we'll notice its natural umami more. If we grill or roast it, there will be delicious browning with a hint of bitter complexity. And if we sprinkle those enchiladas with aged Mexican cheese (*queso añejo*), we've sprinkled on what amounts to irresistible umami dust.

My Most Relied-on Pantry Items for Creating Great Flavor

My essential great-flavor pantry items are mostly Mexican, though a couple can be used in any style of cooking. The Mexican pantry items—and there really aren't that many—contribute an unmistakable flavor, one that Mexican food lovers will gravitate toward wherever they find it. It's a Mexican pantry, however, not a Mexican-American one, so it relies less on cumin, sour cream, shredded melting cheese and sweet-tangy salsas. Here are the bare necessities, my "must have on hand" for a well-stocked Mexican pantry:

♦ **Dried ancho chiles,** to add sweet-smoky complexity and a gentle spiciness. I always have powdered dried ancho on

ancho chiles

hand, too, because it comes in handy for making a super-fast red chile *adobo* and a few other dishes. Look for shiny, supple chiles with a lot of aroma and store them in a closed container for up to six months.

◆ **Dried guajillo chiles,** to provide bright earthiness and an attractive spiciness. In Mexican markets you can find powdered dried guajillo, which can be mixed into an *adobo* or sprinkled on pozole or fruit or a steak destined for the grill. Whole dried guajillos should be shiny, supple and aromatic. They can be stored for six months or so in a closed container.

◆ **Canned chipotle chiles *en adobo*,** to introduce a whole host of sweet-smoky flavors and an invigorating spiciness. Once opened, the chipotles can stay for a week or so in the refrigerator.

◆ **Fresh hot green chiles** (serranos, jalapeños or pretty much any other small green chile) to add that grassy-green-flavored bright heat. In the vegetable bin of your refrigerator, fresh hot green chiles will last a week or more.

◆ **Fresh poblano chiles,** for that unmistakably complex green chile flavor and a gentle spiciness. Like fresh hot green chiles, poblanos will last for a week or more in the refrigerator.

guajillo chiles

poblano chiles

- **Mexican *añejo* cheese** (or perhaps another garnishing cheese, like Romano or Parmesan), for a walloping punch of salty, complex umami.
- **Canned fire-roasted tomatoes,** because besides being packed with thrilling umami, fire-roasted tomatoes resonate with the flavors of central and southern Mexico, flavors that taught me how delicious food could be. Unless it's the height of the season and you can roast vine-ripened farmers' market tomatoes, I suggest you buy some of the fire-roasted canned tomatoes on the market for the fullest flavor.
- **Dried shiitake (or other) mushrooms,** because they (and their soaking liquid) add depth and savoriness at a moment's notice. Because they keep for six months or so in a tightly closed container, I always have them around.
- **Fresh tomatillos,** because without them it is impossible to create very many truly Mexican-tasting dishes. Tomatillos offer a bright and complex tanginess unlike any other; they're not really citrusy or vinegary but offer a distinctive tang that's unique to the Mexican kitchen. Choose unblemished ones and store them loose in your vegetable bin. Though the papery husk may begin to deteriorate after a week or two, the

tomatillos can last a month or two, depending on how fresh they are when you buy them.

tomatillos

- ***Masa harina,*** the dehydrated and powdered corn *masa* from which corn tortillas are made. While I'm not the biggest fan of tortillas made from the dehydrated stuff, I always have *masa harina* on hand to thicken sauces or warm beverages like *atole* and *champurrado,* as well as to make quick *tamal* dough. Store it well wrapped at room temperature if you're keeping it for only a few weeks, in the freezer if it'll be around longer.

◆ **Onions and garlic,** for their complex sweetness, which forms the backbone of so many Mexican sauces and salsas. In Mexico, only white onions are used for general cooking. Garlic is often the more pungent purplish variety with rather small cloves.

◆ **Cilantro and other Mexican herbs, such as oregano, epazote, *hoja santa* and banana leaves,** because without their beautiful herbiness, many of us wouldn't recognize certain dishes as Mexican. Cilantro is most common; I like to store it (and fresh parsley) rolled up in a spread-out layer on barely damp paper towels, placed in a plastic bag and kept in the refrigerator. Epazote can be stored the same way, though it's hard to find outside Mexican groceries (it's very easy to grow, though); dried epazote is a medicinal herb and offers no flavor for cooking. *Hoja santa* is very common in southern Mexico but not in U.S. groceries, even Mexican ones. It grows wild in Texas, is available from some restaurant herb purveyors and can be grown in warm climates (mine resides in my small greenhouse during the winter); otherwise it'll be beyond your reach. Banana leaves, however, are much more widely

available at Mexican, Asian and well-stocked grocery stores, typically in the freezer section (they freeze well). Keep them frozen until you need them to add their special gentle herbiness.

hoja santa

◆ ***Crema, crème fraîche* or Greek-style yogurt,** because they all soften and embrace so many of the bolder flavors of the Mexican kitchen. The best *crema* in Mexico is very much like the French *crème fraîche*; in Mexican groceries in the States, what's called *crema* is often leaner, mildly tangy and artificially thickened. American sour cream is also leaner, but it's way tangier than the Mexican classic. If that's the flavor I'm after, I typically use Greek-style yogurt rather than sour cream (because I usually have some in my refrigerator) and thin it with a little milk if it's going to be spooned on top of a dish.

♦ **Worcestershire sauce,** because it adds something similar to Asian soy and fish sauces: that element that draws you back to a dish bite after bite, that indescribable depth and deliciousness. A little Worcestershire makes pretty much anything it graces that much more attractive.

♦ **Bacon,** because—and I know I'll get both lauded and slammed for this—bacon really does make most things taste better. Besides being an umami bomb, as is any cured pork product, it has a sweet smokiness that is welcome practically anywhere.

Four secret weapons (from left): Quick Red Chile *Adobo*, Green Chile *Adobo*, Roasted Garlic *Mojo*, Sweet-Sour Dark Chipotle Seasoning

Four Secret Weapons I Always Have in My Refrigerator

◈◈

I f you could buy these four preparations in the grocery store, I'd have listed them above with my essential pantry items. Though they're not available (yet), each is very simple to make and they all keep for months in your refrigerator. Having them on hand means you can always have beautiful Mexican flavor at easy access. They include two marinade-like *adobos* (a green chile–herb *adobos* I think of as a relative of pesto, and a bright red chile *adobos*), a slow-roasted garlic *mojo* (which provides delectable oil as well as sweet garlic solids) and a sweet-spicy-tangy-smoky chipotle flavoring. They all have dozens of uses and make my simple, everyday cooking really outstanding.

GREEN CHILE *ADOBO* • *Adobo de Chile Verde*

You'll find this to be one of the most useful seasonings, because it offers a way to preserve fresh herb flavor—underscored with a little spicy green chile and roasted garlic. Think of it as a kind of Mexican pesto. And since the marriage of green chile and cilantro is iconic in the Mexican kitchen, I find myself utilizing this seasoning frequently as a way to get those flavors into my simple everyday cooking. This recipe has a good amount of oil, which will rise to the top and solidify when the mixture is refrigerated. That oil preserves color and freshness. After removing a spoonful of the solids to stir into your eggs or toss with pasta, make sure to smear the oily part flat again (or add more oil) to re-create that protective covering.

Makes about 1½ cups

½ head garlic, separated into unpeeled cloves

4 to 5 fresh serrano chiles, stems removed

1 large bunch cilantro (thick bottom stems cut off), roughly chopped (about 2 cups loosely packed)

1 large bunch flat-leaf parsley, thick bottom stems cut off, roughly chopped (about 2 cups loosely packed)

1 cup olive oil

2 generous teaspoons salt

Set a large (10-inch) skillet over medium heat. Lay in the garlic and chiles and roast, turning regularly, until soft and browned in spots, about 10 minutes for the chiles and 15 for the garlic. (If you're really short on time, you can soften them in a microwave: Cut a slit in each garlic clove and combine with the chiles in a microwavable bowl. Cover with plastic wrap, poke a few holes in the top and microwave at 100% for 30 seconds.) Cool until handleable, then slip off the garlic's papery husks. Roughly chop everything (no need to remove the chile seeds).

In a blender or food processor, combine the garlic and chiles with the cilantro, parsley, olive oil and salt. Process, stopping to scrape down the sides if necessary, until nearly smooth (it should look a little like pesto). Transfer to a pint-size jar and store, covered, in the refrigerator, where it will last several months.

The Simplest Uses for Green Chile *Adobo*
   1. Toss with pasta and a little grated Mexican *queso añejo*, Parmesan or Romano
   2. Mix into eggs before scrambling or making an omelet
   3. Mix into sour cream (and/or mayonnaise) for a dip or sandwich spread
   4. Whisk into a simple vinaigrette or creamy dressing
   5. Smear over grilled or roasted vegetables (especially any beautiful summer squash you find in the farmers' market)
   6. Drizzle on bean dip or hummus
   7. Mix with sashimi-grade raw fish and lime juice for an instant ceviche
   8. Stir into meatloaf before baking

Recipes in *More Mexican Everyday* that use Green Chile *Adobo*
   Skillet Tacos (page 93)
   Roasted Chayote with Herbs and Tofu (or Goat Cheese) (page 142)
   Creamy Rice and Beans in Three Classic Flavors (page 250)

Green Chile *Adobo* (page 33)

Quick Red Chile *Adobo* (page 37)

QUICK RED CHILE ADOBO • *Adobo Rápido de Chiles Secos*

Any sauce or marinade made primarily from dried ancho or guajillo or pasilla chiles is destined to be one of my favorites. I'll be bolder and say it straight out: in my opinion, dried chile sauces, whether simple or elaborated into complex *moles*, are the crown jewel of Mexican cuisine. Unfortunately, for most American cooks, the dried chiles used to make them either seem impossibly foreign or are just plain unavailable. That's why I figured out this super-easy, super-useful version of the classic red chile *adobo*. This version makes that beautiful dried chile flavor easily accessible to any American cook. It relies on the easier-to-work-with pure ancho *powder*, which looks like regular chili powder but contains no extra spices—only the powdered ancho chile. (If you can't find powdered ancho at the grocery store, you can easily order it online.) If you cover ancho powder with boiling water, a velvety texture returns. And once you've worked in the rest of the *adobo* ingredients, you've got a beautiful, complex, dried chile marinade/seasoning, almost indistinguishable from one made with dried chile pods.

Two notes: If you fall in love with this *adobo*, feel free to double the recipe. And if you like a sweeter, toastier flavor, roast the garlic cloves (still in their papery skins) in a dry skillet over medium heat, turning them regularly until soft and blotchy black, about 15 minutes. Cool, peel and blend with the other ingredients.

Makes about 1⅓ cups

A scant ½ cup good-quality ancho chile powder (the amount you'll get from a typical 2-ounce spice jar)

8 garlic cloves, peeled

½ teaspoon ground cinnamon, preferably Mexican *canela*

¼ teaspoon ground black pepper

⅛ teaspoon ground cumin

1 teaspoon dried oregano, preferably Mexican

3 tablespoons apple cider vinegar

1½ teaspoons salt

Scoop the chile powder into a blender or small food processor. In a medium saucepan, bring 1¼ cups water to a boil. Pour the hot water over the chile powder, *loosely cover* the blender or secure the top of the processor and pulse to create a smooth slurry. Let cool.

Collect the garlic in a microwavable bowl, cover with water and microwave at 100% for 1 minute. Drain and add to the blender or food processor along with the spices, oregano, vinegar and salt. Process to a smooth puree. If necessary, stir in some water, a splash at a time, until the *adobo* is the consistency of barbecue sauce. Transfer the *adobo* to a pint jar and store, covered, in the refrigerator, where it will last for a couple of months.

Prefer to work with whole dried chiles?
If you don't have any pure powdered ancho chile, you can make this simple *adobo* from pods. Remove the stems and seeds from 4 medium dried ancho chiles and toast in a dry skillet over medium heat for a minute or so (until very aromatic). When they have cooled, tear the chiles into small pieces, scoop into a blender and proceed with the recipe, blending the pods with boiling water, garlic, spices, oregano, vinegar and salt.

The Simplest Uses for Quick Red Chile *Adobo*
1. Use as a marinade for fish, scallops, shrimp, chicken or pork destined for the grill or skillet
2. Mix with ground pork for a quick Mexican chorizo
3. Add to pretty much any brothy soup for depth and interest
4. Use to season sautéed greens or potatoes
5. Use in simple vinaigrette to drizzle over a salad made with tomatoes, melon or apples
6. Add a little to rice as it cooks

Dishes in *More Mexican Everyday* that use Quick Red Chile *Adobo*
Skillet Tacos (page 93)
Red Chile Roast Chicken (page 112)
Eggs Poached with Ancho Chile, Kale, Potatoes and Fresh Cheese (page 134)
Chipotle Rice with Shrimp (page 260)
Red Chile Pozole with Pork (page 276)
Lamb or Beef *Barbacoa* (page 294)
Slow-Grilled Pork Shoulder with Ancho Barbecue Sauce (page 300)
Grilled Red-Chile Ribs (page 308)
Chicken *Barbacoa* (page 324)

ROASTED GARLIC MOJO • *Mojo de Ajo Asado*

I've written many different versions of this super-useful sweet garlic seasoning, from the laborious hand-minced garlic version, simmered slowly and carefully in olive oil until soft and golden, to the whole-clove, oven-baked version, which requires little more than an hour of your time. This version illustrates another approach, this one the absolute simplest—and the most roasted in flavor. Simply roast unpeeled garlic cloves in a dry skillet, slip them from their papery skins and pulse in a food processor with oil and seasonings. Make it with the larger quantity of oil if you, like me, want plenty of the garlicky oil to skim off the top for sautéing potatoes, basting grilled vegetables, making an omelet or a dressing, whipping into mayonnaise—pretty much anything you can dream up. Most of my *mojo* recipes call for a little chile. I've left it out here, so that you can add whatever seems appropriate when you're using it.

Makes about 2 cups

4 heads of garlic, separated into unpeeled cloves

1½ to 2 cups olive oil

¼ cup fresh lime juice

1 teaspoon salt

Set a very large (12-inch) skillet over medium heat. Lay in the garlic and roast, turning regularly, until soft and browned in spots, about 15 minutes. Cool until handleable, then peel, place in a food processor and pulse until the garlic is roughly chopped. With the machine running, pour the olive oil through the feed tube in a slow, steady stream. Stop the machine, add the lime juice and salt and pulse to incorporate. Transfer the *mojo* to a pint-size jar and store, covered, in the refrigerator, where it will last for several months.

The Simplest Uses for Roasted Garlic *Mojo*

1. Use the oil to sauté shrimp or chicken, then spoon on the garlic just before serving

2. Toss with pasta, chile flakes, a handful of arugula and a little grated Parmesan

3. Spread a little on bread before you grill it or before you use it to build a sandwich

4. Spoon it onto roasted or grilled vegetables (especially good on mushrooms with a sprinkling of cilantro and some crumbled goat cheese)

5. Drizzle on popcorn, then sprinkle with grated Mexican *añejo* cheese and cilantro

6. Stir into mashed potatoes (or any other mashed root vegetables or winter squash)

7. Mash with avocado and roasted poblano for a delicious winter guacamole

8. Use in pretty much any stir-fry

Dishes in *More Mexican Everyday* that use Roasted Garlic *Mojo*

Pan-Roasted Summer Squash with Garlic *Mojo* and Güero Chile (page 182)

Roasted Sunchoke Salad with Creamy Garlic *Mojo* and Herbs (page 196)

Roasted Garlic Chicken with Mushrooms, Potatoes and Spinach (page 296)

SWEET-SOUR DARK CHIPOTLE SEASONING • *Salsa Negra*

Don't think of this Veracruz specialty as a typical salsa, in spite of its Spanish name; it's more of a seasoning paste, with deep, dark richness and smoldering heat—just right for adding depth and complexity to the simplest of dishes. The traditional version of this salsa is so involved (oil-roast the chiles and garlic, soak in raw-sugar water, puree and cook slowly in an oily pan for an hour or more) that no one really makes it at home. Which is the reason I worked on a quick cheater version, but one that, to my taste, is pretty darn close to the original.

Makes about 2 cups

Two 7½-ounce cans chipotle chiles *en adobo* (canning liquid and all)

2 tablespoons molasses

¼ cup balsamic vinegar or sweet sherry vinegar

¼ cup (packed) dark brown sugar

¼ cup soy sauce

Salt

Place the two cans of chiles (and their canning liquid), molasses, vinegar, sugar and ½ cup water in a blender and process until completely smooth. Scrape into a small saucepan and set over medium heat. Let the mixture come to a brisk simmer, then turn the heat to medium-low and continue simmering, stirring regularly, until the mixture is the consistency of tomato paste, about 30 minutes. Remove from the heat and stir in the soy sauce. If necessary, add some water, a splash at a time, until the

Roasted Garlic *Mojo* (page 39)

Sweet-Sour Dark Chipotle Seasoning (page 40)

salsa is the consistency of runny ketchup. Cool, taste and season with salt; it may not need any, depending on the saltiness of your soy sauce. (That said, keep in mind that *salsa negra* should be seasoned highly, both to preserve it for longer storage and to make it useful as a seasoning.) Transfer the salsa to a pint-size jar and store, covered, in the refrigerator, where it will last for a month or two.

The Simplest Uses for Sweet-Sour Dark Chipotle Seasoning
   1. Spoon onto raw oysters or add to cocktail sauce for shrimp
   2. Toss with nuts and a little oil and bake for a delicious nibble
   3. Toss with shrimp or smear on chicken after sautéing or grilling
   4. Use as a glaze for practically anything off the grill. It's particularly good on tuna, mackerel and sardines, as well as eggplant.
   5. Believe it or not, it's good on peanut butter–banana sandwiches
   6. Use instead of Worcestershire and hot sauce for a spicy bloody Mary
   7. Stir into cream cheese with crumbled bacon for an amazing bagel spread
   8. Stir into caramel sauce and use as a dip for apples
   9. Add to the pot when braising shortribs

Dish in *More Mexican Everyday* that uses Sweet-Sour Dark Chipotle Seasoning
Spicy Chipotle Eggplant with Black Beans (page 215)

GO-TO MEALS
TO KNOW BY HEART

Creamy Roasted Poblano *Rajas* and Two Delicious Dishes to Make from Them **47**

♦ Creamy Zucchini, Corn and Roasted Poblanos **52**

♦ Roasted Poblano Cream Soup **53**

Roasted Tomato Salsa and Three Delicious Dishes to Make from It **57**

♦ *Huevos Rancheros* **60**

♦ Salsa-Braised Fish (or Tofu or Eggplant) **64**

♦ Tomato–Green Chile Seafood Rice **67**

Roasted Tomatillo Sauce Base and Three Delicious Dishes to Make from It **69**

♦ Roasted Tomatillo Enchiladas **73**

♦ Tomatillo-Sauced *Chilaquiles* **77**

♦ Pork (or Chicken) with Roasted Tomatillos, Poblanos and Potatoes **79**

Carne Asada Dinner **86**

Skillet Tacos **93**

Pork and Black Bean Dinner **100**

Weekend Dish: Red Peanut *Mole* with Chicken **105**

Red Chile Roast Chicken **112**

Chipotle Meatballs **117**

roasted, sliced poblano chiles

garlic cloves

white onion

Mexican *crema*

dried Mexican oregano

Ingredients for Creamy Roasted Poblano *Rajas* (page 47)

Creamy Roasted Poblano *Rajas* and Two Delicious Dishes to Make from Them

Rajas Poblanas con Crema

◇◇◇

I could write riffs on this marriage of roasted poblano chiles and cream all day long. It can be made into the perfect creamy accompaniment to a piece of grilled fish or steak. It's delicious spooned onto a grilled chicken taco. It's perfect when blended with chicken broth (with maybe a little corn thrown into the blender) for a delicious soup that welcomes crispy tortilla chips or roasted zucchini or something luxurious like crab or shrimp. If you keep your creamy blended poblano mixture on the thicker side, it's a crowd-pleasing sauce for crowd-pleasing sautéed chicken breasts. And when it's made with the red poblanos that make an appearance at our farmers' market every fall, the result is beyond delicious. You quickly get the picture: roasted poblanos and cream is one of the most versatile and delicious starting-point preparations I know.

An average poblano chile weighs about 4 ounces, and for every pound of poblanos (typically 4) you need about ¾ cup cream (Mexican *crema*, *crème fraîche* or heavy cream). That's really all you need to know. Adding garlic, onions, herbs, other vegetables, broth—that's up to your taste, mood and, ultimately, what role your *crema poblana* is going to play.

Makes about 2 cups

No matter how I'm ultimately going to use my roasted poblanos and cream, I start by making classic *Rajas Poblanas con Crema*. If a gas flame (or charcoal fire) is available to me, I roast directly over high heat, turning frequently,

4 (about 1 pound total) medium fresh poblano chiles

I want the heat intense so the tough skin of the chiles will blister and blacken before

Roasting a poblano chile on the stovetop

the flesh has softened too much. It shouldn't take much more than 5 minutes to roast a chile on an open flame. (When using only one burner, I roast the poblanos in batches.) If only an electric stove is available, I heat the broiler, adjust the shelf as high as it will go, lay the chiles on a baking sheet and slide them under the broiler. As they blister and blacken, I turn them until all are uniformly charred, about 10 minutes. (Broiler-roasting works fine, though the chiles' flesh tends to get a little more cooked and takes on less smoky flavor than when flame-roasting.)

Whether the chiles are broiler- or flame-roasted, when they are evenly blackened, I collect them in a bowl and cover it with a kitchen towel to trap a little steam to loosen the charred skin. (Some cooks put them in a plastic bag, but for me, that traps too much steamy heat, leading to flesh that's softer—more cooked—than I like.) When the chiles have cooled enough to be handleable, I rub off their charred skin, remove the seedpods, then rinse the peeled, seeded flesh *briefly* under cool water. Last, I slice the roasted chiles into ¼-inch strips.

Peeling the roasted poblano

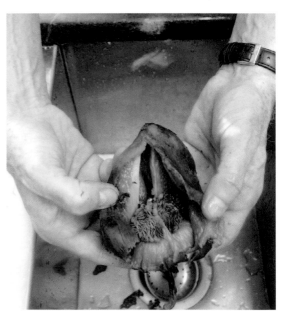

Seeding the poblano

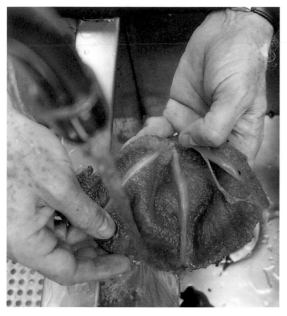

Rinsing the poblano

Slicing the roasted poblano

Poblano in all stages of preparation

To finish the *rajas a la crema*, I heat over medium-high in a very large (12-inch) skillet
   2 tablespoons vegetable or olive oil

When hot, I add
   1 large white onion, sliced ¼-inch thick

Slicing a white onion

Sliced onion

and cook, stirring regularly, until the onion is richly browned but still a little crunchy, about 7 minutes. Then I stir in
   2 garlic cloves, peeled and finely chopped
   ½ teaspoon dried oregano, preferably Mexican

After a minute or so, when the garlic is fragrant, I stir in the chile strips and
   ¾ cup Mexican *crema*, *crème fraîche* or heavy cream (if I'm planning on turning the *rajas* into soup, Greek-style yogurt is also an option)

When the cream has thickened enough to coat the chiles nicely, which takes only a couple of minutes over medium-high heat, though they need to be stirred nearly constantly,

Cooked *rajas* mixture before adding the *crema*

I taste the mixture and season it with salt, usually about ½ teaspoon. This is the perfect accompaniment for grilled meat or fish tacos, for steak or pork chops, or for grilled, sautéed or broiled fish or chicken.

A RECAP OF WHAT YOU NEED:

4 (about 1 pound total) medium fresh poblano chiles

2 tablespoons vegetable or olive oil

1 large white onion, sliced ¼-inch thick

2 garlic cloves, peeled and finely chopped

½ teaspoon dried oregano, preferably Mexican

¾ cup Mexican *crema*, *crème fraîche* or heavy cream

Salt

CREAMY ZUCCHINI, CORN AND ROASTED POBLANOS • *Calabacitas y Elote con Rajas y Crema*

Makes about 4 cups, enough for 12 generous tacos

When I want a vegetarian soft taco filling, I heat in a very large (12-inch) skillet over medium-high

1 tablespoon vegetable or olive oil

When really hot, I add

4 (about 1 pound total) zucchini, cut into cubes a little smaller than ½ inch

I cook the zucchini, stirring and turning the pieces frequently, until they are richly browned all over. That's when I add

Creamy Zucchini, Corn and Roasted Poblanos

1 cup fresh or frozen corn kernels

and I let that brown, too (which takes just a couple of minutes). I scrape in the 2 cups of *rajas*, along with

1 sprig epazote, leaves removed and thinly sliced (if I have it)
OR ¼ cup chopped cilantro

When everything comes to a simmer over medium heat, I add a couple more table-spoons of *crema* (or one of its stand-ins) if I think the mixture needs it, taste the dish for salt and scrape it into a serving bowl. Though it's not absolutely necessary, the mixture is delicious sprinkled with

¼ cup crumbled Mexican *queso fresco* or other fresh cheese such as feta or goat cheese

A RECAP OF WHAT YOU NEED IN ADDITION TO *RAJAS*:

1 tablespoon vegetable or olive oil

4 (about 1 pound total) zucchini, cut into cubes a little smaller than ½ inch

1 cup fresh or frozen corn kernels

1 sprig epazote, leaves removed and thinly sliced

OR ¼ cup chopped cilantro

¼ cup crumbled Mexican *queso fresco* or other fresh cheese such as feta or goat cheese

ROASTED POBLANO CREAM SOUP • *Crema Poblana*

Makes about 6 cups, serving 4 to 6

When I want a soup, I add to the skillet with the *rajas*

1 medium (4 ounces) red- or white-skin boiling potato, peeled and grated
OR ½ cup fresh or frozen corn kernels

and cook the mixture, stirring regularly over medium heat, until the potato is tender (the corn just has to heat through), about 4 minutes. Then I scrape the mixture into a blender or food processor, cover (*loosely* for the blender), process until smooth, scrape into a large (4-quart) saucepan and stir in

2 cups vegetable broth, chicken broth, seafood broth or milk

I taste the soup for salt (it usually needs ½ teaspoon, depending on the saltiness of the broth), set it over medium heat and decide what I want to add: vegetables, chicken or shellfish. You need about 2 cups total (a little more if you're using shrimp). If you're just adding one item, I'd suggest

2 cups (about 8 ounces) coarsely shredded, boneless grilled or rotisserie chicken

OR 2 cups vegetables (fresh or frozen corn kernels; steamed, cubed potatoes or zucchini)

OR 3 cups (about 1 pound) peeled, deveined, and cooked small to medium shrimp or bay scallops

I'm sure you can think of other additions (cooked cubes of chayote or parsnips, coarsely chopped spinach or kale or chard, butternut or other winter squash when you make the soup with red poblanos). This is a very versatile soup, one that can serve four as a first course or two for dinner (with extra left over for lunch the next day).

Roasted Poblano Cream Soup (page 53)

I ladle the soup into bowls and top each one with one or more of the following:

Crisp-fried tortilla strips or broken chips

Crumbled Mexican *queso fresco* or other fresh cheese such as feta or goat cheese

Mexican *crema*, sour cream, *crème fraîche* or Greek-style yogurt

A RECAP OF WHAT YOU NEED IN ADDITION TO *RAJAS*:

1 medium (4 ounces) red- or white-skin boiling potato, peeled and grated
OR ½ cup fresh or frozen corn kernels

1½ cups vegetable broth, chicken broth, seafood broth or milk

2 cups (about 8 ounces) coarsely shredded, boneless grilled or rotisserie chicken OR 2 cups vegetables (fresh or frozen corn kernels; steamed, cubed potatoes or zucchini) OR 3 cups (about 1 pound) peeled, deveined, and cooked small to medium shrimp or bay scallops

Crisp-fried tortilla strips or broken chips
Crumbled Mexican *queso fresco* or other fresh cheese such as feta or goat cheese
Mexican *crema*, sour cream, *crème fraîche* or Greek-style yogurt

Bonus: Simple Poblano Cream Sauce

For a smooth poblano cream sauce, I simply scrape the Creamy Roasted Poblano *Rajas* into a blender or food processor while warm, cover (*loosely* for the blender), process it until smooth, scrape it into a saucepan, thin it with a little more *crema* (or one of its stand-ins) or a little broth or water and taste for salt. (I know a lot of you might think that using water will result in a watered-down sauce. It doesn't. In fact, using water gives the sauce the cleanest, toastiest *rajas* flavor.)

Simple Poblano Cream Sauce over chicken breasts

ripe tomatoes

sliced white onion

unpeeled garlic cloves

fresh jalepeño chiles

Raw ingredients for Roasted Tomato Salsa (page 57)

Roasted Tomato Salsa and Three Delicious Dishes to Make from It

Salsa de Molcajete y Tres Platillos Deliciosos que la Utiliza

◇◇

I n the United States, homemade salsa often means a chopped *pico de gallo*–style fresh tomato version. What we buy in jars is more like Mexico's very common *molcajete* salsa, the best ones (in Mexico and in American jars) being made from roasted tomatoes, jalapeños and garlic. Given the fact that the best off-season tomatoes you can buy never compare with the farmers' market variety, I only make chopped, fresh tomato salsas in the summer, when tomatoes are at their peak.

Roasted Tomato Salsa is something else entirely. Because we can all lay our hands on decent fire-roasted tomatoes in a can when farmers' market tomatoes aren't around, this is a recipe that can be made year-round. And besides being a good salsa for tacos and chips, it can be relied on for many other dishes such as great *huevos rancheros,* salsa-baked fish (or chicken or tofu or vegetables) or a simple but dressy *arroz a la tumba* (salsa-infused rice with seafood). Classic, available and useful—that's why it's one of my go-to recipes.

Makes a generous 2 cups

If I have **fresh tomatoes**, I heat a broiler, adjust the rack as high as it will go, and spread onto a rimmed baking sheet

1 pound (about 2 medium-large round or 4 to 5 plum) ripe tomatoes

3 unpeeled garlic cloves

1 to 2 small fresh jalapeño chiles, stemmed

½ small white onion, sliced ½-inch thick

After sliding them onto the high rack, I roast everything until the tomatoes are softening, blackened and blistered on one side, usually about 6 minutes, then I turn *everything* and roast the other side. The tomatoes, garlic and chiles should be soft to create the best texture and flavor in the salsa. When cooled, I roughly chop the chiles (no need to remove the seeds), slip off and discard the papery skin of the garlic and peel off most of the skin from the tomatoes. In the classic, 3-cup-capacity lava-rock mortar (*molcajete*), I crush the garlic and chiles to a paste. Then, one by one, I add the tomatoes and crush them to a coarse puree, adding any juices from the baking sheet. This takes a

Roasted ingredients for the salsa

Peeling roasted tomatoes

Peeled roasted tomatoes

little patience (as well as practice), but you'll get the sweetest and richest flavor by using a mortar. (No mortar? I pulse the garlic and roughly chopped chiles in a food processor until finely chopped, then I add the tomatoes with any juices from the baking sheet and pulse a few times until I have a coarse puree.)

I scrape the salsa into a bowl, then chop the roasted onion into small pieces (I like ones about ¼ inch) and stir them in. I usually need to stir in about ¼ cup water to give it an easily spoonable consistency. Last, I taste the salsa and season it with salt (usually about ¾ teaspoon)

Roasted jalapeño and garlic in a *molcajete*

Crushing the jalapeño and garlic

Crushing in the roasted tomatoes

Salsa de Molcajete

For **canned fire-roasted tomatoes,** I follow all the same steps—broiler-roasting garlic, chiles, onions—but instead of the roasted and peeled fresh tomatoes I use

    One 15-ounce can diced fire-roasted tomatoes, undrained

A RECAP OF WHAT YOU NEED:

1 pound (about 2 medium-large round or 4 to 5 plum) ripe tomatoes OR one 15-ounce can diced fire-roasted tomatoes, undrained

3 unpeeled garlic cloves
1 to 2 small fresh jalapeño chiles, stemmed
½ small white onion, sliced ½-inch thick
Salt

HUEVOS RANCHEROS

This recipe is about as archetypal as it comes. Most cooks either use steamy-soft just-baked corn tortillas for their *huevos rancheros* or they soften ones that have cooled and stiffened by quick-frying them on both sides in an oily skillet. Since most of us use cold corn tortillas, I've spelled out a simpler, less oily way to heat them. Top the tortillas with sunny-side-up eggs, spoon on warm Roasted Tomato Salsa, scatter on a few garnishes if that appeals and the meal is ready. In my opinion, *huevos rancheros* are perfect any time of day.

Heated tortillas

Serves 4

First I turn on the oven to 350 degrees, then lay out on my countertop

    8 corn tortillas, preferably from a local tortilla factory

I spray or lightly brush both sides of each tortilla with a little oil, stack them up, slip them into a plastic bag, fold it over and microwave them at 100% for 1 minute. I let them stand for a minute (to uniformly absorb the heat).

Huevos Rancheros
(page 60)

In a very large (12-inch) heavy skillet (preferably nonstick), I heat over medium
Enough vegetable or olive oil to coat the bottom lightly

When it is quite warm—not smoking hot—I crack in
8 eggs

The fresher the eggs are, the less they'll run, making them easier to fit into the skillet. (If I don't have a 12-inch skillet, I do them in batches, sliding them onto a plate when they're done, then reheating them in the oven just before serving.) I sprinkle them generously with salt and let them cook slowly, lowering the heat if necessary, until the whites are set but the yolks are still bright yellow and runny; that takes about 6 minutes.

When the eggs are ready, I open up the hot, soft tortillas, lay 2 tortillas overlapping on each of 4 warm plates and top with 2 eggs. I immediately return the skillet to high heat and add
2 cups Roasted Tomato Salsa (page 57)

When it comes to a boil, I stir in a little more water (usually about ¼ cup) to give it a saucy consistency, then spoon the sauce over the eggs, leaving the yolks exposed. Before carrying them to the table, I like to sprinkle the plates with

Thinning Roasted Tomato Salsa with water

Finished Roasted Tomato Salsa sauce

About ¼ cup crumbled Mexican *queso fresco* or other fresh cheese such as feta or
goat cheese
A handful of cilantro leaves

A RECAP OF WHAT YOU NEED:

8 corn tortillas, preferably from a local
tortilla factory

Vegetable or olive oil

8 eggs

Salt

2 cups Roasted Tomato Salsa (page 57)

About ¼ cup crumbled Mexican *queso
fresco* or other fresh cheese such as feta
or goat cheese

A handful of cilantro leaves

Spooning on Roasted Tomato Salsa to make *Huevos Rancheros*

SALSA-BRAISED FISH (OR TOFU OR EGGPLANT) • *Pescado Horneado con Salsa de Molcajete*

This preparation, which might look like "smothered" fish if you were raised in the South, has a place among those I think you should know by heart, because you can make it anywhere that has a burner, any time of the year, with practically anything you can scrounge up to stand in the center of the plate: fish, shrimp, chicken, pork chops, tofu, vegetables. Though it's hands-down the best with homemade salsa crafted from farmers' market tomatoes, I've made it with canned fire-roasted tomatoes, or, in a pinch, good-quality jarred salsa. If you're eating light, a salad alongside is enough. Usually I like to have rice or beans or roasted potatoes to fill out the meal.

Serves 4

First I choose what's going in the center of the plate:

> **Four 5-ounce (1¼ pounds total) skinless fish fillets (snapper, halibut, walleye, even salmon), preferably about 1 inch thick**
>
> **OR one 14-ounce package firm tofu, cut into 8 slices**
>
> **OR 8 slices cut from a medium (about 14 ounces) eggplant—2½ to 3 inches in diameter**

In a very large (12-inch) skillet, I heat over medium-high

> **Enough vegetable or olive oil to lightly coat the bottom of the pan**

When it's very hot, I dry off the fish, tofu or eggplant with paper towels, sprinkle it generously on both sides with salt and lay it in the pan. When it's richly browned on one side, about 3 minutes, I flip it over and brown the other side. Then I spoon over everything

> **2 cups Roasted Tomato Salsa (page 57)**

and immediately reduce the heat to low, cover the pan and let the fish/tofu/eggplant coast to perfect doneness, about 2 minutes.

I carefully scrape the salsa off the top and divide the fish/tofu/eggplant among 4 warm dinner plates. Usually the salsa in the pan has thickened more than I like, so I stir in a few tablespoons water, taste it for salt, then spoon it over the plates. This is best when sprinkled just before serving with

> **Several tablespoons chopped cilantro**

Salsa-Braised Fish (page 64)

Tomato–Green Chile Seafood Rice (page 67)

A RECAP OF WHAT YOU NEED:

Four 5-ounce (1¼ pounds total) skinless fish fillets (snapper, halibut, walleye, even salmon), preferably about 1 inch thick

OR one 14-ounce package firm tofu, cut into 8 slices

OR 8 slices cut from a medium (about 14 ounces) eggplant, 2½ to 3 inches in diameter

Vegetable or olive oil

Salt

2 cups Roasted Tomato Salsa (page 57)

Several tablespoons chopped cilantro

TOMATO–GREEN CHILE SEAFOOD RICE • *Arroz a la Tumbada*

The first time most of my American friends taste this dish, they describe it as a brothy paella: rice, seafood, some tomato, a little spice and herb and enough broth to make it soul-satisfyingly soupy. At my house, everything for making *arroz a la tumbada* is always there, except, of course, the fish, shrimp and mussels or clams, which I insist on procuring the same day I make the dish. For me, the mussels or clams are pretty much a must: as they open in the pot of cooking rice, they release their beautiful seaside flavor, making the chicken broth taste pretty much like fish broth. I have on occasion doubled the mussels or clams and skipped the fish and shrimp altogether. Everything else is up for grabs. If either the shrimp or the fish isn't available (or doesn't look like something I want to eat), I replace whatever's MIA with more of the other. In just a few minutes more than it takes to cook a pot of rice, you can have a company-worthy dinner on the table, which is why this classic, Veracruz-style dish is one you should know by heart.

Serves 4

In a large (4-quart) saucepan, I heat over medium-high

   2 tablespoons oil (olive oil tastes great here, but vegetable oil will do)

When it's hot, I scoop in

   2 cups Roasted Tomato Salsa (page 57)

and I stir it as it cooks down until the mixture starts looking shinier; that'll take about 5 minutes. This fuses the flavors and enhances the sweetness of the tomatoes. That's when I add

   1 cup rice (my preference is for the meatier texture of medium-grain rice, though long-grain rice will work fine)

and stir it slowly for 2 minutes with a wooden spatula, scraping the bottom of the pan so that nothing burns or sticks. Then it's time to add almost everything else:

4 cups chicken broth

½ pound meaty, skinless fish fillet (mahimahi, halibut, sea bass), cut into ½-inch cubes

12 big mussels (about 6 ounces) or small clams (about 12 ounces), scrubbed, any beards pulled out

1 big sprig of epazote (if I have it)

I season the whole thing with salt (about ½ teaspoon if the broth is salted, 1 teaspoon if it's not). When the liquid comes to a simmer, I reduce the heat to medium-low, cover the pot and set the timer for 15 minutes. When it goes off, I taste a little of the rice: if it's still a little crunchy at the center, I re-cover the pot and cook it for a few minutes longer, then test again. When the rice is just barely cooked through—don't let it cook any longer, or both the fish and the rice will take on a mushy, overcooked texture—I turn off the heat and gently stir in

12 medium-large (about 8 ounces) shrimp, peeled and deveined, if you wish

I re-cover the pot, set the timer for 5 minutes, then give the broth a taste and season it with a little more salt if necessary. And if I didn't use any epazote (or even if I did), I stir in

About ½ cup chopped cilantro or flat-leaf parsley

After ladling the mixture into big bowls, I carry it to the table and serve it with

1 lime, cut into wedges

for each person to squeeze on *al gusto*.

A RECAP OF WHAT YOU NEED:

2 tablespoons oil

2 cups Roasted Tomato Salsa (page 57)

1 cup medium-grain or long-grain rice

4 cups chicken broth

½ pound meaty, skinless fish fillet (mahimahi, halibut, sea bass), cut into ½-inch cubes

12 big mussels (about 6 ounces) or small clams (about 12 ounces), scrubbed, any beards pulled out

A big sprig of epazote (if you have it)

Salt

12 medium-large (about 8 ounces) shrimp, peeled and deveined, if you wish

About ½ cup chopped cilantro or flat-leaf parsley

1 lime, cut into wedges

Roasted Tomatillo Sauce Base and Three Delicious Dishes to Make from It

Salsa de Tomate Verde Asado con Tres Platillos Deliciosos que la Utiliza

◇◇

No other cuisine on our planet uses tomatillos the way Mexico does. In fact, most people don't even know what tomatillos are, which to my way of thinking is a pity. They're wonderfully citrusy and herby, with a nice amount of complexity, especially when they're roasted. Plus, they create the most beautiful, near velvety consistency in any sauce they grace. For me, tomatillo sauce is an icon of the Mexican kitchen, and this base is the foundation of a great one.

Makes 2 cups

For any tomatillo-sauced dish, I first make a roasted tomatillo base. On a rimmed baking sheet, I spread out

1 pound (6 to 8 medium) tomatillos, husked and rinsed

4 unpeeled garlic cloves

1 or 2 fresh serrano chiles

1 small white onion, sliced ½-inch thick

I slide the baking sheet as close up under my preheated broiler as possible. After 4 or 5 minutes, when everything is blotchy black and softening, I turn the vegetables and roast the other side. I'm looking for everything to cook through (they should be soft) while taking on an attractive bit of rustic char. Once the vegetables are roasted, they need to cool a little on the countertop.

When the vegetables have cooled down enough to handle, I slip the skins off the garlic and pull the stems off the chiles. In a blender, I combine the tomatillos (and any juice on the baking sheet), garlic, chiles, onion and a scant teaspoon salt and blend everything to a coarse puree. I now have the base for a great roasted tomatillo-sauced dish.

To turn this base into a simple tomatillo sauce, I heat 2 tablespoons of vegetable or olive oil over medium-high, add the base and let it reduce and concentrate for about 4 minutes. When it's thicker than tomato sauce, I stir in 1½ cups chicken broth, vegetable

Raw ingredients for Roasted
Tomatillo Sauce (page 69)

husked tomatillos

sliced white onion

fresh serrano chiles

unpeeled garlic cloves

Roasted ingredients for Roasted Tomatillo Sauce

broth or water and ¼ cup chopped cilantro or flat-leaf parsley. I season the sauce with about ½ teaspoon salt, turn the heat down and let it simmer until I need it.

A RECAP OF WHAT YOU NEED:

1 pound (6 to 8 medium) tomatillos, husked and rinsed

4 unpeeled garlic cloves

1 or 2 fresh serrano chiles

1 small white onion, sliced ½-inch thick

Salt

Roasted Tomatillo Enchiladas (page 73)

ROASTED TOMATILLO ENCHILADAS • *Enchiladas Verdes*

Enchiladas, like *chilaquiles* and scrambled egg tacos, provide quick, sure-fire comfort for me. They're the perfect balance of toothsome texture (supple corn tortillas and a little meat, seafood or vegetables), brightness (tomatillo sauce), savoriness (Mexican cheese) and freshness (onions and cilantro). Enchiladas, when well made, are simple perfection, which is why I've included them in my go-to meals.

Serves 4

First I make the sauce. In a large (10-inch) skillet over medium-high heat I measure

> **2 tablespoons vegetable oil, olive oil, bacon drippings or freshly rendered pork lard**

When it's hot, I add

> **2 cups Roasted Tomatillo Sauce Base (page 69)**

I let the sauce reduce and concentrate, stirring it frequently, for about 4 minutes. When it's thicker than spaghetti sauce, I stir in

> **1½ cups chicken broth, vegetable broth or water**
> **¼ cup chopped cilantro or flat-leaf parsley**
> **OR a large sprig of epazote**

I season the sauce with salt (usually a generous ½ teaspoon, depending on the saltiness of the broth), turn the heat down to medium-low and let it simmer while I prepare the filling.

Though these enchiladas are good filled with 1 pound of raw ground beef, pork or turkey that's been cooked in a little oil with chopped onion in a skillet until browned and seasoned with salt, I like them better with coarsely shredded cooked chicken, pork, beef or fish. Even shredded melting cheese or goat cheese is good. I measure out

> **2¾ cups (12 ounces) cooked, coarsely shredded, boneless chicken, pork or beef (this is a good place for rotisserie chicken or leftover roasted or braised meats)**
> **OR 3 cups (12 ounces) shredded Mexican melting cheese (such as Chihuahua, quesadilla or asadero) or Monterey Jack, brick or mild cheddar**
> **OR 1½ cups (12 ounces) goat or dryish ricotta cheese**

When I'm ready to start building my enchiladas, I turn on the oven to 400 degrees. I spray or brush with oil both sides of

8 corn tortillas, preferably from a local tortilla factory

Then I stack them up, slip them into a plastic bag, fold it over and microwave them at 100% for 1 minute. I let them stand for a minute (to uniformly absorb the heat) while I stir a little sauce into the meat to moisten it (the cheese needs no sauce). Then I lay out the tortillas on the counter, top them each with a portion of the meat or cheese, roll them up and fit them into a 13x9-inch baking pan. I spoon the hot sauce over them (covering the whole tortilla to keep the ends from drying out), slide them into the oven and bake just until heated through, about 4 minutes. Longer in the oven means mushy enchiladas.

To serve the enchiladas, I simply use a spatula to transfer them to dinner plates. They're better, however, when I garnish them with a dairy product (for a little richness, umami and balance to the tomatillos' natural tang), such as

Dollops of Mexican *crema*, sour cream, *crème fraîche* or Greek-style yogurt thinned with a little milk

Filling tortillas with chicken

Rolling enchiladas

OR A few tablespoons grated Mexican *queso añejo* or other garnishing cheese such as Romano or Parmesan
OR a handful of shredded Mexican melting cheese (such as Chihuahua, quesadilla or asadero) or Monterey Jack, brick or mild cheddar; you can sprinkle it over the enchiladas before they go into the oven

and a final sprinkling of
A few slices of white onion
A handful of cilantro leaves (if I have them)

A RECAP OF WHAT YOU NEED:

2 tablespoons vegetable oil, olive oil, bacon drippings or freshly rendered pork lard

2 cups Roasted Tomatillo Sauce Base (page 69)

1½ cups chicken broth, vegetable broth or water

¼ cup chopped cilantro or flat-leaf parsley OR a large sprig of epazote

Salt

2¾ cups (12 ounces) cooked, coarsely shredded, boneless chicken, pork or beef OR 3 cups (12 ounces) shredded Mexican melting cheese (such as Chihuahua, quesadilla or asadero) or Monterey Jack, brick or mild cheddar

OR 1½ cups (12 ounces) goat or dryish ricotta cheese

8 corn tortillas

Dollops of Mexican *crema*, sour cream, *crème fraîche* or Greek-style yogurt thinned with a little milk

OR a few tablespoons grated Mexican *queso añejo* or other garnishing cheese such as Romano or Parmesan

OR a handful of shredded Mexican melting cheese (such as Chihuahua, quesadilla or asadero) or Monterey Jack, brick or mild cheddar

A few slices of white onion

A handful of cilantro leaves (if you have them)

Chilaquiles (page 77) topped with a fried egg, white onion and cheese

TOMATILLO-SAUCED *CHILAQUILES* • *Chilaquiles Verdes*

I may be overstating this, but it seems to me that pretty much every cook in Mexico can make *chilaquiles*, those crispy tortilla chips softening in sauce, pretty much at a moment's notice. Like macaroni and cheese, this is comfort food, the kind of dish you want to be able to put on the table whenever people are hungry. *Chilaquiles* are frequently made with tomato sauce, though it's been my experience that tomatillo sauce is even more common. A red chile version, while less known, is very appealing, too.

Chilaquiles are a common *almuerzo* (brunchy lunch) dish, though they make a perfect light dinner as well. They're rich (like a well-made mac 'n' cheese), so I eat them less frequently than I do, say, grilled chicken tacos. I think they make a great accompaniment to grilled steak, chicken or fish, as well as a meatless main dish with some *frijoles refritos* and a salad.

The skeleton of the dish is simply sauce and crispy tortillas. Typically, they're embellished with a drizzle of *crema*, a sprinkling of aged *queso añejo*, and a few coarse shreds of chicken or a fried egg. I like to make them with greens and other vegetables, as well.

Serves 4

The most important part of making good *chilaquiles* is the chips. My ideal version starts with chips I've fried myself from medium-thick tortillas (see page 79). My second choice is thicker chips from a local tortilla factory (I've found them all over the United States). I've made *chilaquiles* from Tostitos, though, and you know what? They were passable, as long as I didn't let them sit at all. Because the volume of 8 ounces of tortilla chips varies widely depending on the thickness of the tortilla, weight is the best measurement. I make or measure out

8 ounces (10 to 12 cups) corn tortilla chips

To make the sauce, I measure into a medium (4-quart) heavy pot (preferably a Dutch oven) set over medium-high

2 cups Roasted Tomatillo Sauce Base (page 69)
2 cups chicken broth or vegetable broth
A large sprig of epazote (if I have it)

When the sauce comes to a boil, I add the tortilla chips and stir to coat the chips uniformly. I cover the pan (a baking sheet is useful here if a lid isn't at hand), turn off the heat and set the timer for 4 minutes.

Chilaquiles just before cooking

When the timer sounds, I stir the mixture to distribute the sauce evenly, then I divide the *chilaquiles* between 4 warm plates. Last, I top the *chilaquiles* with a drizzle or sprinkle of

> ¼ cup Mexican *crema*, sour cream, *crème fraîche* or Greek-style yogurt thinned with a little milk
>
> A few tablespoons grated Mexican *queso añejo* or other garnishing cheese such as Romano or Parmesan
>
> A few slices of white onion
>
> A handful of cilantro leaves (if I have them)

Riffs on *Chilaquiles*:

This could go on and on, but it's common to stir some coarsely shredded cooked chicken, pork or beef into the mix (a great way to use up leftovers). For a special-occasion brunch dish, I serve *chilaquiles* with fried eggs (on top) or scrambled eggs (stirred in). I also like to add a big handful of stemmed spinach or chard along with the chips. You can make an even richer version by stirring in a big handful of shredded cheese when the timer sounds.

A RECAP OF WHAT YOU NEED:

8 ounces (about 12 cups) corn tortilla chips

2 cups Roasted Tomatillo Sauce Base (page 69)

2 cups chicken broth or vegetable broth

A large sprig of epazote (if you have it)

¼ cup Mexican *crema*, sour cream, *crème fraîche* or Greek-style yogurt thinned with a little milk

A few tablespoons grated Mexican *queso añejo* or other garnishing cheese such as Romano or Parmesan

A few slices of white onion

A handful of cilantro leaves (if you have them)

HOMEMADE TORTILLA CHIPS

TO MAKE 9 OUNCES TORTILLA CHIPS: Open a 10-ounce package of corn tortillas (preferably medium-thick ones from a local tortilla factory), separate them and cut each into 6 wedges. Lay the wedges out in a single layer on your countertop and let them air-dry for 15 minutes. While the tortillas are drying, warm 1 inch vegetable oil (I like safflower oil that's made for high heat) in a large (10-inch) skillet over heat that's between medium and medium-high. When the oil reaches 360 degrees (it'll look shimmery across the surface, but it's best to determine this with a thermometer), start frying the tortilla wedges a few at a time, letting them float around in the oil until the bubbling nearly subsides, about 1 minute depending on the exact temperature of the oil. Use a spider or skimmer to remove the chips to a paper towel–lined plate. Continue until all the chips are fried. You'll have about 9 ounces of chips, a little more than you need for the *chilaquiles*.

PORK (OR CHICKEN) WITH ROASTED TOMATILLOS, POBLANOS AND POTATOES • *Lomo de Puerco (o Pollo) en Salsa Verde con Papas*

There are few preparations I've turned to more through the years: browned pork or chicken braised in the classic tanginess of roasted tomatillo sauce with rich green-chile flavor and the always satisfying texture of waxy boiling potatoes. When they are at hand, greens such as sliced chard, sliced kale or picked purslane make the dish even better, added, of course, toward the end of cooking. No matter whether I use pork loin, pork tenderloin, pork shoulder, chicken thighs or chicken breasts, and no matter whether the dish is cooked in a skillet, Dutch oven or slow cooker, this is a traditional-tasting crowd pleaser. It's uniquely Mexican because the sauce is all about the flavor of tomatillos and chiles, with compelling, rustic flavor added by the browning. Yet at the same time the dish appeals on every American table because, yes, it's basically meat and potatoes.

Pork with Roasted Tomatillos,
Poblanos and Potatoes (page 79)

Serves 4 generously

I'm going to explain to you how you can make this dish with pork (loin, tenderloin, shoulder) and chicken (thighs, breasts). Certain versions are finished in a skillet, others in a Dutch oven. For all of them, I start with the vegetables.

If a gas flame (or charcoal fire) is available to me, I roast directly over high heat, turning frequently,

1 large fresh poblano chile

I roast it until the tough skin blisters and blackens but take it off before the flesh has softened too much; it shouldn't take more than 5 minutes. If only an electric stove is available, I heat the broiler, adjust the shelf as high as it will go and roast, turning, until the chile is uniformly charred, about 10 minutes.

When the chile is evenly blackened, I place it in a bowl and cover it with a kitchen towel to trap a little steam to loosen the charred skin. (Some cooks put roasted chiles in a plastic bag, but for me, that traps too much steamy heat, leading to flesh that's softer—more cooked—than I like.) When the chile has cooled enough to be handleable, I rub off the charred skin, remove the seedpod by pulling firmly on the stem, then rinse the peeled, seeded flesh *briefly* under cool water.

While the poblano is roasting, I collect in a microwavable bowl

1½ pounds (about 10) small red- or white-skin boiling potatoes (I like ones that are about 1 inch across; if they're larger I cut them in halves or quarters), peeled if I'm in the mood

I sprinkle them with a tablespoon of water, cover tightly with plastic wrap, poke a few holes in the top and microwave at 100% for 4 minutes.

Now to the meat choices.

For pork loin or shoulder, I choose

1½ pounds well-trimmed pork loin roast

OR 1½ pounds well-trimmed pork shoulder cut into 2-inch cubes (often labeled "pork for stew" in the meat case)

Browned pork shoulder

Adding remaining ingredients, ready to braise

After I turn on the oven to 325 degrees, I heat a medium (4-quart) heavy pot (preferably a Dutch oven) over medium-high and add

Enough vegetable oil, olive oil, bacon drippings or freshly rendered pork lard to coat the bottom

When hot, I dry off the meat with paper towels, sprinkle it generously with salt and lay it in the pan (an uncrowded layer for the cubed shoulder). When brown on all sides—this takes 5 to 10 minutes—I remove the meat to a plate and add to the pan

2 cups Roasted Tomatillo Sauce Base (page 69)

I let the sauce reduce and concentrate, stirring it frequently, for about 4 minutes.

Braised pork shoulder with roasted tomatillos, poblanos and potatoes

Then I roughly chop the poblano and add it to the pot along with the potatoes. Finally, I stir in

1 cup chicken broth, pork broth, vegetable broth or water
Several tablespoons chopped epazote or cilantro leaves

I return the meat to the pot, cover it and slide it into the oven. If I have chosen **pork loin**, I cook it until it reaches 145 degrees on an instant-read thermometer (about 30 minutes), then remove the meat to a plate, loosely cover with foil and let it rest for 10 minutes to re-absorb the juices that would run onto the cutting board if I sliced it right away. When I'm ready to serve, I reheat the sauce over medium, taste and season it with salt (usually about 1 teaspoon), slice the meat, lay the slices overlapping on 4 warm deep dinner plates, then spoon the sauce and potatoes over and around it. If I have chosen **pork shoulder**, I cook it until it's tender (that takes about 1 hour), season the sauce with salt, then spoon the delicious braise into deep plates and it's ready. Either one benefits from a fresh garnish of cilantro leaves.

For pork tenderloin, chicken breast or thighs, I choose

1½ pounds (usually 1 large or 2 very small) pork tenderloins
OR 1½ pounds (4 medium-small) boneless, skinless chicken breast halves
OR 1½ pounds (8 medium) boneless, skinless chicken thighs

In a very large (12-inch) heavy skillet set over medium-high, I heat

Enough vegetable oil, olive oil, bacon drippings or freshly rendered pork lard to coat the bottom

When hot, I dry off the meat with paper towels, sprinkle it generously with salt and lay it in an uncrowded single layer in the pan. When brown on all/both sides, 5 to 10 minutes, I remove the meat to a plate and add to the pan

2 cups Roasted Tomatillo Sauce Base (page 69)

I let the sauce simmer and reduce, stirring it frequently, for about 4 minutes. Then I roughly chop the poblano and add it to the pan along with the potatoes. Finally, I stir in

1 cup chicken broth, pork broth, vegetable broth or water
Several tablespoons chopped epazote or cilantro leaves

I return the meat to the pan, immediately reduce the heat to medium-low, cover it and let the meat coast slowly toward doneness, about 20 minutes for the pork tenderloins, 15 minutes for the chicken breasts and thighs.

When the meat is done, I remove the pork to a cutting board or the chicken directly to 4 warm, deep dinner plates. I bring the sauce to a full boil, then taste and season it with salt (usually about 1 teaspoon). I like to cut the tenderloin into thick oval slices on the diagonal and lay them overlapping on the plates (chicken pieces can be left whole). The sauce and potatoes get spooned over and around the meat before I carry the plates to the table. Cilantro leaves add freshness to the finished dish.

A RECAP OF WHAT YOU NEED:

1 large fresh poblano chile

1½ pounds (about 10) small red- or white-skin boiling potatoes

1½ pounds well-trimmed pork loin roast

OR 1½ pounds well-trimmed pork shoulder cut into 2-inch cubes

OR 1½ pounds (usually 1 large or 2 very small) pork tenderloins

OR 1½ pounds (4 medium-small) boneless, skinless chicken breast halves

OR 1½ pounds (8 medium) boneless, skinless chicken thighs

Vegetable oil, olive oil, bacon drippings or freshly rendered pork lard

Salt

2 cups Roasted Tomatillo Sauce Base (page 69)

1 cup chicken broth, pork broth, vegetable broth or water

Several tablespoons chopped epazote or cilantro leaves

WARMING PLATES

I don't care how simple the meal, I like to serve hot food on warm plates so that it doesn't cool to room temperature too quickly. Most of us think of warming plates in the oven, but it takes time to heat the oven (or maybe it's in use already) and plates heat slowly in it. I use the microwave to heat plates most of the time. Four plates take 2 minutes to heat in my microwave.

Carne Asada Dinner
(page 86)

Carne Asada Dinner

Cena Completa de Carne Asada

◇◇

I would wager that when most of us think of *carne asada*, the much-loved Mexican steak dinner with guacamole, salsa, and beans, we're thinking of a big-deal summer cookout, budget-busting steaks, and a crowd that's larger than normal at our table. None of that's necessary. *Carne asada* can be made indoors or out, from expensive steaks or ones that are reasonable and flavorful, and for a small group or large. That's why it's a good recipe to have in your back pocket, to take out whenever you need it, whether it's a Saturday night with friends or a Wednesday night with family.

Serves 4

First choose your steaks. If it's a really special occasion, rib-eye and strip steak or tenderloin are tender and enjoyable choices. But even on some special occasions I'll reach for skirt steak: it has great flavor, stays tender even when cooked medium and beyond, and is typically a cheaper cut in the butcher's case. Here's what I buy for four people:

4 *outer* skirt steaks, each about ½-inch thick (I typically buy about 6-ounce steaks)

For outdoor cooking, I heat my grill (between medium and medium-high for gas or a thick bed of coals that are quite hot and covered in white ash) and lay on a perforated grill pan (lacking this, lay on a square of foil, 2 or 3 layers thick, and poke holes in it). I scatter onto it

1 pound (6 to 8 medium) tomatillos, husked and rinsed

1 large head of garlic, separated into unpeeled cloves

Hot fresh green chiles to taste (I usually like 3 serranos or 2 small jalapeños), stems removed

I roast all the vegetables, turning them regularly, until they are blotchy black and soft (about 15 minutes for the tomatillos, 10 to 15 minutes for the garlic and 10 minutes for the chiles). Grill-roasting these flavorful ingredients adds a beautiful, gentle smokiness. (For indoor cooking, I roast everything, turning regularly, to a rich roasty sweetness—it will take about the same amount of time—on a rimmed baking sheet set about 4 inches below a preheated broiler.)

Marinating the steaks

When the garlic is cool enough to handle, I make a simple marinade: I peel it (the soft cloves easily slip from the skins), drop it into a food processor, chop it as fine as possible, scoop *half* into a small bowl and leave the rest in the food processor. I stir into the bowl

- ¼ **cup fresh lime juice**
- ¼ **cup vegetable or olive oil**
- **2 teaspoons dried oregano, preferably Mexican (rubbed between your palms if leaves are whole)**
- **1 teaspoon salt**
- ½ **teaspoon ground black pepper (I like it coarsely ground here)**

I set aside 2 tablespoons of the garlicky marinade and smear the rest on both sides of the steaks, lay them in a deep plate and set them aside at room temperature (for quick penetration) while preparing the rest of the ingredients.

For the Salsa, I add the tomatillos and chiles (they should be nearly cool by now) to the garlic in the food processor, along with

½ **cup roughly chopped cilantro**

After pulsing the mixture until it looks like salsa, I scoop *half* of it into a serving bowl.

To make the Guacamole, I scoop the remaining *half* of the salsa into a medium mixing bowl. Using a potato masher (or large fork or back of a spoon), I mash in

2 **ripe avocados, pitted and flesh scooped from the skin**

Then I taste and season both the guacamole and the salsa with salt—it usually takes about ¾ teaspoon for each one. The guacamole benefits from being covered with plastic wrap directly on the surface and refrigerated until serving time.

Avocados for guacamole

Mashing the avocados

Guacamole

I prepare *frijoles puercos* (porky beans) in a large (4-quart) saucepan over medium heat, by first cooking

    2 or 3 thick slices (2 to 3 ounces) bacon, cut crosswise into ½-inch pieces

      OR ¼ cup (or more) fresh Mexican chorizo sausage, casing removed

When I've stirred the bacon or chorizo until it has rendered its fat and is beginning to brown, I stir in

    Two 15-ounce cans pinto beans, most of the canning liquid drained

    1 cup beer, chicken broth, beef broth, vegetable broth or water

When the beans reach a simmer, I turn the temperature to low, cover the pan and keep the beans warm until I'm ready to serve.

Cooking the bacon

Beans, bacon and beer, before simmering

It's time to grill the steaks. For *outdoor grilling*, re-stoke the charcoal fire if necessary to get it quite hot; whether charcoal or gas, I make sure that there is a very hot section of the grill for searing and a cooler section for letting the steaks finish cooking without burning. For *indoor grilling*, I heat a grill pan (I like cast iron best) between medium and medium-high for about 10 minutes to ensure it's heated thoroughly. I turn on the oven to 250 degrees and set up a wire rack on a rimmed baking sheet.

I remove the steaks from the marinade, letting as much marinade as possible drip back onto the plate, and lay them on the hottest part of the charcoal or gas grill or in the grill pan. After a minute or so, depending on the temperature and thickness of the steaks, I use a pair of tongs to check if they are ready to flip: all meat initially sticks to the grill (and some marinades are stickier than others) but will more or less release itself when it's ready to flip. If I can't easily lift the steaks off the grate, I leave them a little while longer until they release themselves more. Then I flip them (they should have rich brown grill marks on one side) and cook the other side. To my taste, outside skirt steaks are best served medium (they're too chewy for me when rare), which should take 7 to 10 minutes total, depending on the temperature of your grill pan or grill. (If you prefer your skirt steaks medium-rare, take them off the grill 2 minutes earlier.) Skirt steaks are tasty at medium-well, too, but to ensure that they stay juicy and don't burn, you'll want to move them to the cooler part of the grill. The same times generally apply to grill-pan steaks, though to tell the truth, I like to mark them on the grill pan, transfer them to the rack and finish them in the oven. The cooking is slower (so I have a longer period to judge their doneness) and the meat comes out juicier.

Grilling the skirt steaks

When the steaks are done, I brush them with the reserved marinade. All steaks are juiciest when I let them rest on a cooling rack set on a rimmed baking sheet and slide them into the very low oven or cover them with a loose tent of foil. That's when I finish the beans and get everything on the table.

The beans should be a little brothy. If they aren't, I stir in a little water, taste them for salt (they usually need a little) and stir in

2 tablespoons roughly chopped cilantro

I ladle the beans into individual bowls to serve alongside the steaks. I pass the salsa and guacamole separately, for each person at the table to use *al gusto*. A big salad is always welcome with *carne asada* at my house.

A RECAP OF WHAT YOU NEED:

4 *outer* skirt steaks, each about ½-inch thick (I typically buy about 6-ounce steaks)

1 pound (about 8 medium) tomatillos, husked and rinsed

1 large head of garlic, separated into unpeeled cloves

Hot fresh green chiles to taste (3 serranos or 2 small jalapeños), stems removed

¼ cup fresh lime juice

¼ cup vegetable or olive oil

2 teaspoons dried oregano, preferably Mexican

Salt

½ teaspoon ground black pepper

½ cup roughly chopped cilantro, plus more for the beans

2 ripe avocados, pitted and flesh scooped from the skin

2 or 3 thick slices (2 to 3 ounces) bacon, cut crosswise into ½-inch pieces OR ¼ cup (or more) fresh Mexican chorizo sausage, casing removed

Two 15-ounce cans pinto beans

1 cup beer, chicken broth, beef broth, vegetable broth or water

SKIRT STEAK 101

Though it's not always labeled, there is inner skirt steak (typically about ¾-inch thick and tough enough to need tenderizing) and outer skirt steak (typically about ½-inch thick and tender enough to serve as a steak). You can choose among select, choice and prime grades (tenderness increasing as you go up that ladder) and between conventional and the harder-to-find grass-fed beef (the latter being better for our bodies but typically fuller in flavor and sometimes a little less tender). And any meat that's aged to increase its tenderness can be wet-aged in vacuum packages or dry-aged to give it a more mature, developed flavor. As a rule of thumb, the longer the aging, the more tender and flavorful the meat.

Shrimp Skillet Tacos (page 93) with Green Chile *Adobo* and caramelized onions

Skillet Tacos

Tacos al Sartén

◇◇

Typically, when people in the United States say they're making tacos, they mean one of two things. One group browns up some ground beef with a little onion, adds a dry spice packet and serves it to the whole family with, more times than not, crispy shells or flour tortillas, shredded lettuce, sour cream, shredded cheese and salsa. Is there hot sauce? Some would say "Absolutely!" while others would insist on chopped tomato, cilantro leaves, avocado or whatever they think makes those tacos taste like tacos *should* taste.

The second group makes tacos that are closer to one of two other well-known categories of tacos in Mexico: *tacos a la plancha* (griddle-seared meat tacos) or *tacos al carbon* (grilled meat tacos). They marinate some skirt steak, pork or chicken breast, griddle-sear or grill it, slice or chop it, and serve it on corn tortillas if they're being really authentic, flour tortillas if that's what they prefer. They often accompany those tacos with any or all of the accompaniments the ground-beefers put out. Which, though delicious, can make them taste distinctively American compared to their simpler Mexican counterparts. In Mexico, griddle-seared or grilled meat tacos are pretty much just that: a smallish pile of sliced or chopped grilled meat or poultry (maybe with a little caramelized onion) on steamy fresh corn tortillas (two if they're thin), with several salsas to choose from. Grilled knob onions, a little simple guacamole, maybe a side of roasted poblano *rajas* are what you might order to add more interest and a bit of luxury.

The tacos I think you should know by heart are a different type. They're my personal hybrid between a griddle-seared or grilled meat taco and one from the tradition of *tacos de cazuela*, the stewy mixtures that are set out in earthenware *cazuelas* in little hole-in-the-wall eateries all across Mexico. To me, these tacos offer the Mexican equivalent of Spanish tapas, with tortillas instead of bread: you peruse the offerings (many of them are vegetable preparations), point out the ones that appeal, watch as each is spooned onto a fresh corn tortilla and then fold them up and pop the deliciousness into your mouth.

For this preparation, I'm first searing chicken, shrimp or meat in a way that would be appealing for those who love traditional meat tacos. Then I'm adding a saucy flavoring (an herby-spicy-bright Green Chile *Adobo* in the main recipe, the garlicky-mellow Quick Red Chile *Adobo* in the variation) plus some caramelized onions. A brief simmer gives me pure

Mexican flavor, meaty enough for the folks who think tacos equal meat in a tortilla and saucy enough to resonate with those who know tacos in a wider (and, for me, more appealing) context.

I've called for chicken breast or thigh, peeled shrimp, skirt steak or boneless pork chop, but pretty much cut labeled steak can be made to work, as can pieces of fish like halibut, bass and walleye (among many others) and other cuts of pork, such as tenderloin. Cooking times will vary, however.

Serves 4

First, I start by making a batch of Green Chile *Adobo*. I set a large (10-inch) skillet over medium heat and lay in

½ head garlic, separated into unpeeled cloves
4 to 5 fresh serrano chiles, stems removed

and roast, turning regularly, until soft and browned in spots, about 10 minutes for the chiles and 15 for the garlic. When the chiles and garlic have cooled, I slip the skins off the garlic, roughly chop everything (no need to remove the chile seeds) and scoop it into a blender or food processor. To that I add

1 large bunch cilantro (thick bottom stems cut off), roughly chopped (about 2 cups loosely packed)
1 large bunch flat-leaf parsley (thick bottom stems cut off), roughly chopped (about 2 cups loosely packed)
1 cup olive oil
2 generous teaspoons salt

I process it all, stopping to scrape down the sides if necessary, until it's nearly smooth and looks a little like pesto. Last, I scoop out ⅓ cup of the *adobo*, combine it with 2 tablespoons water and set it aside. (I cover the remaining *adobo* and keep it in the refrigerator for another use.)

Before I start the final cooking, I heat

12 corn tortillas

according to the instructions on page 60. I let them sit while I finish the rest of my taco filling.

By this time, I've decided whether I'm using

1 pound boneless skinless chicken breasts or thighs

OR 1 pound shrimp, peeled and, if you like, deveined

OR 1 pound skirt steak, trimmed of excess fat and silverskin and cut into 3-inch pieces

OR 1 pound thin-cut (½ inch or a little less) boneless pork chops (I prefer the ones from the blade end)

Whether I've chosen poultry, shrimp or meat, I pat it dry with paper towels and season with a generous sprinkling of salt.

Adding shrimp and onion to the hot skillet

In a very large (12-inch) heavy skillet set over medium-high, I heat

2 tablespoons vegetable oil, olive oil, bacon drippings or freshly rendered pork lard

When I see the first wisp of smoke, I lay in the chicken, shrimp or meat in a single layer and strew onto the open spots

1 medium onion, cut into ¼-inch slices

As the protein sears, I nestle in the onion slices, turning them as they brown. When the protein is browned on one side (2 to 3 minutes for shrimp, about 5 minutes for everything else), I turn it over, brown the other side, then remove just the protein to a plate. I like the onions really caramelized, so I leave them in the pan a little longer, stirring regularly for several minutes, until they're richly browned.

While the onion is cooking, I cut the meat or poultry into ¼-inch slices (skirt steak must be sliced *across* the grain), add it back to the pan and stir in the reserved Green Chile *Adobo* mixture. If the mixture looks like it needs to be saucier, I add a little more water, then I taste everything and season it with salt if it needs some.

Adding Green Chile *Adobo* to the shrimp

Shrimp, onions and Green Chile *Adobo*

After scooping the mixture into a warm serving bowl, I carry it to the table, along with the warm tortillas wrapped in a towel. These tacos are perfect topped with

¼ cup crumbled Mexican *queso fresco* or *queso añejo* or other fresh or aged garnishing cheese like fresh farmers' cheese, dry goat cheese, Romano or Parmesan

A big handful of cilantro leaves

and accompanied by a simple salad and some fried beans.

A Red Chile Riff on the Green Chile Skillet Tacos:

When making these tacos with beef or pork, I am drawn to using the Quick Red Chile *Adobo* (page 37) instead of the herby Green Chile *Adobo* called for above. Add ¼ to ⅓ cup of it to the onions when they're caramelized, stir for 2 to 3 minutes, then stir in about ⅓ cup water (enough to give it the consistency of barbeque sauce). After it has simmered for a couple of minutes, add the sliced protein and warm it through. You're ready to eat.

A RECAP OF WHAT YOU NEED:

*For the **Green Chile** Adobo:*

½ head of garlic, separated into unpeeled cloves

4 to 5 fresh serrano chiles, stems removed

1 large bunch cilantro (thick bottom stems cut off), roughly chopped (about 2 cups loosely packed)

1 large bunch flat-leaf parsley (thick bottom stems cut off), roughly chopped (about 2 cups loosely packed)

1 cup olive oil

Salt

*For the **tacos**:*

12 corn tortillas

1 pound boneless, skinless chicken breasts or thighs

OR 1 pound shrimp, peeled and, if you like, deveined

OR 1 pound skirt steak, trimmed of excess fat and silverskin and cut into 3-inch pieces

OR 1 pound thin-cut (½ or a little less) boneless pork chops (I prefer the ones from the blade end)

Salt

2 tablespoons vegetable oil, olive oil, bacon drippings or freshly rendered pork lard

1 medium onion, cut into ¼-inch slices

¼ cup crumbled Mexican *queso fresco* or *queso añejo* or other fresh or aged garnishing cheese like fresh farmers' cheese, dry goat cheese, Romano or Parmesan

A big handful of cilantro leaves

REHEATING CORN TORTILLAS

In a microwave oven: Dribble 3 tablespoons water over a clean kitchen towel (or paper towel), then wrap your cold tortillas in it. Slide the package into a microwavable plastic bag and fold the top over—don't seal it. Microwave at 50% power for 4 minutes to create a steamy environment around the tortillas. Let stand for 2 or 3 minutes before serving.

With a vegetable steamer: Set up a vegetable steamer (one without that little post sticking up). Pour about ½ inch water into the bottom. Wrap the cold tortillas—no more than 12 at a time—in a clean kitchen towel. Lay the package in the steamer, set the lid in place and set the pot over high heat. When steam comes puffing out, set a timer for 1 minute. Then turn off the heat and let the tortillas sit in the steam for 10 minutes. They're ready.

Pork and Black Bean Dinner (page 100)

Pork and Black Bean Dinner

Frijol con Puerco

◇◇

For me, this is the perfect cold-weather dinner, which seems a little odd, since the only place in Mexico that claims it as a big-deal regional specialty is the always-warm Yucatán. Most of the time I let it simmer away all day in a slow cooker, filling the house with its remarkable earthy-sweet aroma, though it's just as easy to do a faster braise on the stovetop. My cold-weather association with soul-satisfying, stick-to-your-ribs pork and black beans has led me to call for canned fire-roasted tomatoes here. Should I be moved to make a summer version, I'd use fresh tomatoes from my garden or the farmers' market—fresh tomatoes that are roasted and blended for the braise and simply chopped in the salsa to serve alongside.

The dish is pretty complete by itself, though you may want to prepare either white rice or a leafy salad, perhaps both, as accompaniments.

Serves 6 to 8

To ensure that the dish has the richest taste, I first brown the pork. In a very large (12-inch) skillet or the removable, stovetop-safe insert to my slow cooker, I heat over medium-high

> **2 tablespoons vegetable oil, olive oil, bacon drippings or freshly rendered pork lard**

When hot, I add in a single, uncrowded layer

> **1½ pounds boneless pork shoulder, cut into 1-inch cubes and trimmed of extraneous fat**

I sprinkle it generously with about a teaspoon of salt, and as the cubes brown, I turn them until they're browned on all sides, about 10 minutes. I either scrape the meat into the slow cooker or transfer the slow-cooker insert to its base, then add

> **1½ quarts water**
>
> **1 pound (about 2¼ cups) dry black beans, picked over to remove any stones or debris**
>
> **1 medium white onion, chopped into ½-inch pieces**
>
> **A big sprig of epazote (if I have it)**

Ingredients for Pork and Black Bean Dinner, ready for cooking

Cooked Pork and Black Bean Dinner

I cover the slow cooker and turn it on to high. The beans and meat will be done in about 6 hours, though you can hold it for longer. (My slow cooker can be programmed to switch from high after 6 hours to a low keep-warm temperature for another 6 hours. Some slow cookers click to keep-warm automatically; others need to be switched manually.)

(A quick parenthesis: If I'm making this on the stovetop, I brown the pork in a 4-quart Dutch oven, then add 2 quarts water and the beans. I partially cover the pot and cook it at a simmer over medium-low for 2½ hours, stirring every half hour or so and adding more water when the liquid drops below the level of the beans.)

While the meat and beans are cooking, I make the tomato–green chile sauce. In a very large (12-inch) skillet, I heat over medium-high

2 tablespoons vegetable oil, olive oil, bacon drippings or freshly rendered pork lard

When hot, I add

1 medium white onion, chopped into ½-inch pieces

and stir until it begins to brown. While the onion is cooking, I pour into a blender

One 28-ounce can fire-roasted diced tomatoes in juice, undrained

and pulse it a few times until coarsely pureed. I pour the puree into the pan with the onions. Then I add

2 fresh serrano or jalapeño chiles, stemmed and roughly chopped into small pieces (in Yucatán, they'd use ½ to 1 habanero)

and cook, stirring regularly, until the mixture is thick enough to hold its shape in a spoon.

I season the sauce with salt (it usually takes ½ teaspoon) and stir *half* the mixture into the beans. Then I season the meat and beans, usually with 1½ teaspoons more salt.

Coarsely pureed tomatoes

Cooking tomato–green chile sauce

Adding tomato–green chile sauce to pork and beans

After a few minutes of simmering, the dish is ready to serve. I ladle it into bowls, spoon a little of the remaining sauce on top and, if I feel like it, dot with

**1 large ripe avocado, pitted, flesh scooped from the
 skin and cut into ½-inch pieces**
A handful of cilantro leaves
A handful of sliced radishes

I know lots of you will automatically reach for the sour cream, but in Mexico that would be considered . . . well, a bit odd.

A RECAP OF WHAT YOU NEED:

4 tablespoons vegetable oil, olive oil, bacon drippings or freshly rendered pork lard (divided use)

1½ pounds boneless pork shoulder, cut into 1-inch cubes and trimmed of extraneous fat

Salt

1 pound (about 2¼ cups) dry black beans, picked over to remove any stones or debris

2 medium white onions, chopped into ½-inch pieces (divided use)

A big sprig of epazote (if you have it)

One 28-ounce can diced tomatoes in juice, preferably fire-roasted, undrained

2 fresh serrano or jalapeño chiles, stemmed and roughly chopped into small pieces

1 large ripe avocado, pitted, flesh scooped from the skin and cut into ½-inch pieces

A handful of cilantro leaves

A handful of sliced radishes

canned fire-roasted diced tomatoes

Ingredients for Red Peanut *Mole* with chicken (page 105)

chicken broth

torn firm white bread

canned chipotle chiles *en adobo*

roasted peanuts

ground cinnamon

ground allspice

Weekend Dish: Red Peanut *Mole* with Chicken

Mole de Cacahuate con Pollo

◇◇

Putting classic *mole* in a book that's dedicated to simple, approachable and speedy dishes is a little foolhardy. *Mole* is, after all, one of the most laborious dishes in the world, especially when made from scratch in the traditional, pull-out-the-fiesta-stops versions you find in the classic kitchens of Puebla, Oaxaca, Veracruz and so on.

It's the thought of those days-long preparations that have led many Mexican cooks to start their fiesta cooking with prepared *mole* pastes—made from all of the not-quickly-perishable *mole* ingredients that are toasted, blended and cooked slowly into a thick mass that's stable and long-lasting at room temperature. While some work well as the base for a good *mole*, those are not usually the ones that make it north of the border. Most have rough edges that require a lot of sugar to smooth out.

That said, this relatively simple, from-scratch *mole* may at first glance seem suspect. Not as suspect, though, as a chef friend's strategy, explained to me earnestly, for tackling *mole* in his restaurant: start with peanut butter, stir in a lot of chili powder, thin with chicken stock and sweeten with chocolate sauce. No, this recipe starts with traditional *mole* ingredients but tips the proportions toward peanuts to temper the dried chiles (they typically need long, slow cooking on their own to beautifully integrate their flavor into the sauce). The recipe is based on one I culled from an old Mexico City cookbook, a volume dedicated to honest, simple cooking. It could legitimately be called a *pipián* rather than *mole*, because of the focus on the nuts. But you'll recognize that hauntingly delicious *mole* flavor and be happy you can make it in about an hour.

Serves 6, with about 1 quart of *mole*

In a medium-large heavy pot or Dutch oven (it's easiest to work through all the steps in a pan that's 8 to 10 inches wide and holds 4 to 6 quarts), I heat over medium

> **2 tablespoons vegetable oil, olive oil, bacon drippings or freshly rendered pork lard**

When it's hot, I add

> **2 medium dried ancho chiles, stemmed, seeded, and torn into 5 or 6 flat pieces**
> **½ small white onion, sliced ¼-inch thick**
> **2 garlic cloves, peeled**

I cook the mixture for 5 or 6 minutes, stirring frequently, until the onion and garlic have softened and browned and the chile is toasty-looking and aromatic. Then I scrape it all into a blender jar (setting the pan aside unwashed). To the blender I add

⅔ of a 15-ounce can (1 cup) diced tomatoes, preferably fire-roasted, with juice

1 cup dry- or oil-roasted peanuts

2 slices firm white bread, roughly torn into pieces

2 canned chipotle chiles *en adobo*

¼ teaspoon ground allspice

½ teaspoon ground cinnamon, preferably Mexican *canela*

1½ cups chicken broth

Browned onion and garlic, toasted ancho

Blending all the ingredients

and blend until as smooth as possible. That takes a couple of minutes with most blenders; I know it's ready when a drop of the puree rubbed between my fingers doesn't feel gritty. Unless I've used a powerful high-speed blender like a Vitamix, I always pass the mixture through a medium-mesh strainer to remove chile skins and anything else that didn't get thoroughly blended.

To cook the *mole*, I return the pan to the heat, this time medium-high, and add

2 more tablespoons vegetable oil, olive oil, bacon drippings or freshly rendered pork lard

When the fat is hot enough to make a drop of the sauce sizzle fiercely, I add it all at once. When the puree hits the hot fat, it's important to stir constantly for 7 or 8 minutes until it has reduced by two thirds of its original volume and darkened to a thick, rusty-orange paste (about the consistency of tomato paste). This is the critical step that fuses the disparate flavors into a harmonious sauce. When the mixture begins to splatter, I lay a cookie sheet or splatter screen over most of the pot and stir from the side; my implement of choice is always a blunt-end wooden spatula that won't conduct heat and will thoroughly scrape the bottom of the pan.

Cooked-down *mole* paste

To my cooked-down *mole* paste, I stir in

2 more cups chicken broth

Then I decide whether I want the dish to tip toward the sweeter side, which focuses on the flavor of the chiles and chocolate (it'll taste more *mole*-like to many), or the savory side, which focuses on the nuts (it'll taste more *pipián*-like).

For a sweeter *mole*, I stir in

¼ cup (about 1½ ounces) finely chopped Mexican chocolate

For a more savory *mole*, I whisk in

½ cup red wine

2 bay leaves

1 tablespoon vinegar (cider vinegar is good here)

I partially cover the pot, turn the heat to low and let it simmer, stirring occasionally, for as long as I have. A half hour is good, but an hour is better; making the *mole* a day ahead and refrigerating produces the best flavor.

For the final sauce seasoning, I start with

> **Salt (it usually takes about 1½ teaspoons for the savory version, 2½ teaspoons for the sweeter one)**

After I've tasted the sauce and feel it has the right amount of salt, I season with

> **Sugar (usually about ½ teaspoon for both)**

I know most folks who cook from a European perspective (and that's most of us) will immediately think of sugar as a crutch: "Sweetness will make the *mole* taste mainstream American." "Sweetness is used only to mask poor cooking techniques." "Sweetness is for sissies who can't take the heat and bitterness." None of it is true. Adding a small amount of sugar won't produce a *mole* that's perceptibly sweet, even when added to the savory version of this sauce. What it will produce is a *mole* in which the dried chiles fully play their flavorful role. No sugar equals dead chile flavor.

I make sure the consistency resembles that of smooth bean soup, and if it is thicker than that, I stir in a little more broth or water to make it right. (If I've made the *mole* the day before and refrigerated it, I re-warm it and adjust the consistency and seasonings if necessary.)

The easiest way to serve the *mole* is to bake it with chicken. I turn on the oven to 350 degrees, then arrange in a 13 x 9-inch baking dish

> **6 boneless, skinless chicken breast halves (each about 8 ounces)**
> **OR 12 boneless, skinless chicken thighs (each about 4 ounces)**

I always choose thighs when I know the dish may have to sit for a while or possibly be re-warmed; they stay moister than chicken breasts. Cooking either one with the bones still in will offer maximum flavor, but skin, baked in the sauce, will render a lot of fat and result in a less-than-appealing texture.

I ladle the hot *mole* over the chicken, slide it into the oven and bake until the chicken is just cooked through, about 35 minutes. I use tongs to transfer the chicken to warm dinner plates, then whisk the *mole* to ensure that all the chicken juices are thoroughly incorporated and ladle it over. A sprinkling of chopped peanuts and a few parsley leaves are welcome garnishes. Classic Mexican white rice (especially if it contains cubes of fried sweet plantain) is the perfect, traditional accompaniment, though black beans are excellent with *mole*, too.

Red Peanut *Mole* with Chicken (page 105)

A RECAP OF WHAT YOU NEED:

4 tablespoons vegetable oil, olive oil, bacon drippings or freshly rendered pork lard (divided use)

2 medium dried ancho chiles, stemmed, seeded, and torn into 5 or 6 flat pieces

½ small white onion, sliced ¼-inch thick

2 garlic cloves, peeled

⅔ of a 15-ounce can (1 cup) diced tomatoes, preferably fire-roasted, with juice

1 cup dry- or oil-roasted peanuts

2 slices firm white bread, roughly torn into pieces

2 canned chipotle chiles *en adobo*

¼ teaspoon ground allspice

½ teaspoon ground cinnamon, preferably Mexican *canela*

3½ cups chicken broth (divided use)

¼ cup (about 1½ ounces) finely chopped Mexican chocolate

OR ½ cup red wine, 2 bay leaves and 1 tablespoon vinegar (cider vinegar is good here)

Salt

Sugar

6 boneless, skinless chicken breast halves (each about 8 ounces)

OR 12 boneless, skinless chicken thighs (each about 4 ounces)

Red Chile Roast
Chicken (page 112)

Red Chile Roast Chicken

Pollo Adobado y Rostizado

◇◇◇

Everybody needs a roast chicken recipe for that simple weeknight meal when you want to fill the kitchen with a beautiful aroma and the plate with flavors that capture all your attention. Now, while I'm all for the drama of carving a whole chicken at the table, I'm realistic enough to know that few of us feel comfortable with it. So this is a recipe for roasted chicken *parts*. I prefer breasts and thighs cooked with the bones in and skin on—both skin and bone contribute immeasurably to the finished flavor. But you can use this approach with chicken legs and wings, too. I am giving you directions for brining the chicken because brining ensures the best flavor and texture. It takes an hour. When I don't have an extra hour to invest, I buy a kosher chicken, because the koshering process includes a light brine.

Serves 4

To brine the chicken, I place 1 quart cool water in a large bowl, then add

> **¼ cup salt**

and stir until dissolved. Then I slip in

> **2 large bone-in, skin-on chicken breast halves**
> **4 large bone-in, skin-on chicken thighs**

I cover and refrigerate the chicken for 1 hour.

Usually I have a batch of Quick Red Chile *Adobo* in my fridge. But if I don't, I make a half batch for this recipe. In a blender or small food processor I combine

> **A scant ¼ cup good-quality ancho chile powder**

with ⅔ cup boiling water. I *loosely* cover the blender or secure the top of the food processor and pulse to create a slurry. While I wait for it to cool, I scoop into a microwavable bowl

> **4 garlic cloves, peeled**

I cover the cloves with water and microwave at 100% for 30 seconds.

When the ancho mixture and the garlic are cool, I put them both in a blender or small food processor along with

¼ teaspoon ground cinnamon, preferably Mexican *canela*

⅔ teaspoon ground black pepper

A big pinch of ground cumin

½ teaspoon dried oregano, preferably Mexican

2 tablespoons apple cider vinegar

¾ teaspoon salt

I process all that into a smooth puree, scoop the now-finished *adobo* into a bowl and set it aside.

After heating the oven to 400 degrees, I remove the chicken from the brine, dry it on paper towels, then transfer it to a large, microwave-safe bowl and add

about ⅓ cup Quick Red Chile *Adobo* (half of what you made)

I toss the chicken with the *adobo* until it's all lightly coated, then spread it into an uncrowded layer on half of a rimmed baking sheet, leaving some *adobo* in the bowl. Next the chicken goes into the oven. I set the timer for 35 minutes and immediately start the potatoes.

Into the chicken-tossing bowl (unwashed), I scoop

1½ pounds (about 10) red- or white-skin boiling potatoes (I like ones that are about 1 inch across; if they're larger I cut them in halves or quarters), peeled if I wish

I sprinkle in a little salt and olive oil and toss it all together. (The potatoes pick up a bit of the *adobo*, and that's exactly the point.) I add a tablespoon of water to the

Adding the *adobo* to the chicken

bowl, cover it tightly with plastic wrap, poke a few holes in the top and micro-wave it at 100% for 5 minutes, until the potatoes are almost done. I open the oven and spread the potatoes on the uncov-ered side of the baking sheet.

While the chicken and potatoes are roast-ing, I stir together

about ⅓ cup Quick Red Chile *Adobo* (the other half of what you made)

2 tablespoons honey, agave nectar or brown sugar

1 tablespoon vegetable oil

When the timer goes off, I remove the bak-ing sheet, brush the chicken pieces evenly with this sweet chile glaze, then return the baking sheet to the oven. I roast the

Tossing the chicken with the *adobo*

chicken until the thickest part of one of the breasts reaches 150 degrees on an instant-read thermometer, usually about 3 minutes more. That's when I remove the sheet pan from the

Microwaving tossed potatoes

oven, very loosely tent the chicken with foil and let it rest 10 minutes for the chicken to re-absorb the juices and finish cooking. (I test the potatoes to make sure they're done; if not, I remove the chicken and return the sheet pan of pota-toes to the oven.) I cut the breasts in half with a large knife and serve a piece of breast, a thigh and a spoonful of potatoes on each of 4 warm dinner plates. A simple leafy green salad is the perfect accom-paniment.

A RECAP OF WHAT YOU NEED:

*For the **Quick Red Chile** Adobo:*

A scant ¼ cup good-quality ancho chile
  powder

4 garlic cloves, peeled

¼ teaspoon ground cinnamon, preferably
  Mexican *canela*

⅛ teaspoon ground black pepper

A big pinch of ground cumin

½ teaspoon dried oregano, preferably
  Mexican

2 tablespoons apple cider vinegar

¾ teaspoon salt

*For the **Red Chile Roast Chicken:***

Salt

2 large bone-in, skin-on chicken breast
  halves

4 large bone-in, skin-on chicken thighs

1½ pounds (about 10) red- or white-skin
  boiling potatoes

Olive oil

2 tablespoons honey, agave nectar or
  brown sugar

1 tablespoon vegetable oil

Chipotle Meatballs (page 117)

Chipotle Meatballs

Albondigas al Chipotle

◇◈◇

There's a reason I'm going back to this very traditional preparation (the versions in *Mexican Everyday* and *Authentic Mexican* have been very popular among my readers). Including it in the small group of go-to, committed-to-memory recipes enables me to explain the big-picture basics that led me to the exact proportions I use to make great meatballs when I walk into the kitchen. Plus, knowing these basics allows me to vary the outcome based on who I'm cooking for, what I have on hand or what I've found at the farmers' market or grocery.

A basic meatball is typically a combination of ground meat, something to soften the meat's tendency toward firmness and something else to keep it from falling apart. In Mexico, the meat is typically ground pork, beef or a combination of the two, though I have made this recipe very successfully with ground lamb, turkey and chicken thigh. The typical softener in Mexico is cooked rice (fresh breadcrumbs work well, too), and an egg helps hold it together. Besides salt, the typical seasoning for the meat in Mexico is chopped fresh mint (other herbs, such as oregano or parsley, are good alternatives); like many Mexican cooks, I like to add garlic, too. Another great addition is chopped fresh bacon.

Browning the meatballs in a large skillet and adding the simple ingredients of a tomato-chipotle sauce turns out one of the most crowd-pleasing dishes I know. I like to serve meatballs with rice or mashed potatoes and a salad.

Serves 4

First I mix together in a bowl

1 pound ground beef or pork, or a combination of the two

1 egg

2 garlic cloves, peeled and finely chopped

1 teaspoon salt

2 to 3 tablespoons chopped fresh mint leaves (if they are available)

and then I add a tenderizing ingredient:

½ cup (packed) cooked, cooled rice (I like to break up the grains by spreading the rice on a cutting board and giving it a rough chop)

OR ¾ cup (packed) fresh breadcrumbs, made with a soft, caky bread such as Pepperidge Farm white sandwich bread

Ingredients for Chipotle Meatballs

Using my fingers or a spoon, I mix everything together, being careful to get an even distribution without beating or compacting the mixture too much (which turns out a dense meatball). Then I form the mixture into 12 meatballs, rolling them gently between my palms without pressing too hard. (Meatballs made with rice will be a little wet at this stage, but they cook up lighter, which is why I prefer them.)

Next, in a very large (12-inch) skillet (I like to work in heavy cast iron or nonstick), I heat over medium

2 tablespoons vegetable oil, olive oil, bacon drippings or freshly rendered pork lard

When it's hot, I add the meatballs in a single uncrowded layer. As they brown on one side, I turn them with tongs or a spatula, continuing until they're evenly and richly browned all over, 6 to 8 minutes.

Mixing Chipotle Meatballs ingredients

Forming the meatballs

Meatballs ready to be cooked

While the meatballs are browning, I combine in a blender jar

One 15-ounce can diced tomatoes, preferably fire-roasted, with juice

1 to 2 (or more, if I want the sauce really spicy) canned chipotles *en adobo*, stemmed and optionally seeded

1 tablespoon chipotle canning sauce

1 scant teaspoon dried oregano, preferably Mexican
OR 2 tablespoons chopped fresh flat-leaf parsley

2 garlic cloves, peeled and halved

and pulse until coarsely pureed.

When the meatballs are ready, I pour the sauce mixture evenly over the top, making sure to coat the meatballs evenly and loosen any that may be sticking a little.

Chipotle sauce in the blender

After covering the pan and reducing the heat to medium-low, I let the meatballs cook for about 10 minutes more, until they're cooked through.

To serve the meatballs, I remove them to 4 dinner plates, leaving behind as much of the sauce as possible. I raise the temperature under the skillet to medium-high and stir in

⅓ cup water, beef broth, chicken broth, beer or wine

and let the sauce simmer for a minute or two. I season the sauce with salt (it usually takes about 1 teaspoon) and spoon it over the meatballs, and my *albondigas* are ready.

A RECAP OF WHAT YOU NEED:

1 pound ground beef or pork, or a combination of the two

1 egg

2 garlic cloves, peeled and finely chopped

Salt

2 to 3 tablespoons chopped fresh mint
   leaves (if they are available)

½ cup (packed) cooked, cooled rice
   OR ¾ cup (packed) fresh breadcrumbs,
   made with a soft, caky bread such as
   Pepperidge Farm white sandwich bread

2 tablespoons vegetable oil, olive oil,
   bacon drippings or freshly rendered pork
   lard

One 15-ounce can diced tomatoes,
   preferably fire-roasted, with juice

1 to 2 canned chipotles *en adobo*,
   stemmed and seeded

1 tablespoon chipotle canning sauce

1 scant teaspoon dried oregano, preferably
   Mexican
   OR 2 tablespoons chopped fresh flat-leaf
   parsley

2 garlic cloves, peeled and halved

⅓ cup water, beef broth, chicken broth,
   beer or wine

VEGETABLES AT THE HEART OF THE MEXICAN KITCHEN

2

COOKING GREENS

Greens and Beans with Red Chile and
Fresh Cheese **126**

Mustard Greens Soup with Poblanos
and Almonds **129**

Crispy Cakes of Greens, Potato and
Green Chile **132**

Eggs Poached with Ancho Chile, Kale,
Potatoes and Fresh Cheese **134**

"Sturdy Greens" Salad with Mango
and Habanero **138**

Greens and Beans with Red Chile and Fresh Cheese

Frijoles y Quelites en Chile Guajillo con Queso Fresco

◇◇◇

This is my go-to taco when I need a bite that's comforting and time-tested. Sure, greens and beans have had the reputation of being old-fashioned, of being peasant food, but now we're awakening to the fact that there's nothing truly more satisfying to our spirits and bodies than food the not-so-affluent have nourished themselves with for centuries. Plus, when you season those greens and beans with the bright, earthy flavor of dried guajillo chiles and garlic, the result tastes so iconically Mexican that each mouthful feels like a big hug from the Pueblan or Oaxacan or *veracruzana* grandmother I never had.

In my quick, everyday cooking, I often turn to the Quick Red Chile *Adobo* (page 37) for red chile seasoning. You can use it in this recipe, too: Heat 2 (not 3) tablespoons oil in your saucepan over medium and fry ½ cup of Quick Red Chile *Adobo* in the oil, stirring nearly constantly, for about 2 minutes, until it is darker and aromatic. Add the ¾ cup water and continue with the recipe, remembering that Quick Red Chile *Adobo* already contains salt. But if you have or can easily lay your hands on dried guajillo chile pods, use them in this recipe. You'll be surprised at how simple and satisfying the outcome is.

Serves 4

3 tablespoons vegetable oil

8 medium-large (about 2 ounces) dried guajillo chiles, stemmed, seeded and torn into large, flat pieces

3 garlic cloves, peeled and roughly chopped

½ teaspoon dried oregano, preferably Mexican

¼ teaspoon ground black pepper

Salt

Sugar

1 medium bunch (about 12 ounces) black (aka Tuscan or dinosaur) kale, stems removed, cut crosswise into ½-inch strips (about 6 cups)

One 15-ounce can black beans, drained

¼ cup crumbled Mexican *queso fresco* or other fresh cheese such as feta or goat cheese

Heat the oil in a large (4-quart) saucepan over medium. Fry the chiles one or two at a time, until they're aromatic and change color (they'll lighten a little on the inside and brown on the outside), 10 seconds or so on each side. Remove to a bowl, cover with hot tap water, weight with a plate to keep them submerged and rehydrate for about 20 minutes. Set the pan aside.

Scoop the chiles into a blender jar, along with ⅔ *cup* of the soaking water.

Add the garlic, oregano and pepper and blend to a smooth puree. (If the mixture won't move through the blender blades, add a little more of the soaking liquid to loosen it up.)

Return the oily pan to medium-high heat. When hot, set a medium-mesh strainer over the pan and press the chile mixture through. Discard the skins and seeds left in the strainer. Cook, stirring nearly constantly, until the mixture has the consistency of tomato paste, about 4 minutes. Pour in ¾ cup water, reduce the heat to medium-low and simmer, stirring regularly, until the sauce takes on a medium consistency, about 5 minutes. Taste and season highly with salt, usually about 1 teaspoon; adding about ½ teaspoon sugar will bring out the natural fruitiness of the chile and balance the heat a little.

Add the kale and beans to the sauce all at once, tossing to coat with the guajillo sauce. Cook, stirring often, until the kale wilts, about 3 minutes. Transfer the mixture to a warm serving bowl. Sprinkle the *queso fresco* (or one of its stand-ins) on top and you're ready to serve, along with warm tortillas if you're making tacos.

Greens and Beans with Red Chile
and Fresh Cheese (page 126)

Mustard Greens Soup
with Poblanos and Almonds

Crema de Quelites de Mostaza, Chile Poblano y Almendra

Yes, this is soup is a cousin of the poblano cream I've included in Go-To Meals to Know by Heart (page 53). But it's substantially different in two ways. First, it really celebrates the flavor of spicy mustard greens rather than poblano chile. And second, this unctuous soup is vegan (you may decide to make it the first time for someone who's vegan, then find yourself turning to it over and over when there are no vegans at the table—it's that good). It's made creamy with potato and enriched with the wonderful flavor of toasted almonds.

Makes about 6 cups, serving 4 to 6

⅔ cup (about 3 ounces) blanched peeled almonds (I always keep the slivered ones on hand, but you can use whole ones as well), plus a few extra for garnish if you wish

2 fresh poblano chiles

Salt

2 medium (about ½ pound total) unpeeled boiling potatoes (the red- or white-skin variety or the multi-purpose Yukon Gold, which are typically larger), cut into ½-inch cubes

4 garlic cloves, peeled

1 bunch (about 8 ounces) mustard greens, tough stems cut off

3 cups vegetable stock or water, plus a little more if needed

Heat your oven to 325 degrees, spread the almonds on a baking sheet, slide them into the oven and toast them until they are nutty-smelling and pale golden, about 15 minutes.

While the almonds are toasting, roast the poblanos over an open flame or (when the almonds are done) close up under a preheated broiler, turning regularly until blistered and blackened all over, about 5 minutes for the open flame, 10 minutes for the broiler. Place the chiles in a bowl, cover with a kitchen towel and cool until handleable. Rub off the blackened skin and pull out the stems and seedpods. Briefly rinse the chiles to remove bits of skin and seeds.

While you're waiting for the poblanos to cool, bring a large (4-quart) saucepan of heavily salted water to a boil over medium-high. Scrape the toasted almonds into it, boil for about 5 minutes, until noticeably softened, then use a slotted spoon to scoop them into a blender jar. Add the potatoes and garlic to the pot and cook until the potatoes are fork-tender, about 6 minutes.

When the potatoes are ready, use a slotted spoon to scoop the potatoes and garlic into a bowl. Pick out the garlic cloves and add them to the blender, along with *half* of the potatoes. Add about *two-thirds* of the mustard greens to the pot and cook for 1 minute, just until they soften and turn even brighter green. Use tongs or a slotted spoon to transfer the greens to the blender jar. Add *one* of the poblanos (torn into smaller pieces) and the vegetable stock (or water). Process until completely smooth. With a high-powered blender, this should take about 2 minutes; ordinary blenders will take longer. Pour the blanching water out of the pot, then pour in the soup.

Chop the remaining poblano into ¼-inch pieces and add to the soup, along with the remaining *half* of the potatoes. (You can reserve a tablespoon or two of poblano for garnish if you want.) Slice the remaining mustard greens into ½-inch pieces and add to the soup. Simmer the soup for a minute or two—the mustard greens need to soften to a pleasant tenderness—then season with salt, usually about 1½ teaspoons. If the soup seems a little thicker than you'd like, thin it with a little extra vegetable stock or water. Divide the soup among warm bowls and top each with a few pieces of poblano (and chopped toasted almonds if you made extra).

Riffs on Mustard Greens Soup:

You can replace the mustard greens with spinach, chard, kale or collard greens or with wild greens like nettles and lamb's quarters. If this soup is the main dish of your meal, you may want to add cubes of tofu or coarse shreds of cooked chicken just before serving. Poaching shrimp in the soup makes it very special.

Crispy Cakes of Greens, Potato and Green Chile (page 132)

Crispy Cakes of Greens, Potato and Green Chile

Tortitas de Quelites, Papa y Chile Verde

◇◇◇

t takes only a bite or two of these substantial cakes of robust greens, green chile, sweet garlic and umami-packed *añejo* cheese to know why our restaurant staff gets so excited when they go on the menu. Yes, they're vegetarian, but that's not generally cause for staffwide enthusiasm. I think folks love them because they're plain-and-simple delicious and as satisfying as any heartier, meatier dish. Plus, it doesn't hurt that they're golden and crispy. Served with the bright counterpoint of store-bought salsa (you could even use the Roasted Tomato Salsa on page 57) and a spoonful of beans or a tuft of lime-dressed arugula, they make a memorable meal.

Thank goodness panko crumbs are now widely available. They make a big difference in the crispiness of the finished cakes. Though you can simply press those crumbs into the cakes to coat them before frying, the simple flour-egg-crumb coating I outline here produces a wonderful crispness.

Makes 12 cakes, serving 4 as a light main dish

1 pound greens (kale, chard and mustard greens, or a mix of the three, are my favorites here; to my taste, spinach is a little too soft), stems removed, leaves cut crosswise into ½-inch strips, about 8 loosely packed cups

3 medium (12 ounces total) red- or white-skin boiling potatoes, peeled if you wish

2 garlic cloves, peeled

1 fresh green chile (serranos and jalapeños both work), stemmed, seeded if you wish and roughly chopped

½ cup grated Mexican *queso añejo* or other garnishing cheese such as Romano or Parmesan, plus more for garnish

Salt

About ½ cup flour

2 eggs

About 1 cup breadcrumbs, preferably panko

About ¾ cup vegetable oil for frying

About 1½ cups of any salsa you love, for serving

Collect the greens in a large, microwave-safe bowl, sprinkle on a couple of tablespoons of water, cover tightly with plastic wrap, poke a couple of holes in the top and microwave at 100% for about 2 minutes, until the greens are just barely tender. Uncover, being careful of the trapped steam, and remove them to a plate to cool. Cut the potatoes into 1-inch pieces, scoop them into that same bowl, add a little water and cook them in the microwave in the same manner (they will take about 5 minutes). Uncover and let cool.

Place the garlic in a small microwave-safe bowl, cover with water and microwave at 100% for 1 minute. Uncover, drain and transfer to a food processor. Add the chile and pulse until both are finally chopped. Next, add the potatoes (leaving behind as much of their cooking liquid as possible), the cheese and ½ teaspoon salt. Pulse the machine (1-second pulses) until the mixture becomes homogenous (there will still be small pieces of potato). Last, add the greens and pulse until they are incorporated into the potato mixture. I don't like to chop the greens very much—just enough so the mixture holds together when pressed. If it doesn't, pulse a few more times.

Form the greens mixture into 12 patties, each about 2½ inches across and 1 inch thick.

Set up the coating: Spread the flour onto a plate. In a deep, wide plate or shallow bowl, beat the eggs with 1 tablespoon water. Spread the breadcrumbs on another plate. One by one, lay the cakes in the flour, turning them and tossing the flour to coat them lightly all over. Next, lay each cake in the egg and flip it to coat all over. Finally, lay it in the breadcrumbs, flip it, then pat the crumbs all over, coating evenly.

Turn the oven on to its lowest setting. In a large (10-inch) skillet, heat about ½ inch of the oil over medium-high. When hot enough to make an edge of one of the greens cakes sizzle sharply, fry the cakes in 3 batches, cooking them until brown and crisp on both sides, about 4 minutes per side. When a batch is done, drain it on paper towels and keep warm in the low oven while you fry the next batch.

Once all are fried and drained, divide the golden cakes among four plates, sprinkle with *añejo* cheese and serve with your chosen salsa.

Eggs Poached with Ancho Chile, Kale, Potatoes and Fresh Cheese

Huevos Pochados con Chile Ancho, Berza, Papas y Queso Fresco

This is the perfect brunch (or breakfast-for-dinner) dish for folks who like rustic and bold rather than sweetness and light: each deep plate nestles an egg poached in an impish brothy sauce infused with the bright, self-assured flavors of ancho chiles, garlic and sweet spices. There are wilted greens, potatoes and cubes of fresh cheese, plus bacon if you want it. I'm the guy who always wants savory for breakfast, and for me this is the ultimate.

Serves 4

4 thick slices (4 ounces) bacon, cut into ½-inch pieces (this is optional: for those who want to keep the dish vegetarian, replace the bacon fat with 1 tablespoon vegetable or olive oil)

½ cup Quick Red Chile *Adobo* (recipe follows)

2 cups chicken or vegetable broth

3 medium (12 ounces total) red- or white-skin boiling potatoes, peeled if you wish and cut into ¼-inch pieces

Salt

4 eggs

1 small bunch (about 6 ounces) black (aka Tuscan or dinosaur) kale, stems removed, leaves cut crosswise into ½-inch strips (about 3 cups)

6 ounces Mexican *queso fresco, panela* or *quesillo* or other fresh cheese, such as dryish fresh goat cheese, not-too-salty feta or fresh mozzarella, cut into roughly ½-inch cubes or coarsely shredded or crumbled

In a large (10-inch) skillet (I have a straight-sided one that works great here), cook the bacon over medium heat, stirring regularly, until crispy, about 10 minutes. Scoop out onto paper towels, leaving the fat behind. (If not using bacon, measure the oil into the pan.)

Raise the heat to medium-high and scrape the *adobo* into the bacon fat (or oil). Cook, stirring nearly constantly, for about 4 minutes to remove any raw flavor from the chile; as the sauce fries it will begin to look shiny. Stir in the broth, reduce the heat to medium-low and let the sauce come to a bare simmer.

While the sauce is heating, collect the potatoes in a microwavable bowl, splash with a couple tablespoons of water, cover tightly with plastic wrap, poke a few holes in the top and microwave at 100% until tender, about 3 minutes.

Taste and season the *gently* simmering sauce with salt (usually about ¼ teaspoon), then crack the eggs into it, each in its own quadrant (the fresher the eggs, the more compact they'll stay). Spoon some sauce over the eggs and use a spatula to gently loosen them from the bottom of the skillet. Cover the skillet and poach until the whites are set but the yolks are soft, about 5 minutes. Use a slotted spoon to scoop out the eggs onto a plate.

Raise the heat to medium-high, add the potatoes (leave any liquid behind) and kale to the pan and bring the sauce to a brisk simmer. Cook until the kale is tender, 6 to 7 minutes, and the sauce has thickened to the consistency of a light cream soup. Stir in *half* the bacon, then divide the mixture among 4 warm, deep plates. Top each with a poached egg, a spoonful of the remaining bacon and a sprinkling of cheese. Brunch is served.

Riffs on Eggs Poached with Ancho Chile:

The Quick Red Chile *Adobo* that gives this dish its character is so simple you can make it in 10 minutes. If, however, you don't have any pure powdered ancho chile, you can make a simple sauce from ancho pods by toasting 2 medium stemmed and seeded dried ancho chiles in a dry skillet for a minute or so (until very aromatic), breaking or tearing them into a blender and adding ⅔ cup boiling water, 2 peeled garlic cloves, a little Mexican oregano and ground black pepper. Loosely cover and blend until smooth, then cook that mixture in the bacon fat (or oil) until it's as thick as tomato paste and continue with the recipe.

Feel free to utilize other greens in this dish—anything from spinach to chard, collards, beet greens, even wild-harvested nettles in the spring.

QUICK RED CHILE *ADOBO*

Scoop **a scant ½ cup powdered ancho chile** into a blender or small food processor. Bring **1¼ cups water** to a boil, pour over the chile, *loosely cover* the blender or secure the top of the processor and pulse to blend thoroughly. In a small microwave-safe bowl, collect **8 peeled garlic cloves**, cover with water and microwave at 100% for 1 minute. Drain and add to the blender or processor, along with ½ **teaspoon ground cinnamon**, ¼ **teaspoon ground black pepper**, ⅛ **teaspoon ground cumin**, **1 teaspoon dried oregano**, **3 tablespoons apple cider vinegar** and **1½ teaspoons salt**. Process until smooth.

"Sturdy Greens" Salad with Mango
and Habanero (page 138)

"Sturdy Greens" Salad with Mango and Habanero

Ensalada de Quelites con Mango y Habanero

◇◇◇

know that some of you will roll your eyes at another massaged kale salad recipe, having lived through the few years during which you couldn't move without bumping into one. The kale fervor, of course, became tiring, as every pop culture craze does, and many of us found ourselves throwing out kale altogether (*so* last year) rather than remembering what made that salad so mouthwateringly attractive in the first place.

So I stand my ground at including this salad recipe here—made with kale, chard, beet greens or, if you're feeling particularly bold, spicy mustard greens, which are a great counterpoint to the sweet mangos. I won't say "It's good for you," because you already know that. I'll just say it's unexpectedly enticing: sweet, sour, spicy and satisfying. At our restaurant, during mango season we'll cycle this onto the menu, garnishing it with smoked homemade fresh cheese (*queso fresco*). Smoked or not, a wonderful creamy fresh cheese offers dimension.

Serves 4

½ fresh habanero chile, stemmed, seeded if you wish

3 garlic cloves, peeled

Zest (colored part only) of ½ orange

¼ cup fresh orange juice

⅓ cup fresh lime juice

½ cup olive oil

¼ cup agave nectar or honey

Salt

1 small white or red onion, thinly sliced

4 cups sliced (about ½ inch is good) sturdy greens (any of those mentioned above; you'll need to start with about 8 ounces of most greens, then pull off or cut out the stems or stalks before slicing)

2 cups (about 3 ounces) frisée leaves (if your frisée is in a head, cut out the core and tear the leaves into rough 1-inch pieces)

1 large ripe mango (I like the yellow-skin Ataulfo—honey Manila—mangos best for flavor and texture), peeled, flesh cut from the pit and chopped into ¼-inch pieces

2 tablespoons crumbled Mexican *queso fresco* or other fresh cheese such as feta or goat cheese

2 tablespoons pine nuts or slivered almonds, toasted lightly in a dry skillet over medium heat until golden and aromatic

In a small microwaveable dish, combine the habanero and garlic. Cover with water and microwave at 100% for 1 minute. Drain and transfer to a blender. Add the zest, juices, oil and agave (or honey). Blend into a smooth dressing. Taste and season highly with salt, usually about ½ teaspoon.

Scoop the onion into a small bowl and stir in a little of the dressing.

Place all the sturdy greens in a large bowl; use your fingers to massage them, making them more tender by breaking up the fibers, until the greens darken a little, 3 to 5 minutes. Add the onion and frisée to the greens. Drizzle on about 3 tablespoons of the dressing (the leftover dressing can be covered and refrigerated for another salad) and toss to coat the greens well. Taste and season with additional salt if you think it's necessary.

Divide the salad among 4 serving plates and spoon over each about a tablespoon of mango (the mango you don't use is yours to snack on). Sprinkle the salads with the cheese and nuts and they're ready to serve.

TRADITIONAL MEXICAN VEGETABLES, NEW IDEAS

Roasted Chayote with Herbs and Tofu (or Goat Cheese) **142**

Fresh Corn in Spicy-Herby Broth **144**

Herby, Spicy Fried Corn **146**

Steamed Roots with Roasted Poblano and Tomatillo **147**

Grilled Tostadas with Bacon, Avocado Mayo and Heirloom Tomatoes **150**

Pickled Tomatillo Salad with Little Gem Lettuce and Pumpkin Seeds **152**

Roasted Knob Onions with *Crema* and Aged Mexican Cheese **154**

Four Seasons Grilled Salad with Smoky Knob (or Green) Onions and Sesame **156**

Jícama-Beet Salad with Radicchio, Peanuts and Lime **160**

Nopal Cactus and Poached Egg in Roasted Tomato–Chipotle Broth **163**

Fresh Fava Bean *Enfrijoladas* **166**

Roasted Chayote with Herbs and Tofu (or Goat Cheese)

Chayote Asado con Hierbas y Tofu (o Queso de Cabra)

◇◇◇

Chayote, with its light, sweet flavor and juicy texture, leaves some people cold. But I contend that they simply don't understand how to bring all its positive attributes to the fore. High-heat roasting does the trick. Underscore it with herbs (use a big handful of cilantro, torn basil or torn sorrel if you can't make the green *adobo*) and a few drops of lime, then fill out the dish with tofu (we have an amazingly flavorful one here in Chicago made from local, organic soybeans) or crumbled goat cheese and you have a wonderful light meal. Served with warm, fresh tortillas, this makes a perfect taco filling, especially layered with black bean *refritos*; served over greens such as baby arugula or watercress, it becomes a robust salad.

Serves 2 as a light main dish, 4 as a side

4 large (about 2½ pounds total) chayotes, peeled if you wish, pitted and cut into ¾-inch chunks

2 tablespoons olive oil

Salt and cracked black pepper

3 tablespoons Green Chile *Adobo* (recipe follows)

2 tablespoons fresh lime (or lemon or other tart citrus) juice, plus a little finely grated zest (colored part only)

8 ounces (about ½ package) fresh silken tofu

OR 4 ounces fresh goat cheese (a not-too-briny feta works well too), broken into large chunks

Turn on the oven to 425 degrees and adjust the rack in the middle. (If your oven has a convection setting, this is a good time to turn it on.)

Toss the chayote with the olive oil and a generous amount of salt (usually about ½ teaspoon) and cracked pepper (usually about ¼ teaspoon). Spread it on a rimmed baking sheet, slide it into the oven and roast, turning the chayote every few minutes, until it is beautifully browned and tender, about 25 minutes.

Remove from the oven and toss with the Green Chile *Adobo*, lime juice and zest (or one of their stand-ins). Divide between warm serving plates and gently fold the tofu into the chayote with a spoon (if you're using cheese, scatter it on top). If you have any leftover parsley or cilantro, sprinkle some on each plate and you're ready to eat.

Riffs on Roasted Chayote with Herbs and Tofu:

If you're trying to go meatless but taking it one step at a time, you may want to add a little delicious cured pork. This dish is *really* good when you cook 4 slices of bacon that you have chopped, use a slotted spoon to remove them to a paper towel, then toss the chayote with the rendered fat instead of olive oil before roasting. Sprinkle the finished dish with the crispy bacon or with some browned chorizo.

GREEN CHILE *ADOBO*

Set a large (10-inch) skillet over medium heat and add ½ **head of garlic,** separated into cloves but not peeled, and **4 to 5 fresh serrano chiles**, stems removed. Roast, turning regularly, until soft and browned in spots, about 10 minutes for the chiles and 15 for the garlic. Cool, slip off the garlic's peels and give it all a rough chop (no need to remove the chile seeds). In a blender or food processor, combine the garlic and chiles with **1 large bunch cilantro**, roughly chopped; **1 large bunch flat-leaf parsley**, roughly chopped; **1 cup olive oil;** and **2 generous teaspoons salt**. Process, stopping to scrape down the sides if necessary, until nearly smooth (it should look a little like pesto).

Fresh Corn in Spicy-Herby Broth

Esquites Caldosos

◇◇◇

I think most folks in the United States would say that grilled corn on the cob is Mexico's most iconic street food, slathered with mayo (in the old days it used to be *crema*, which I still love) and sprinkled with sharp garnishing cheese and ground red chile. As tasty as that is, it's eclipsed by another street corn dish in much of Mexico: a brothy cup of corn kernels simmered with big handfuls of herby epazote. There's often mayo in this version, too, but stirred into the broth, making it creamy, along with a squeeze of lime. The chile can be fresh and green and simmered with the corn, or it can be dried and powdered and sprinkled on, along with the delicious hit of crumbled *fresco* cheese.

But what is it, this street food called *esquites*? A soup? A side dish? North of the border, it's hard to wrap our heads around it. So I just call it a juicy, lazy-guy's version of corn on the cob—no need to chew the kernels from the cob or find a beverage to wash them down. It's all right there to enjoy with a spoon, all the classic Mexican corn-on-the-cob flavors included.

Serves 4 as a snack or side dish

4 large ears corn, husked, silks pulled off

A handful of fresh corn husks

2 big sprigs of epazote (about 12 leaves), if you have them
OR a big handful of flat-leaf parsley or cilantro leaves

2 fresh serrano chiles or 1 large fresh jalapeño, stemmed, seeded and cut into small pieces

Salt

½ cup mayonnaise, for serving

½ cup crumbled Mexican *queso fresco* or other fresh cheese such as feta or goat cheese, for serving

1 or 2 limes, cut into wedges, for serving

Cut the kernels from the ears of corn. Break the newly stripped cobs in half and add them to a large (4-quart) saucepan or medium soup pot. Add the corn husks to the pot and enough water to cover by 1 inch. Bring to a boil, then simmer, partially covered, for 30 minutes to create a corn-infused broth. Pick out the husks and cobs and discard.

Add the corn, epazote (or parsley; if using cilantro, add it at the end), chiles and 1 teaspoon salt to the pot. Return to a simmer and cook, partially covered, for a few minutes (30 minutes will give you good flavor if you have that much time). Check the mixture's consistency: there should be enough broth to cover the corn completely. If there isn't, add enough water to bring it to that level. Taste and add more salt if you think it needs it. (Add the cilantro now, if that's the herb you're using.) Divide the mixture among 4 small bowls. Serve with the mayonnaise, cheese and lime wedges for each guest to add *al gusto*.

A CORN-CUTTING TIP

Flip a small bowl upside down and set it in a very large bowl. Stand a husked ear of corn on the overturned bowl and use a sharp knife to shave the kernels off the cob. The kernels will collect in the bigger bowl, not on the floor.

Herby, Spicy Fried Corn

Esquites Fritos

◇◇◇

As puzzling as it is for most Americans to categorize the brothy *esquites caldosos*, the fried version is easy to figure out. It's basically just fried corn, but not the kind that's spooned alongside that meatloaf I grew up on. No, this version, with its classic flavor of chile, is spooned into cups by street vendors all over Mexico for us to snack on while listening to corner accordion players or searching out bargains from the guys who have carved wooden bowls or the ladies who've made those folkloric-looking little dolls.

Makes about 3 cups, serving 4 to 6 as a side dish

2 tablespoons freshly rendered pork lard, bacon drippings, olive oil or vegetable oil

3 cups fresh corn kernels (just cut from the cob)—you'll need 3 or 4 large ears corn

1 fresh serrano chile, seeded if you wish and finely chopped

3 tablespoons chopped epazote leaves (or cilantro or flat-leaf parsley, if no epazote is available)

Salt

A generous ½ cup crumbled Mexican *queso fresco* or other fresh cheese such as feta or goat cheese

Lime wedges, for serving

In a large (10-inch) skillet, heat the lard (or one of its stand-ins) over medium-high until you see the first wisp of smoke. Add the corn and chile and cook, stirring regularly, until both are richly browned, about 5 minutes. Add the epazote (or cilantro or parsley), stir a few more times, then scrape into a serving bowl. Season with salt (usually ½ teaspoon) and crumble the cheese on top. Serve with wedges of lime for you and your guests to squeeze on *al gusto*.

Steamed Roots with Roasted Poblano and Tomatillo

Camotes de Diferentes Variedades con Chile Poblano y Tomate Verde

◇◇

Potatoes with roasted poblanos, and perhaps a little caramelized onion woven in for natural sweetness, is a frequent and always welcome filling for tacos in Mexico. I like them with a lot of poblano, a big spoonful of herby roasted tomatillo salsa and some *crema* or salty-fresh *fresco* cheese And good tortillas, of course. It's hard to make great tacos with less-than-great tortillas.

This is also good served alongside scrambled or sunny-side-up eggs. Or carried on a picnic to serve cool with roast chicken or pork.

Here I'm taking the blinders off that classic Mexican potato-poblano taco filling: I'm opening it up to welcome a variety of large meaty chiles and any root vegetable that's white—anything from sweet parsnips and white sweet potato to earthy turnips, rutabaga and *ñame* (red beets, orange carrots and the like aren't great with green chiles, in my opinion). And I've combined the salsa with fresh-tasting dairy. Greek yogurt adds a distinctive and beautiful brightness, though of course you can use Mexican *crema*, sour cream or *crème fraîche*, if that appeals more.

Serves 4

1 medium onion, sliced ¼-inch thick

3 large (about 12 ounces) fresh red or green poblano chiles
OR about 12 ounces any fresh chile/pepper that you'd roast—think Anaheims, New Mexicos, cubanelles, lipsticks, anything that's large and thick-fleshed enough (and, for me, medium spicy) to roast and peel

4 unpeeled garlic cloves

8 ounces (3 to 4 medium) fresh tomatillos, husked and rinsed

1 pound boiling potatoes (I prefer Yukon Gold or something waxy like red-skins), parsnips, white-fleshed sweet potatoes, small (mild) turnips, rutabaga, taro or *ñame* (a kind of yam), peeled and cut into ½-inch pieces

Salt

About ¼ cup roughly chopped cilantro

3 tablespoons Greek-style yogurt

Turn on the broiler and adjust the rack to its highest setting. Spread the onion, chiles, garlic and tomatillos on a rimmed baking sheet. Slide into the oven and roast, turning everything regularly, until the chiles are blistered and blackened all over, the garlic is soft, the onions are lightly caramelized and the tomatillos are darkened and soft, about 10 minutes. Remove and cool.

Scoop the potatoes (or whichever root vegetable you've chosen) into a microwave-safe bowl, sprinkle with 2 tablespoons water, cover with plastic wrap, poke a few holes in the top and microwave at 100% until completely tender, about 5 minutes for potatoes and parsnips, slightly longer for the denser vegetables. Carefully uncover (steam will escape!), tip off any water and roughly mash the vegetables with an old-fashioned potato masher, large fork or whatever's at hand that will do the job.

When the chiles are cool enough to handle, rub off the skin, pull out the stems and seedpods, then briefly rinse to remove stray seeds and bits of skin. Chop into ¼-inch pieces, set aside ¼ *cup* to use in the salsa, then scrape the rest in with the root vegetable. Chop the onion, too, add it to the bowl and stir everything together. Taste and season with salt, usually about 1 teaspoon.

Peel the garlic and scoop it into a blender with the tomatillos (plus any juice they've exuded) and the reserved roasted chile. Blend to a coarse puree, then measure in the cilantro and yogurt. Pulse to combine, scrape into a serving bowl and season with salt (it usually takes ½ teaspoon).

Warm the filling in the microwave (1 minute at 50% power) and serve with the salsa, plus, of course, a stack of warm tortillas if you're making tacos.

Grilled Tostadas with Bacon, Avocado Mayo
and Heirloom Tomatoes (page I50)

Grilled Tostadas with Bacon, Avocado Mayo and Heirloom Tomatoes

Tostadas Asadas a la Parilla con Tocino, Mayonesa de Aguacate y Tomates "Heirloom"

◇◇◇

About the most compelling dish in Oaxaca—a region of compelling dishes—is a *tlayuda*. Huge leathery corn tortillas are crisped on a charcoal fire, brushed with the roasty-flavored dark lard called *asiento*, splashed with salsa (plus or minus brothy beans) and strewn with chorizo or pork *cecina* or beef *tasajo*. It's smoky, rustic and appealing beyond words. Nobody doesn't love a good *tlayuda*.

Back in the States, a good *tlayuda* is almost unreachable, unless you live in parts of Los Angeles or other places where lots of Oaxaqueños have imported those special tortillas. They're made from corn that's perfect (unlike our American corn) for creating that unique size and texture. But we can lift a page from Oaxaca's playbook and grill tortillas to crispiness, giving them touches of rustic char, then brush them with a little fat and top them with things that make sense where we live. In the summer, I basically create BLT flavors, focusing on great bacon and heirloom tomatoes. An avocado mayo with a good amount of cilantro finishes my midwestern tostada by way of Oaxaca.

Serves 4 to 6

12 good corn tortillas (it's best to use factory-made tortillas here, especially ones meant for serving at the table, not the super-thin, coarse-ground kind that are best for frying into chips)

2 egg yolks

1 tablespoon fresh lime juice

1 cup vegetable oil

½ avocado, flesh scooped from the skin and roughly chopped

Fresh hot green chile to taste (1 to 2 serranos or 2 to 3 jalapeños), seeds removed if you wish, chopped into small pieces

About ¼ cup finely chopped cilantro, plus a few leaves for garnish

Salt

About 10 thick slices (10 ounces) bacon, cut crosswise into ½-inch pieces

A generous pound of mixed heirloom tomatoes (different colors and sizes will make your finished dish more interesting), cored, seeded if you wish, cut into ¼-inch slices or pieces

Lay the tortillas in a single layer, cover with a dish towel or napkin and let them dry for about 30 minutes (depending on their moistness) until they are leathery. This will enable them to crisp thoroughly on the grill.

Meanwhile, in a food processor or blender, combine the egg yolks and lime juice and pulse until blended. With the machine running, slowly drizzle in the oil (the yolks and oil should emulsify and become creamy). Turn the machine off, add the avocado, green chile and cilantro and run the processor or blender for another 20 seconds to ensure that these ingredients are incorporated. You may have to stop the machine once or twice to scrape down the sides. Taste and season with salt, usually about 1 teaspoon. Scrape the mayonnaise into a bowl and set aside.

In a large (10-inch) skillet set over medium heat, cook the bacon, stirring occasionally, until crispy, about 10 minutes. Remove the bacon and drain on paper towels. Pour the fat into a small bowl. You need about ¼ cup bacon fat; if you don't have that much, add vegetable oil to bring it to that quantity.

When the tortillas are ready, turn on a gas grill to medium or light a charcoal fire and let the coals burn until medium hot and covered with gray ash. When you're about ready to serve, lay several tortillas on the grill and turn every 20 seconds or so until they're golden brown all over and cracker-crisp; this will take 5 to 10 minutes, depending on the heat of your fire. Brush the top of each tortilla generously with the bacon fat and let the tortillas crisp a little longer, then remove them to a serving platter. Spread on some spicy avocado mayo and top with a portion of the tomatoes. Sprinkle each tostada with about 1 tablespoon bacon, garnish with cilantro leaves and immediately serve to your guests while you make the next round.

Riffs on Grilled Tostadas:

Sky's the limit here, once you've crisped your tortillas on the grill. I always choose something creamy (avocado mayo, guacamole, mashed beans), then add a vegetable (grilled zucchini or eggplant, snow peas or broccolini or baby artichokes, everything cut into small pieces), then something meaty (coarsely shredded chicken, chorizo sausage, shrimp, leftover shreds of roast). Then maybe I splash on a salsa and, occasionally, sprinkle on fresh cheese (Mexican *queso fresco*, crumbled goat cheese, dryish feta). Really, the sky *is* the limit.

Pickled Tomatillo Salad with Little Gem Lettuce and Pumpkin Seeds

Tomates Verdes Encurtidos con Lechuguita Orejona y Pepitas

◇◇

I never expected that I'd be able to put one of our full-on restaurant recipes in a book about simple, dynamic dishes for the home kitchen. But here it is: the Frontera salad, just the way we've done it for a few years now. And none of us wants to change it, because we can't think of anything better than sweet-sour pickled tomatillos, a creamy, citrusy dressing and my favorite little romainelike leaf. (Feel free to use any lettuce you like, though one with a crunchy texture works well with the tomatillos.)

This salad isn't the only place that pickled tomatillos work—their distinctive tang is great in lots of other salads, or even tucked into sandwiches. To have extras on hand, double the recipe and keep the remainders in a jar, immersed in the vinegar, in the refrigerator; they'll be good for at least a week. No matter what size batch you go with, the tomatillos require a little planning, because they take a minimum of 6 hours to pickle. Start them in the morning before work or, if you're really thinking ahead, the night before.

Serves 4

For the pickled tomatillos:

⅔ cup sugar

Salt

3 tablespoons light vinegar (I like rice wine vinegar here)

8 ounces (3 to 4 medium) tomatillos, husked, rinsed and cut into eighths

For the dressing:

½ cup fresh lime juice

¾ cup (3 ounces) toasted pumpkin seeds (*pepitas*), plus a few tablespoons more for sprinkling over the salad

½ to 1 small fresh serrano chile, stemmed, seeded and roughly chopped

¼ cup vegetable or olive oil

Salt

4 medium heads Little Gem lettuce, leaves separated

OR 2 hearts of romaine, leaves separated, larger ones torn into smaller pieces

OR 1 large head Boston or Bibb lettuce, leaves separated

2 to 3 tablespoons grated Mexican *queso añejo* or other garnishing cheese such as Romano or Parmesan

In a small saucepan, combine ⅔ cup water, the sugar and 4 teaspoons salt. Set over high heat. Swirl the pan until the sugar is dissolved, then remove from the heat and stir in the vinegar. When cooled to room temperature, add the tomatillos. Transfer to a resealable 1-quart plastic bag, press out the air, seal and refrigerate for 6 hours or, better, overnight.

To make the dressing, pour the lime juice and 2 tablespoons water into a blender. Add the pumpkin seeds and chile and blend until smooth; then, with the motor running, drizzle in the oil. (If you happen to have it, this is a great place to add a teaspoon or so of dark pumpkin seed oil.) Taste and season with salt, usually about ½ teaspoon.

Drain the tomatillos. In a large bowl, toss the lettuce with 2 to 3 tablespoons of the dressing and the cheese, coating all the leaves evenly. (Refrigerate the remaining dressing, covered, for another salad; it will last for several weeks.) Divide between 4 salad plates, sprinkle with the pickled tomatillos and a few pumpkin seeds and serve right away.

Pickled Tomatillo Salad as a Passed Appetizer:

When you want something delicious and light to pass around at a party or the beginning of a nice dinner, choose small inner leaves of Little Gem or Boston lettuce and line them up on a platter. Slice more leaves crosswise a little wider than ¼ inch. Toss with dressing and cheese, then divide the sliced lettuce "salad" among the leaves on the platter. Top each with small pieces of pickled tomatillos, a little more cheese and a few pumpkin seeds. This is one of my favorite bites to serve as a snack with drinks.

Roasted Knob Onions with Crema and Aged Mexican Cheese

Cebollitas Rostizadas con Crema y Queso Añejo

◇◇

I f you think of this dish as a distant cousin of those creamy Thanksgiving pearl onions, you'll be on the right track. Knob onions are a little bigger and fresher than pearl onions (and don't have to be peeled!), and the cultured cream and aged garnishing cheese make them taste more dynamic. Sure, they're rich, but put them on the table with a taco (or turkey, or steak) feast and nobody will complain. I've left this recipe chile-neutral, because I think of it as a "go with" dish. You could easily stir in a little chopped fresh serrano or jalapeño or some canned chipotle chile *en adobo* to add greater definition to the flavor.

Serves 4 as a side dish

2 pounds (4 to 6 bunches, about 15 onions total) knob onions, 1 to 2 inches in diameter, trimmed of roots and withered leaves

2 tablespoons olive oil, butter, freshly rendered pork lard or bacon drippings

¼ cup Mexican *crema*, *crème fraîche* or heavy cream

3 tablespoons grated Mexican *queso añejo* or other garnishing cheese such as Romano or Parmesan

Salt

Turn on the oven to 425 degrees. Cut the white knobs from the onions where they connect to the greens. Separate a small handful of the green parts, cut them crosswise into ¼-inch pieces and set aside. Cover and refrigerate the remaining greens for another dish (they are delicious in scrambled eggs and potato soup).

Heat the oil (or its stand-in) over medium in a large (10-inch) skillet with a heatproof handle. When hot, add the onion bulbs and cook, shaking the skillet and turning them regularly, until you notice the first sign of browning, about 3 minutes. Immediately slide the skillet into the oven and roast, shaking the skillet every couple of minutes to turn the onions, until they're richly browned and tender but still retain a little crunch, 15 to 20 minutes.

Remove from the oven, add the *crema* (or one of its stand-ins) and chopped green onion tops, and set over medium heat. Stir regularly, spooning the *crema* over the onions, until the *crema* has taken on some of the onions' golden color and reduced enough to coat the onions richly. Stir in the cheese, taste and season with a generous sprinkling of salt. Scrape into a bowl and they're ready to serve.

Four Seasons Grilled Salad with Smoky Knob (or Green) Onions and Sesame

Ensalada a la Parilla "Cuatro Estaciones" con Cebollitas Ahumaditas y Ajonjolí

◇◇

In this recipe, I describe how to make a delicious year-round dressing, one that starts by developing flavor with green onions (and I hope you'll find the bulbous ones common in Mexican groceries and farmers' markets, the ones we call knob onions). The white part is used fresh for sparkle; the green part turns sweet and smoky when grilled. Add a chipotle chile, some toasty-nutty sesame seeds and sesame oil, a little dark vinegar and a few cloves of sweet garlic, and you have a dressing that makes anything you've grilled—vegetables, fish, chicken—taste even better. And yes, I grill in the winter, but usually on a grill pan in the warmth of my kitchen. That's when I make this salad with the ever-available chayote. In summer I grill tomatoes outside as the salad's main focus. In fall it's beets (sometimes I use sliced butternut, too). And in spring, though it doesn't sound typically Mexican, I fire up the charcoal and make this salad with our local asparagus.

Serves 4

3 garlic cloves, peeled

1 to 2 chipotle chiles *en adobo*, stemmed, seeded and roughly chopped

½ cup vegetable or olive oil, plus a little extra for grilling the vegetables

2 teaspoons toasted sesame oil

¼ cup balsamic or sweet sherry vinegar OR 3 tablespoons red wine vinegar plus 1 tablespoon Worcestershire sauce

Salt

2 knob onions (ones with a 1-inch bulb have the best taste and texture, in my opinion) or green onions, trimmed of roots and withered leaves removed

2 pounds (about 4 medium-large) firm-ripe round tomatoes, cored and sliced ½-inch thick

OR 2 pounds (about 8 medium-small) any color beets, peeled and sliced ¼-inch thick

OR 1 pound asparagus, woody bottom sections cut off

OR 2 pounds (about 4 medium) chayote, peeled if you wish, pitted and sliced ¼-inch thick

A couple tablespoons toasted sesame seeds (either buy them toasted—easily available at Asian groceries—or toast them over medium heat in a small dry skillet, stirring until golden and aromatic), for serving

Place the garlic in a small, microwave-safe dish, cover with water and microwave at 100% for 1 minute. In a blender, combine the garlic, chipotles, oils and vinegar (and Worcestershire sauce if you're using it). Blend until smooth and pour into a small bowl. Taste and season highly with salt, usually a scant teaspoon.

Heat one side of a gas grill to medium-high and the other side to low, or light a charcoal fire and let it burn until the charcoal is medium-hot and covered with white ash; bank most of the coals to one side. Cut the onions in two where the green meets the white. Thinly slice the white, scoop into a small bowl and stir in the dressing. Using a brush or an oil sprayer, lightly oil the green onion tops and both sides of each vegetable slice or all the asparagus. First grill the onion tops, starting them on the hot side of the grill to brown, then moving them to the cooler side to coast along to a beautifully soft sweetness. Chop them into ¼-inch pieces and add to the dressing bowl. Next, sprinkle both sides of the vegetable pieces or the asparagus with salt and grill them. I grill the tomatoes on the hottest part of the grill, 1 to 2 minutes per side, making sure they're well oiled (if the tomatoes are soft-ripe, they are harder to work with on the grill). I grill all the other vegetables until richly grill-marked on both sides, then I move them to the cool side of the grill and let them cook until as soft as I like, usually about 5 minutes for the asparagus, slightly longer for the beets and chayote. (If you're using a grill pan, heat it over medium-high and cook the vegetables until richly grill-marked, then transfer them to a rimmed baking sheet in a 325-degree oven to finish cooking.)

Arrange a portion of the grilled vegetable (warm or cooled to room temperature) on each of 4 plates. Stir the dressing and onions well and spoon on as much as you like (cover and refrigerate the rest for another salad). Sprinkle with the toasted sesame seeds and you're ready to eat.

Riffs on Four Seasons Grilled Salad:

When the salad needs to play a role larger than side dish, I add a big handful of coarsely crumbled Mexican *queso fresco* or *panela*, goat cheese or tofu. If greens are an essential when you think of salad, nestle the grilled vegetable in a bed of watercress, baby wild arugula, torn frisée, mesclun greens or the like. Though some of you may cry "cultural whiplash" when I say this, any of the four versions (with or without the cheese/tofu) is delicious over steamed rice.

Jícama-Beet Salad with Radicchio,
Peanuts and Lime (page 160)

Jícama-Beet Salad with Radicchio, Peanuts and Lime

Ensalada de Jícama, Betabel, Radicchio, Cacahuates y Limón

A t Frontera, this kind of salad, inspired by Mexico's classic Christmas Eve salad, shows up only on our holiday menus. Which, of course, is too narrow a window of enjoyment for a combination this enticing. The classic salad includes romaine (instead of radicchio) and orange or tangerine (instead of just lime). You can do the same if you wish, though I encourage you to try this deliciously sophisticated cousin first. The unrefined peanut oil (which, unlike the refined stuff, tastes strongly of peanuts) is worth seeking out.

Makes 6 cups, serving 6

1 pound (about 4 medium) any color beets, peeled and cut into French fry–size batons (in chef-speak)

2 tablespoons olive oil or unrefined peanut oil (I really like the peanutiness of Spectrum brand unrefined peanut oil)

2 tablespoons fresh lime juice plus a little finely grated lime zest (colored part only)

About 1 teaspoon agave nectar (optional)

Salt

½ pound (about ½ medium) jícama, peeled and cut into batons that match the beets

½ head (about 5 ounces) radicchio, cored and sliced crosswise about ¼-inch thick

A generous ¼ cup roasted peanuts, roughly chopped

Scoop the beets into a microwave-safe bowl, sprinkle on a couple tablespoons of water, cover tightly with plastic wrap, poke a few holes in the top and microwave at 100% for about 3 minutes, until the beets are tender but not falling apart. While the beets are cooking, in a small bowl whisk together the oil, lime juice and zest and agave nectar (if you're using it). Taste and season highly with salt, usually about ½ teaspoon. Uncover the beets, tip off the water, spoon on *half* the dressing and toss to coat the beets well. Cool completely.

In a large bowl, combine the beets (and any pooled dressing), jícama and radicchio. Whisk the remaining dressing again, then drizzle it over the salad and toss to combine. Divide among 6 plates, sprinkle with the peanuts and a little salt, and the salad's ready.

Nopal Cactus and Poached Egg in Roasted
Tomato–Chipotle Broth (page 163)

Nopal Cactus and Poached Egg in Roasted Tomato–Chipotle Broth

Nopales Navegantes

◇◇◇

This *nopales* "soup,"—with a beefy red chile broth punctuated by bits of tangy cactus and crunchy onion, is a wonderful excuse to visit a Mexican grocery store (which is still the most likely place to find *nopal* cactus paddles). It's also a great reason to expand your *nopales* horizons and move beyond the simple, ubiquitous cactus salad. When you break into the poached egg, the yolk beautifully enriches the broth as it does in every classic Spanish (and Mexican) garlic soup. I love the richness of beef broth here, but feel free to make the soup vegetarian by using vegetable broth.

Makes 6 cups, serving 4 as a substantial starter or light main dish

1 pound (4 to 6 medium) uncleaned fresh *nopal* cactus paddles, cleaned of their spines (see page 164 for directions on how to clean them)
  OR 12 ounces cleaned fresh *nopal* cactus paddles (many Mexican groceries sell them cleaned)

1 large onion, sliced about ⅛-inch thick

2 tablespoons vegetable or olive oil

One 15-ounce can fire-roasted tomatoes, drained

1 to 2 chipotle chiles *en adobo* (use 2 only if you want the soup really spicy)

2 garlic cloves, peeled and roughly chopped

1 quart beef broth

Salt

4 large eggs

1 cup broken tortilla chips, for serving

Flat-leaf parsley or cilantro leaves, if you have them, for serving

Cut the *nopal* cactus into strips a little narrower than ½ inch, then cut the strips into 2-inch lengths. In a medium-large (6-quart) Dutch oven or wide soup pot (it needs to be about 10 inches across to accommodate the egg poaching), combine the *nopal* and onion, then drizzle with the oil and mix to coat. Set over medium heat, cover the pot and cook for about 4 minutes. Uncover and take a look—the mixture will probably look a little sticky. Continue to cook, stirring regularly, until all the sticky stuff has evaporated and the mixture is sizzling in the oil and beginning to brown, about 5 minutes.

While the cactus is cooking, combine the tomatoes, chipotles and garlic in a blender jar and blend to a smooth puree. Add it to the cooked cactus mixture along with the broth. Bring to a boil over high heat, then reduce the heat and simmer for 15 minutes minimum, though I like the soup best after the flavors have simmered together for 45 minutes to an hour. Taste and season with salt, usually about 1 teaspoon, depending on the saltiness of your broth.

Just before serving, crack the eggs into the *barely* simmering soup, each in its own quadrant (the fresher the eggs, the more compact they'll stay). Spoon some of the soup over the eggs and use a spatula to gently loosen them from the bottom of pot. Cover the pot and poach until the whites are set but the yolks are soft, about 5 minutes. (Test doneness by lifting an egg out of the liquid with a slotted spoon and touching it for firmness). When the eggs are ready, use a slotted spoon to scoop each into a warm, deep soup plate or bowl. Ladle on a portion of the soup, garnish with a handful of chips and a sprinkling of herbs if you're using them. Carry to the table without hesitation.

CLEANING CACTUS PADDLES

Hold the cactus paddle carefully between the nodes of the prickly spines—they're sharper than they look!—and trim off the edge that outlines the paddle, including the blunt end where it was cut from the plant. Slice or scrape off the spiny nodes from both sides. The paddle is now ready to slice whatever way you like.

Fresh Fava Bean
Enfrijoladas (page 166)

Fresh Fava Bean *Enfrijoladas*

Enfrijoladas de Haba Fresca

◇◇◇

Think of anything called an *enfrijolada* as an enchilada finished with a bean sauce, rather than one made of dried chiles, say, or tomatillos. *Enfrijoladas* are incredibly soul-satisfying: corn tortillas rolled around a filling (or not), doused with any kind of bean sauce, and served with a little something dynamic on top. Since corn and beans combine to form a complete protein, this is a perfect recipe for when you're going meatless. (Though I rarely think about food as a jumble of macronutrients, eating all-vegetable meals that offer complete protein satisfies me longer.) Beyond that, I've given you several filling options, from spinach and scrambled eggs to meaty chicken.

And about those favas: they're not beans in the Mexican sense, since they're not from the *phaseolus vulgaris* species that's native there. Favas and lentils and chickpeas were all brought by the Spaniards and are from completely different species. Somehow, though, they got lumped together linguistically with beans from the New World. It surprises me that I've never had *enfrijoladas* made with fresh fava bean sauce in Mexico. It seems like a natural.

Lately I've seen vacuum-sealed, all-natural cooked fresh fava beans in the refrigerated case of my natural foods grocery. This is a perfect place to use them. And because you don't have to peel off the outer skin of the favas, you get to capture the flavor of the fresh beans without much work.

When I start with fresh favas in their big pod, I buy a generous 3 pounds, break open the pod, remove the fava beans and blanch them in salted water for about 3 minutes, until they're just tender.

Serves 4

4 garlic cloves, peeled

About 1 pound (2½ cups) cooked fresh fava beans (my grocery sells them in the produce department in ½-pound, vacuum-sealed pouches—no need to remove the light-colored outer skin from each bean)

Salt

2 tablespoons olive oil, butter, freshly rendered pork lard or bacon drippings

1 large onion, sliced ¼-inch thick

12 ounces (about 10 cups loosely packed) spinach, stems removed and cut roughly into 1-inch pieces

OR 8 large eggs
OR about 2 cups coarsely shredded
roasted or grilled chicken
12 corn tortillas
A little vegetable oil for the tortillas
Mexican hot sauce (like Tamazula or
Valentina, or choose your favorite hot
sauce), for serving

2 to 3 cups loosely packed fresh greens
(sliced romaine hearts, wild arugula,
sturdy mesclun mix, torn frisée,
watercress tops and cilantro leaves are
all good here)
About ½ cup grated Mexican *queso añejo*
or other garnishing cheese such as
Romano or Parmesan

Place the garlic in a small microwave-safe bowl, cover with water and microwave at
100% for 1 minute. Drain and scoop into a blender jar. Add the fava beans and 3 cups
water. Blend until smooth, then pour into a large (4-quart) saucepan. Bring to a boil
over high heat, reduce the heat to medium-low, partially cover and simmer 15 minutes.
Taste and season with salt, usually a generous teaspoon.

In a large (10-inch) skillet, make your filling of choice: Heat the oil or other fat over
medium (if you're using eggs, a nonstick skillet is highly recommended). Add the onion
and cook, stirring regularly, until the onion is soft and richly caramelized, about 10
minutes. If you're using spinach, stir it in, let it cook for a minute, then remove from the
heat and season with salt, usually about a scant ½ teaspoon. If you're using eggs, crack
in the eggs, break the yolks, sprinkle with a scant ½ teaspoon salt, then start to stir
the mixture slowly as the eggs scramble to your perfect doneness; immediately remove
from the heat. If using chicken, remove the onions from the heat and stir in the chicken;
season with salt, usually about ¼ teaspoon.

When you're ready to serve, reheat the sauce to a simmer and set the filling over
low heat. The sauce should be the consistency of a light cream soup; if it isn't, add
water to reach that consistency. Brush (or spray) both sides of each tortilla with a little oil, slide them into a plastic bag, fold over (don't seal) and microwave at 100% for 1
minute. Let stand 1 minute, then make the *enfrijoladas* and serve without hesitation:
lay 3 tortillas on your work surface, spoon a portion of the filling down the center
of each one, roll them up and arrange on a warm dinner plate. Ladle sauce over and
around the filled tortillas (cover every bit of the tortillas to keep them from drying
out). Garnish with splashes of hot sauce, a few greens and a dusting of cheese.
Enfrijoladas wait for no one.

Riffs on *Enfrijoladas*:

I make white bean *enfrijoladas* with canned beans (cannellinis are particularly good): replace the cooked favas with 2 drained 15-ounce cans of white beans. Garbanzos can replace the white beans which are replacing the favas. In my farmers' market, what are called shell beans are sold most of the summer. They're fully mature beans that are still in their pods—they look like overgrown green beans. But their texture (and flavor) is fresh, not dried. Most cooks find them a real pain to work with, since you have to buy and shell about 3 or 4 pounds to get the 2½ cups you need for the sauce (a mindless task to do while you're watching television). The shelled beans need to be cooked in boiling water as you would the just-shucked fresh favas.

WINTER SQUASH, SUMMER SQUASH, BLOSSOMS AND A RELATIVE

Butternut with Bacon, Tomatillo and Chipotle **174**

Weekend Dish: Fettuccine with Butternut Squash and Red Poblano *Crema* **177**

Kuri (or Butternut or Pumpkin) Soup with Ancho and Apple **180**

Pan-Roasted Summer Squash with Garlic *Mojo* and Güero Chile **182**

Spaghetti Squash *Fideos* with Chipotle, Chorizo, *Crema* and Avocado **185**

Charred Cucumber Salad with Red Chile and Lime **188**

Squash Blossom Soup **190**

Ribbon Salad with Creamy Two-Chile *Vinagreta* **192**

WHERE HAVE ALL THE TACOS GONE?

To quote Secondo from *Big Night*, one of the greatest food movies in my opinion, "Sometimes the spaghetti wants to be alone." Sometimes it doesn't need the meatballs. Sometimes the barbeque doesn't benefit from the bun. Sometimes the taco filling doesn't gain from being wrapped in the tortilla.

That's why I've chosen not to fill the section of vegetable-centric recipes with titles like "Tacos of Greens and Beans with Red Chile" or "Tacos of Charred Summer Squash with Roasted Garlic *Mojo*" in spite of the fact that, depending on your mood and menu, the end result of well over half of what I've included here could be wrapped in a tortilla and very legitimately called a taco. And it would be a damn good one.

So when Taco Tuesday rolls around, I encourage you to be creative. Think beyond the steak, chicken or ground beef, and know that delicious tacos can be made from a lot of preparations. To get you started, here is a list of dishes included in these pages that I think are particularly good served as tacos:

Creamy Roasted Poblano *Rajas* (page 47)
Skillet Tacos (page 93)
Greens and Beans with Red Chile and Fresh Cheese (Page 126)
Roasted Chayote with Herbs and Tofu (or Goat Cheese) (page 142)
Steamed Roots with Roasted Poblano and Tomatillo (page 147)
Pan-Roasted Summer Squash with Garlic *Mojo* and Güero Chile (page 182)
Shell Beans and Artichokes with Roasted Tomatillos, Cilantro and *Añejo* Cheese (page 201)
Yellow *Mole* with Grilled Fennel and Portobello Mushrooms (page 204)
Tangy Sorrel *Salsa Verde* with Stir-Fried Shrimp (page 210)
Braised Artichokes with Tomatoes, Jalapeños, Olives and Capers (page 218)
Pork Carnitas Dinner (page 280)
Green Chile–Braised Beef with Potatoes and Caramelized Onions (page 291)
Lamb or Beef *Barbacoa* (page 294)
Slow-Grilled Pork Shoulder with Ancho Barbecue Sauce (page 300)
Green Chile Chicken Thighs (page 305)
Chicken *Barbacoa* (page 324)

Butternut with Bacon, Tomatillo and Chipotle (page 174)

Butternut with Bacon, Tomatillo and Chipotle

Calabaza Enchipotlada

◇◇

Here's what I consider a perfect light dinner: this tangy, sweet-and-smoky, soul-satis-fying butternut braise accompanied by a simple salad and a few slices of soft-ripened goat cheese from our local Prairie Fruits Farm, or maybe cheddar from Wisconsin's Pleasant Ridge. The butternut braise is remarkably easy to make. And it's comfortable in a variety of roles, from support for a grilled pork chop or chicken breast to a special-occasion side dish on the Thanksgiving table.

Serves 2 to 3 as a main course, 4 to 6 as a side dish

3 garlic cloves, peeled

8 ounces (3 to 4 medium) tomatillos, husked, rinsed and cut in half around the equator

1 to 2 canned chipotle chiles *en adobo*, stemmed

½ small (2-pound) butternut squash, peeled, seeded and cut into 1-inch chunks (about 3 cups)

2 to 4 thick slices (2 to 4 ounces) bacon, cut crosswise into ½-inch pieces

Salt

About 1 tablespoon grated Mexican *queso añejo* or other garnishing cheese such as Romano or Parmesan

Set a large (10-inch) skillet (nonstick or lined with foil) over medium-high heat and lay in the garlic and tomatillos, cut side down. When the tomatillos are well browned, about 4 minutes, flip everything over and brown the other side. (The tomatillos and garlic should be soft.)

In a blender, combine the garlic, tomatillos, chipotles and 1 cup water. Blend to a coarse puree.

Place the butternut pieces in a microwave-safe bowl, cover tightly with plastic wrap, poke a few holes in the top and microwave at 100% for 4 minutes, until about halfway cooked. Meanwhile, in a large (10-inch) skillet (use the tomatillo skillet, cleaning it if necessary) set over medium heat, cook the bacon, stirring occasionally, until crispy, about 10 minutes. Add the butternut and tomatillo sauce to the pan, raise the heat to medium-high and bring the sauce to a brisk simmer. Cook until the butternut is fork-tender and the sauce has reduced by about half its volume, 10 to 15 minutes. Taste and season with salt (it will need only about ¼ teaspoon because of the bacon's saltiness). Scrape into a serving bowl and finish with a generous sprinkling of the *queso*.

Riffs on Butternut with Bacon, Tomatillo and Chipotle:

Though this is sweet, creamy, and delicious with butternut, it's also great made with pumpkin (especially pie pumpkin), red kuri, kabocha, dumpling, acorn or delicata squash; you need about 3 cups of peeled cubes. Not in the bacon-makes-everything-better camp? This dish is very good without it.

Fettuccine with Butternut Squash and
Red Poblano *Crema* (page 177)

Weekend Dish: Fettuccine with Butternut Squash and Red Poblano Crema

Pasta con Calabaza, Chile Poblano Rojo y Crema

◇◈

This recipe is on the rich side and requires a little dedication, which is why I've labeled it a Weekend Dish. First you have to thin-slice the neck of a butternut squash so that it resembles fettuccine, then you make a sauce of roasted red poblanos and thick cream. When the butternut "pasta" and real pasta are *al dente*, you warm them together with the sauce, sprinkle on a little punchy cheese and prepare for a blissful moment. This dish is that good.

A Note About Red Poblanos: We get red poblanos only in the fall, when our local farmers leave them on the plants long enough for them to turn that saturated shade of lipstick red. They can be roasted, peeled and frozen to use through the winter in this and other dishes. You can use an equal weight of fresh red pimientos, red New Mexicos/Anaheims, piquillos or other curiosity-sparking red peppers you find at the farmers' market. I've even made this dish with the flame-roasted piquillos I find in jars in well-stocked and specialty groceries. Of course, you can simply use red bell peppers instead of the red poblanos, but the flavor will be pale by comparison.

Serves 4 as a side dish

3 medium (about 9 ounces total) fresh red poblano chiles (see headnote)

4 unpeeled garlic cloves

Salt

1 small (2-pound) butternut squash, peeled

1 cup heavy cream, Mexican *crema* or *crème fraîche*

8 ounces dried fettuccine

1 cup grated Mexican *queso añejo* or other garnishing cheese such as Romano or Parmesan (divided use)

About ¼ cup coarsely chopped cilantro, for serving

Turn on the broiler and adjust the rack so that it's about 4 inches below the heat. Lay the poblanos and garlic on a rimmed baking sheet and roast, turning occasionally, until they have softened and blackened in spots, about 10 minutes. When cool enough to handle, rub the skins off the poblanos, pull out the stems and seedpods, then quickly rinse to remove stray seeds and bits of skin. Cut 1 poblano into ¼-inch strips and set aside; roughly chop the other 2 poblanos and scoop into a blender. Peel the garlic and add it to the blender, too.

In a large (8-quart) pasta or soup pot, combine 6 quarts water and 2 tablespoons salt. Cover and set over high heat to bring to a boil.

Meanwhile, prepare the squash: Slice through the squash crosswise, separating the rounded bottom from the skinnier neck; reserve the bottom for another use (like the Butternut-Pecan Muffins, page 240). Cut the neck in half lengthwise and use a mandoline to slice each half into thin, ⅛-inch-thick sheets (I use my inexpensive Japanese mandoline, aka Benriner). Slice the sheets lengthwise into ¼-inch-wide strips. You should have about 2 cups of butternut "pasta."

Warm the cream (or one of its stand-ins) in a glass measuring cup in a microwave for 1 minute at 50% power. Pour into the blender jar with the poblanos. Blend until smooth. Taste and season with salt (usually about 1 teaspoon). Pour into a large (10-inch) skillet set over low heat.

Drop the squash strips into the boiling water and cook until *al dente*, 1 to 2 minutes. Remove with a slotted spoon, shaking off the excess water, and add to the skillet with the poblano cream. Add the fettuccine to the boiling water and cook until *al dente*, 10 to 12 minutes. Drain, reserving ¼ cup pasta water. Add the pasta, reserved water and poblano strips to the sauce. Raise the heat to medium-high and bring the sauce to a simmer, all the while tossing the pasta, squash and poblanos together. Stir in ½ cup of the cheese and divide the pasta among 4 warm pasta bowls. Top each bowl with a portion of the remaining cheese and sprinkle each one with cilantro.

Riffs on Fettuccine with Butternut Squash and Red Poblano *Crema*:
If you're putting this much effort into such a beautiful dish, why not serve it with sautéed shrimp? I'd cook them in the large skillet before using it to make the sauce: Heat enough butter or olive oil to coat the skillet over medium-high. Lay in about 1 pound

of peeled, deveined shrimp (I like how they look with the tails left on) in a single layer. Cook until barely browned on one side, flip and brown the other side, then transfer them to an ovenproof plate before they're completely cooked through. Keep warm in a low oven until the pasta is in the pasta bowls. Top the pasta with the shrimp and serve your amazing creation.

You can also transition this dish from red to green by making it with zucchini and green poblano: just cut zucchini to resemble fettuccini (you'll need 2 cups) and replace the red poblanos with the much-easier-to-find green ones.

Kuri (or Butternut or Pumpkin) Soup with Ancho and Apple

Crema de Calabaza con Chile Ancho y Manzana

◇◇

Kuri has such unique, concentrated sweet winter squash flavor that you can turn it into a soup quickly and with little fuss. Dried chile and kuri are a modest, perfect match. Black pepper and cinnamon support the ancho flavor here, as they so often do in Mexico. Apple simply underscores kuri's natural sweetness. And the squash seeds (yes, I've saved them for the soup rather than the compost pile) add nuttiness. With about a half-hour investment (and another half-hour of simmering), you can have a lovely pot of soup to enjoy for several days. I make this soup with water, because I like the purity of flavor. If you want more richness, use chicken or vegetable broth.

Makes 4 cups, serving 4 for lunch or a light supper

1 medium (3-pound) kuri squash or sugar (aka pie) pumpkin
  OR 1 small (2-pound) butternut squash
2 tablespoons butter
1 medium white onion, sliced ¼-inch thick
1 dried ancho chile, stemmed, seeded and torn into flat pieces
  OR 1 tablespoon pure ancho chile powder

1 medium apple (I like a not-too-tart variety here, such as Gala or Fuji), peeled, cored and roughly chopped
½ teaspoon ground black pepper
½ teaspoon ground cinnamon, preferably Mexican *canela*
Salt
Sugar

Cut off the stem end of the squash or pumpkin, then cut it in half from stem to blossom end. Wrap and refrigerate half of whichever squash you chose to use in another dish. Peel the other half, scoop out the seeds and pull off the stringy fibers that entangle them (if a few remain, that's okay). Scoop ¼ cup of the seeds into a small bowl and chop the squash or pumpkin into roughly 1-inch pieces (you should have about 3 cups).

Melt the butter in a medium (3-quart) saucepan over medium heat. Add the seeds and onion and cook, stirring frequently, until the onion is richly golden and the seeds have started to brown, about 10 minutes. Add the chile pieces (or the chile powder) and cook, stirring, for a minute or two, until they are fragrant and lightly toasted. Add the squash or pumpkin, apple, pepper, cinnamon and 1 quart water. Bring to a boil, then reduce the heat and let the mixture simmer until everything is very tender, about 30 minutes. Ladle into a blender, *loosely* cover and blend until completely smooth. (A large, high-powered blender like Vitamix works best here; if yours is smaller, blend in batches. An immersion blender, while easy, will barely blend the seeds.) Set a medium-mesh strainer over the pot and pour the soup through to catch any unblended seeds. Season with salt (usually about 1 teaspoon) and a little sugar (½ teaspoon or so brings out the flavor of the apple). Serve in warm bowls.

Riffs on Kuri Soup with Ancho and Apple:

When the first kuri squash show up in my farmers' market, it's still really warm outside— the perfect weather for a cool soup. And the good news is that this soup is delicious chilled with a spoonful of Mexican *crema*, sour cream, *crème fraîche* or Greek-style yogurt on top; a little crushed, toasted ancho is a great garnish.

For everyday eating, soup as the main dish just isn't enough food for me. I need some coarsely shredded roast chicken or leftover roast pork in the soup. Being a fan of both meatless eating and tofu, I'd be content with a handful of firm tofu cubes in my bowl as well.

Pan-Roasted Summer Squash with Garlic *Mojo* and Güero Chile

Calabacitas Rostizadas al Mojo de Ajo con Chile Güero

◇◇

As my tastes have evolved and I have grown to prefer some dishes to feel both lighter and more rustic when I eat them, the way I prepare the classic summer squash in garlic *mojo* has changed. Instead of using the typical sautéed squash, I now dry-roast or dry-grill it, creating both that lightness (less oil absorbed by the *calabacitas*) and the rusticity from the light charring. Plus, the summer squash tastes sweeter, perfect to pair with the bright flavor of the flame-roasted güero chile. Roasted Garlic *Mojo* is the perfect flavor-packed touch to make the dish soar.

There are so many kinds of summer squash in my farmers' market that during their months-long season I could make this dish every week with a different variety. You can serve it as a soft taco filling. Or spooned across a piece of grilled fish. Or cooled and served as an antipasto with a squeeze of lime. Or layered (warm or cool) on a sandwich with roast pork and mayo.

Serves 4 as a side dish

3 or 4 fresh güero chiles (aka hot or mild banana peppers)

Salt

2 pounds summer squash (the teardrop-shaped, light-skinned tatume and the round ronde de Nice are similar to what's available in Mexico; both have a gentle sweetness and compact texture), skin on, cut into 1-inch cubes

¼ cup Roasted Garlic *Mojo* (recipe follows)

A handful of cilantro leaves, for serving

A few tablespoons grated Mexican *queso añejo* or other garnishing cheese such as Romano or Parmesan, for serving

Roast the chiles over an open flame or close up under a preheated broiler, turning regularly until the skin is blackened and blistered all over, about 4 minutes for an open flame, 6 minutes for a broiler. Cool, then pull off the stems, slice the chiles in half lengthwise, gently scrape out the seeds, then flip the chiles over and scrape off the charred skin. Slice the cleaned chile pieces crosswise into ¼-inch strips.

Lightly salt the squash. In a heavy, dry, large (10-inch) skillet over medium-high heat (or on a grill pan or prepared charcoal or heated gas grill), dry-roast (or dry-grill) the summer squash in a single layer, turning frequently, until lightly charred on all sides but still a little crunchy, about 12 minutes.

When you're ready to serve, combine the summer squash, chiles and the Roasted Garlic *Mojo* in the skillet over medium heat. Stir until hot, then taste and season with salt (usually about ¼ teaspoon). Scrape into a warm serving bowl, then sprinkle with cilantro and cheese. You're ready to serve.

ROASTED GARLIC *MOJO*

In a large (10-inch) dry skillet, roast **4 heads of garlic** (separated into cloves but not peeled) over medium heat, turning regularly until they're soft and blackened in spots, 10 to 15 minutes. Cool, peel, place in a food processor and pulse until roughly chopped. Turn the machine on and add **2 cups olive oil** in a steady stream. Stop the machine, add **¼ cup lime juice** and **1 teaspoon salt** and pulse to incorporate. Store refrigerated in a sealed container.

Spaghetti Squash *Fideos*
with Chipotle, Chorizo, *Crema*
and Avocado (page 185)

Spaghetti Squash *Fideos* with Chipotle, Chorizo, Crema and Avocado

Fideos de Calabaza Espagueti al Chipotle con Chorizo, Crema y Aguacate

◇◇

I've eaten the iconic Mexico City *fideos secos* for years and loved every bite: toasted vermicelli pasta simmered with roasted tomatoes, smoky chipotle chile, chorizo sausage, plus dollops of *crema* and cubes of avocado for richness. Oh, I almost forgot the final punch of umami, in the form of Mexican *añejo* cheese. Not exactly what I think of as an everyday dish.

When you replace the pasta with spaghetti squash, as I have here, the whole thing lightens up. It's still a rich dish, but one that needs to be cycled into the everyday repertory from time to time. It's just too good to pass up.

Serves 6

1 large (about 2½ pounds) spaghetti squash, cut in half from stem to blossom end, seeds scraped out

8 ounces fresh Mexican chorizo sausage, casing removed (about 1 cup)

One 15-ounce can diced fire-roasted tomatoes, drained

1 chipotle chile *en adobo*, seeded, stemmed and roughly chopped

1 tablespoon chipotle canning sauce

2 garlic cloves, peeled and finely chopped

1 cup chicken broth, vegetable broth or water

Salt

About ¼ cup Mexican *crema*, sour cream, *crème fraîche* or Greek-style yogurt

About 1/3 cup grated Mexican *queso añejo* or other garnishing cheese such as Romano or Parmesan (divided use)

1 small ripe avocado, pitted, flesh scooped from the skin and cut into ½-inch cubes

A handful of cilantro leaves, if you have them, for serving

Wrap each spaghetti squash half in plastic wrap, poke a couple of holes in the plastic, place in the microwave and cook at 100% power for 10 minutes, until the squash is soft. (My microwave has a rotating carousel; if yours doesn't, you'll need to rotate the squash every minute or so.) Remove and let cool, still wrapped, for 10 minutes. Remove the plastic and use a fork to scrape at the exposed insides, working in the direction of the "grain," freeing the spaghetti-like strings into a bowl or deep plate. Discard the skin.

In a very large (12-inch) skillet, cook the chorizo over medium heat, stirring to break up any clumps, until it is browned and done through, about 10 minutes. Use a slotted spoon to scoop the chorizo into a small dish, leaving behind as much fat as possible. (You need about 2 tablespoons for the next step; if there's not enough, supplement with vegetable oil.)

In a blender, combine the tomatoes, chipotle and canning sauce and blend until smooth. Set the chorizo-cooking pan over medium heat, add the garlic and stir for a minute or so, until it releases its aroma, then pour in the tomato mixture. Raise the heat to medium-high and cook, stirring almost constantly, until the mixture has darkened and thickened noticeably, 7 or 8 minutes. Stir in the broth or water and bring to a simmer. Taste and season with salt, usually ½ teaspoon, depending on the saltiness of the broth. Add the spaghetti squash, stir carefully to coat it with the sauce, then stir in the *crema* (or one of its stand-ins) and *half* of the cheese. Transfer the *fideos* to a large pasta bowl and top with the remaining cheese and the reserved chorizo. Dot with the avocado, strew on some cilantro leaves if you have them and carry the bowl to the table—you're ready to eat something pretty special.

Going Vegetarian:

You can simply leave out the chorizo (and cook the sauce in vegetable oil), or you can replace it with a generous cup of diced zucchini or other summer squash. Brown the squash in a little olive oil over medium-high heat, scoop it out as you would the chorizo, and continue with the recipe, sprinkling the browned squash over the finished dish.

Charred Cucumber Salad with Red Chile and Lime (page 188)

Charred Cucumber Salad with Red Chile and Lime

Ensalada de Pepino Carbonizado con Chile Seco y Limón

◇〰◇

You're probably asking yourself why in heaven's name I would suggest that you char cucumbers before making them into a salad. I mean, just weaving a little chile, lime and herbs into a simple cucumber salad is plenty good enough, right? You'll have to be the judge of that, but I think charring them first makes a salad that's even more memorable—certainly one that's different, the kind of dish that'll have everyone talking and debating and *paying more attention to their food.* Which is always a plus, to my way of thinking. If you use an unusual variety of cucumber from the farmers' market—I love the Persians, kirbys, lemons, Armenians—you'll have even more to talk about.

Serves 6

1½ pounds cucumbers (Persians, Kirbys, lemon cucumbers—whatever you like or can find)

3 or 4 tablespoons fresh lime juice

½ teaspoon chile flakes (you can buy them or make your own by toasting stemmed arbol chiles lightly in a dry skillet, then pulsing them in an electric spice mill until reduced to flakes)

A generous ½ teaspoon Worcestershire sauce

¼ cup thin-sliced onion (my first choice is the sliced bulbs of knob onions, but small red onions are delicious, too; especially if you can find Tropeas in your farmers' market)

½ cup loosely packed chopped cilantro (or substitute smaller amounts of mint, *hoja santa*, fresh Mexican oregano, thyme, marjoram, even Thai basil)

Salt

First char the cucumbers. You can lay them on an open gas flame turned to high, or over a very hot gas or charcoal fire, and cook, turning almost constantly, until the skin is blackened a little on all sides, about 4 minutes. Or you can char the cucumbers with one of those torches used in kitchens to toast meringue or *crème brûlée.* Either way, the idea is to have the heat high enough for the cucumbers' skins to blacken some before the flesh cooks and softens too much on the inside. And the blackening should be done with a light hand—you're not trying to create charcoal here.

Once the cucumbers are charred, let them cool a bit, then split each one in half lengthwise and slice crosswise into ¼-inch-thick half-moons. Scoop into a bowl, add the rest of the ingredients and toss to combine. Taste and season with salt, usually a scant ½ teaspoon. Let stand for a few minutes to let the flavors mingle, and the salad is ready to serve.

Riffs on Charred Cucumber Salad:

I like to mix chopped cooked shrimp or scallops into the salad and carry it on a picnic. With or without the crustaceans, I like to wrap it in butter lettuce or Little Gem lettuce leaves to eat like a taco.

Squash Blossom Soup

Crema de Flores de Calabaza

◇◇

Squash blossoms are plentiful in Mexico. There, cooks use them with abandon, and they're sold in markets in big bunches at a reasonable price. Here in the States, we see squash blossoms more as a delicacy: they're sold like little jewels, and cooks are expected to stuff each one, batter them and fry them in a more or less Italian style. For this recipe, especially at the height of summer, when farmers' markets are offering them, try to get into the Mexican mindset: the more blossoms, the merrier. If you can procure a surfeit, use more than the number called for here. Double it if you like.

At the farmers' market, I choose blossoms that are unblemished. Once purchased, I store them flat in a wide flat storage container, with paper towels between layers. Tightly covered in the refrigerator, they'll last several days.

Makes about 3 cups, serving 4 as a first course

1 small fresh poblano chile

1 tablespoon butter

1 small white onion, roughly chopped

1 tablespoon *masa harina* or all-purpose flour

2 cups chicken broth

12 to 16 squash blossoms, stamens and sepals removed (divided use)

Kernels cut from 1 ear of corn (usually a generous cup; divided use)

1 small (5-ounce) zucchini or other summer squash, cut into ¼-inch cubes

½ cup Mexican *crema*, sour cream, *crème fraîche* or Greek-style yogurt

About 1 tablespoon of sliced epazote or parsley leaves

Salt

Roast the poblano over an open flame or close up under a preheated broiler, turning frequently, until blackened and blistered all over, about 5 minutes for an open flame, 10 minutes for the broiler. Cover with a kitchen towel and cool until handleable. Rub off the blackened skin, pull out the stem, tear open the chile and scrape out the seeds. Briefly rinse to remove any stray seeds or bits of skin. Chop into ¼-inch pieces.

In a medium (3-quart) saucepan set over medium heat, melt the butter. Add the onion and cook, stirring occasionally, until golden, about 7 minutes. Add the *masa harina* (or flour) and stir for 30 seconds, then add the chicken broth and whisk continuously until it comes to a simmer.

Pour your hot soup into a blender and add *half* the squash blossoms and *half* the corn. Cover *loosely* and blend until smooth. (If you have an immersion blender, this can all be done right in the saucepan.) Return the mixture to the pot and add the zucchini, the poblano and the remaining corn. Cook at a low simmer until the zucchini is tender, about 6 minutes.

Meanwhile, cut the remaining squash blossoms in half lengthwise, then slice them crosswise into ¼-inch strips, bulbous end and all. Stir into the soup along with the *crema* (or one of its stand-ins) and the epazote (or parsley). If you've used sour cream or yogurt, remove from the heat immediately. For *crema* or *crème fraîche,* simmer for a few more minutes, just to let the flavors meld. Taste and season with salt, usually about 1 teaspoon. Divide the soup among warm bowls and it's ready to serve.

Riffs on Squash Blossom Soup:

Feel free to use other roasted chiles in the soup—any shade of green, any shade of red. Each will add something unique. I've made the soup with the just-about-to-open buds of daylilies; it was great but lacked the subtlety of squash blossoms. You can turn the soup into a sauce by simply reducing the broth to 1 cup. Those around your table will be over the moon when you spoon it onto a piece of grilled fish or chicken.

Ribbon Salad with Creamy Two-Chile Vinagreta

Ensalada de Listones con Vinagreta de Dos Chiles

This is a salad about textures, a salad that journeys beyond the simple tenderness of young greens or roasted vegetables. It's a salad that celebrates the resilience of barely softened summer squash and ornery frisée enveloped in a voluptuous dressing. Let me put it this way: it's not a salad that goes unnoticed.

Though you can make the summer squash ribbons with a vegetable peeler, you should think about getting a mandoline to make thin-slicing a breeze. It doesn't need to be the couple-hundred-dollar stainless steel one or even one of the bulky but less expensive options that have come on the market in the past few years. You just need something like the small green Japanese mandoline (aka Benriner) that's sold online for $25 or so. If you want more slicing options, opt for the slightly larger one for $10 or $15 more. With it, you'll be able to whip out a salad like this (or a hundred other thin-sliced or matchstick-cut preparations) in minutes.

My farmers' market has a variety of fresh pimiento- or piquillo-like red peppers that are not too hot, so I always think of making this salad when they come into season. If something similar isn't available, you can use a small red bell pepper (though it won't be as robust in flavor) or some roasted piquillo pepper in a jar. If squash blossoms are in season, tear a few into ribbons and toss them in—they add an intriguing silkiness to the mix.

Serves 4 to 6 generously

1 medium fresh pimiento, piquillo or other fleshy, not-too-hot red pepper

4 garlic cloves, peeled

1 to 2 canned chipotles *en adobo* (or 1 to 2 dried morita chiles that have been lightly toasted in a dry skillet and rehydrated for 20 minutes in water), stemmed and roughly chopped

⅓ cup light vinegar (rice, Cava/ Champagne, distilled white—they all work)

⅔ cup olive oil

2 tablespoons Mexican *crema*, sour cream, *crème fraîche* or Greek-style yogurt

Salt

4 medium (about 1¾ pounds total) summer squash (I love this with yellow squash and zucchini, but your farmers' market will no doubt offer a whole host of options)

1 small red onion, thinly sliced

½ medium head frisée

OR about 2 cups lightly packed sturdy wild arugula or the 2-inch tops of watercress

⅓ cup (about 1½ ounces) sliced almonds toasted in a small skillet over medium-low heat until aromatic

Roast the red pepper over an open flame or close up under a preheated broiler, turning frequently, until blackened and blistered all over, about 5 minutes for an open flame, 10 minutes for the broiler. Cover with a kitchen towel and allow to cool until handleable. Rub off the blackened skin, pull out the stem and scrape out the seeds. Briefly rinse to remove any stray seeds or bits of skin. Place the flesh in a blender.

Place the garlic in a microwave-safe bowl, cover with water and microwave at 100% power for 1 minute. Drain and add to the blender, along with the chipotles (or moritas), vinegar, oil and *crema* (or one of its stand-ins). Blend until smooth, then taste and season with salt, usually about ½ teaspoon.

Cut the summer squash into ribbons (I like ones that are about ⅙-inch thick and a little less than ½-inch wide). You can do this with a mandoline (if yours doesn't offer the width you like, simply thin-slice the squash into sheets, then cut the sheets into strips); or, using a vegetable peeler, cut or peel off strips of squash, rotating the squash a fraction of a turn after each cut (when you get to the seedy center, discard it).

In a large bowl, combine the squash, red onion and a generous ½ cup of dressing. Let stand for about 10 minutes to soften and flavor the vegetables. (At our restaurant, we vacuum-seal the vegetables with the dressing, then release the vacuum immediately, which beautifully softens the squash and onion while deeply flavoring them with the dressing; I highly recommend this if you have a vacuum sealer.)

If you're using frisée, tear off the base, then tear the leaves into natural-looking 2-inch pieces by tearing along the length of the leaf; discard any large stems. Add the frisée (or arugula or watercress) to the squash mixture and lightly toss to distribute. Taste and add more dressing and more salt if you think it needs it, usually ½ teaspoon (pour the leftover dressing into a jar, cover and refrigerate for another salad). Divide between plates, sprinkle each with some toasted almonds and carry to the table.

UNEXPECTED VEGETABLES IN THE MEXICAN KITCHEN

Roasted Sunchoke Salad with Creamy Garlic *Mojo* and Herbs **196**

Grilled Asparagus with Creamy Pasilla Chile **198**

Weekend Dish: Shell Beans and Artichokes with Roasted Tomatillos, Cilantro and *Añejo* Cheese **201**

Yellow *Mole* with Grilled Fennel and Portobello Mushrooms **204**

Celery Root Pancakes with Chipotle *Crema* and Cilantro **208**

Tangy Sorrel *Salsa Verde* with Stir-Fried Shrimp **210**

Banana Pepper–Leek Soup with White Beans and Crispy Chorizo **212**

Spicy Chipotle Eggplant with Black Beans **215**

Braised Artichokes with Tomatoes, Jalapeños, Olives and Capers **218**

Roasted Sunchoke Salad with Creamy Garlic *Mojo* and Herbs

Ensalada de Aguaturma con Ajo Cremoso y Hierbas

◇◇

Sunchokes are the roots of a sunflower native to the Americas. Because of historical quirks and misunderstandings, they are also known as Jerusalem artichokes, which is unfortunate, because they have nothing to do with Jerusalem or artichokes and everything to do with a native American product we can be really proud of. For me, sunchokes roasted with olive oil and sprinkled with coarse salt provide one of the most delectable mouthfuls in the world. Cool them, toss them with a creamy garlic dressing (plus a little chile and a few herbs) and you've got a dynamic salad to serve with grilled halibut or walleye, grilled chicken thighs or pork chops—grilled anything, really. When you have to contribute a dish to a picnic, this will wow people.

Your choice of creamy element (mayonnaise, sour cream or yogurt) will determine whether the salad turns out lusciously creamy, brightly creamy or just plain bright. The limey solids of Roasted Garlic *Mojo* deliver the most flavor here, but if you're short on time you can use 4 roasted, peeled and finely chopped garlic cloves instead (roast them unpeeled in a dry skillet over medium heat, turning regularly until soft and browned, 10 to 15 minutes). If you're thinking about plating this salad individually, I suggest that you nestle it into baby arugula, watercress or frisée.

Serves 6

2 pounds sunchokes (I try to choose the smoothest ones—the ones with the fewest crags and crevices), scrubbed and cut into 1-inch chunks

3 tablespoons olive oil

Salt

2 large fresh poblano chiles OR 2 to 4 canned chipotle chiles *en adobo*, seeded and finely chopped

⅓ cup mayonnaise, sour cream or Greek-style yogurt, or a combination of the three

1 green onion, trimmed of roots and withered leaves, thinly sliced crosswise

1 generous tablespoon solids from Roasted Garlic *Mojo* (recipe follows)

2 or 3 tablespoons chopped cilantro or fresh basil (or a slightly smaller amount of fresh mint, lemon verbena, sage or another herb you like or have on hand)

Turn on the oven to 400 degrees. On a rimmed baking sheet, toss the sunchoke pieces with the olive oil and a generous sprinkling of salt. Slide them into the oven and roast, turning them with a spatula every few minutes, until they are completely tender and beginning to brown, about 45 minutes. Cool.

While the sunchokes are roasting, roast the poblanos (if you're using them) over an open flame or (when the sunchokes are done) close up under a preheated broiler, turning them until they are blackened and blistered all over, about 5 minutes for an open flame, 10 minutes for the broiler. Cover with a kitchen towel and cool until handleable. Rub off the blackened skin, pull out the stems and seedpods, then briefly rinse to remove stray seeds and bits of skin. Chop into ¼-inch pieces and scrape into a medium bowl. (If you're using the chopped chipotle chiles, scrape them into the bowl.)

Add the sunchokes to the bowl, then measure in the mayonnaise (or one of its stand-ins), the green onion, the *mojo* solids and your herb of choice. Stir everything together. Taste and season with salt (the sour cream and yogurt versions will take at least ¼ teaspoon). I think this salad tastes best when the flavors mingle for an hour or two in the refrigerator.

Riffs on Roasted Sunchoke Salad:

Of course, this salad can be made with roasted fingerling or new potatoes, carrots, sweet potatoes, parsnips, little turnips—pretty much any vegetable you can toss with oil and roast.

ROASTED GARLIC *MOJO*

In a large (10-inch) dry skillet, roast **4 heads of garlic** (separated into cloves but not peeled) over medium heat, turning regularly until they're soft and blackened in spots, 10 to 15 minutes. Cool, peel, place in a food processor and pulse until roughly chopped. Turn the machine on and add **2 cups olive oil** in a steady stream. Stop the machine, add ¼ **cup lime juice** and **1 teaspoon salt** and pulse to incorporate. Store refrigerated in a sealed container.

Grilled Asparagus with Creamy Pasilla Chile

Esparragos a la Parilla, Chile Pasilla Cremoso

◇◇◇

Though my most frequent choice for serving grilled asparagus has for years been with the Creamy Roasted Poblano *Rajas* on page 47, this luxuriously rich *crema* made from dried, near-black pasilla chiles, caramelized onion and sweet garlic is quickly eclipsing it. If pasilla chiles aren't on your horizon, you can do the same preparation with ancho chiles, though the flavor won't be as deep and sonorous. Roasting asparagus (a 400-degree oven is ideal) is an alternative to grilling. And replacing olive oil with butter, while not an approach that traditional cooks would likely take, offers an amazing and unexpected flavor.

Of course, this enticing vegetable preparation can be set on a buffet or table with a variety of other dishes (it goes beautifully with grilled fish or poultry), but I like to serve it, individually plated, as a first course, sometimes with thin slices of dry-cured ham ribboned over the top.

I'd love to tell you that the Mexican *crema* or *crème fraîche* could be replaced by sour cream or Greek-style yogurt, but both will curdle when heated. You *could* use heavy cream, but the sauce would be thinner.

Serves 4

2 tablespoons olive oil, plus a little more for the pasilla and asparagus

1 medium white onion, sliced ¼-inch thick

4 garlic cloves, peeled and finely chopped

3 medium (about 1 ounce total) dried pasilla (negro) chiles, stemmed and seeded

½ cup Mexican *crema* or *crème fraîche*

Salt

1 teaspoon vinegar (practically any kind will work here, though a dark one like balsamic will underscore the pasilla flavor)

1 large bunch (about 1 pound) asparagus

In a medium (3-quart) saucepan over medium heat, warm the olive oil, then add the onion and cook, stirring frequently, until very soft and richly golden, about 10 minutes. Add the garlic and cook, stirring nearly constantly, for a minute or so, until soft and very aromatic.

While the onion is cooking, use a pair of kitchen scissors or a sharp knife to cut the pasilla chiles crosswise into thin strips no wider than about ¼ inch.

When the onion-garlic mixture is ready, use a slotted spoon to scoop half of it into a blender jar, the other half into a small bowl, leaving behind as much oil as possible. Add more oil to the pan if necessary to coat the bottom nicely and return to medium heat. Add the chile strips and cook, stirring nonstop, until the chiles have changed color (the interior will lighten noticeably) and they have filled your kitchen with their distinctive toasty aroma, about 30 seconds. Too much toasting will yield bitterness in the sauce; too little toasting won't allow these chiles to give all they have.

Scoop half the toasted chiles into the blender, the other half into the bowl with the onions. Add the *crema* (or *crème fraîche*) to the blender and blend until completely smooth; this will take a minute or two. Scrape your pasilla *crema* back into the saucepan, stir in about 1 tablespoon water to give it an easily spoonable consistency, taste and season with salt, usually about ¼ teaspoon.

Stir the vinegar into the onion mixture in the bowl, taste and season with a sprinkling of salt.

When you're ready to serve, heat a gas grill (or grill pan) to medium or light a charcoal fire and let it burn until medium hot. Trim the bottoms of the asparagus: you can cut off the woody ends with a knife, but my standard method is to hold each spear firmly between my hands and gently bend it until it snaps, which will be exactly at the point where the asparagus starts being really tender (I save the bottoms to blend into soup). Brush or spray the asparagus tops with oil, sprinkle with salt, and grill, turning regularly, until crisp-tender, about 5 minutes.

While the asparagus is cooking, warm the sauce over medium-low heat. Divide the grilled asparagus among 4 plates, spoon the sauce over it, then sprinkle it with the pasilla-onion mixture and you're ready to serve.

Riffs on Grilled Asparagus with Creamy Pasilla Chile:

Think of this sauce when you're going to grill or roast other vegetables, too. It's tasty with grilled green beans (I especially like it with grilled Chinese long beans) or spooned on slow-roasted fennel or even potatoes. You can serve the sauce cool on cool grilled vegetables, too, in which case you can make the sauce with yogurt or sour cream. It is wonderful as a sandwich spread (really) or as a vegetable dip.

Grilled Asparagus with Creamy
Pasilla Chile (page 198)

Weekend Dish: Shell Beans and Artichokes with Roasted Tomatillos, Cilantro and *Añejo* Cheese

Frijoles Frescos y Alcachofas con Tomate Verde Asado, Cilantro y Queso Añejo

When you pick fully mature bean pods, they look like lumpy, overgrown green beans, because the seeds (beans) inside the pods have grown to their full size. You can let them fully dry on the plant, then pick them, shell them and store them for up to a year or so, until you're ready to simmer them slowly to doneness. Or you can pick them when the beans have grown to their full size but not yet dried, shell them right away and simmer them briefly to tenderness. Their flavor and texture is lighter than that of fully dried beans—a truly unique experience. But they take a fair amount of time to shell.

Some say the same thing about baby artichokes: lots of trimming for little yield. Yet, as with shell beans, the flavor and texture of braised or roasted baby artichokes are incredible.

So choose this recipe for a Saturday or Sunday afternoon, when you've been to the farmers' market and have some relaxed kitchen time. Or follow the riff at the end of the recipe for what I call the winter version of this dish—a super-tasty, incredibly quick preparation using canned or vacuum-packed cooked beans and canned artichokes.

Paired with a stack of warm tortillas, this makes for really special vegetarian tacos. But it's just as enticing over pasta or polenta.

How to Trim Baby Artichokes: One by one, pull off all the lower, darker green leaves, revealing a light-green underside. (Those leaves are really tough. It's better to pull off more than you think necessary to avoid serving chewy artichoke.) Cut off the pointy top third of the artichoke. Cut off any stem that continues more than an inch below the bottom of the artichoke. Using a sharp paring knife or vegetable peeler, peel the tough exterior from the stem, then continue peeling up around the base of the artichoke. (There's a lot of tough exterior here. Better to trim a little extra than end up with a mouthful of unchewable fibers.) Now cut the artichokes into quarters and drop them into a bowl of water to which you've added a couple of tablespoons of vinegar or lemon or lime juice. Carbon knives react with artichokes, so use stainless steel.

Serves 4 as a light dinner

2 cups shelled fresh shell beans (think pinto beans, black beans, cranberry beans and the like, but green garbanzos, black-eyed peas and small fava beans work, too; you'll need to start with roughly 1 pound of in-the-shell beans)

Salt

1 pound baby artichokes (about 8 artichokes total), trimmed, quartered and held in acidulated water as described in the headnote

6 garlic cloves, peeled

Hot green chile to taste (I like 1 large serrano or 1 small jalapeño), stemmed

6 medium (about 12 ounces total) tomatillos, husked, rinsed and cut in half crosswise

About ¼ cup chopped cilantro, plus a little extra for serving

A few tablespoons chopped red onion (preferably a fresh-dug one from a farmers' market with the green top still on)

¼ cup grated Mexican *queso añejo* or other garnishing cheese such as Romano or Parmesan

In a medium-large (4- to 6-quart) heavy pot or Dutch oven set over high heat, combine the beans with 6 cups water and 1 tablespoon salt. Bring to a boil, then reduce the heat and simmer until the beans are luxuriously tender, 20 to 30 minutes. Drain the artichokes and add them to the pot and simmer until they, too, are tender, about 5 minutes.

While the beans and artichokes are cooking, make the tomatillo sauce: Set a very large (12-inch) nonstick skillet (or a heavy skillet lined with foil) over medium heat. Lay in the garlic, chile and tomatillos, cut side down. When the vegetables are browned on one side, about 4 minutes, turn everything over and brown the other side, about 4 minutes more. (The tomatillos and garlic should be soft.) Transfer to a blender or food processor. Blend to a coarse puree.

Drain the beans and artichokes and return to the pan. Stir in the sauce and enough water to give it a saucy texture. Bring to a simmer over medium heat, taste and season with salt, usually about 1 teaspoon. Simmer for a few minutes to blend the flavors. Finally, stir the cilantro into the simmering bean and artichoke mixture and transfer everything to a serving bowl.

In a strainer, rinse the chopped red onion under cool tap water, then shake off the excess. Sprinkle the bean and artichoke mixture with the chopped onion, cheese and a little cilantro. A unique culinary experience awaits.

The Winter Version:

Replace the shell beans and artichokes (*and their simmering*): Use 2 cups drained canned or vacuum-packed cooked beans (almost all beans—favas, black-eyed peas, green garbanzos, red kidneys, cannellini—work here) and 1 drained 14-ounce can baby artichokes (sometimes inaccurately labeled "artichoke hearts"). Add these to the sauce and finish as described above.

Other Riffs on Shell Beans and Artichokes with Tomatillos:

The recipe above is really my riff on a Mexican classic of vegetables in roasted tomatillo sauce. Feel free to replace the beans and artichokes with potatoes, chayotes, zucchini or pretty much any light-colored fresh vegetables you run across. They need to be cut into appropriately-sized pieces (small pieces if you're going to serve it as a taco filling) and steamed, blanched or roasted until tender.

Yellow *Mole* with Grilled Fennel and Portobello Mushrooms

Mole Amarillo con Hinojo Asado y Hongo Portobello

◇◇◇

This isn't a complex or time-consuming *mole* but an easily approachable, everyday one with a bright flavor infused with some spices and herbs. And about those spices and herbs, let me put your mind at rest: if any or all of them aren't within reach, just make the *mole* without them (I know cooks in Oaxaca who make very simple yellow *mole*). The classic herb that gives this dish its distinctiveness is *hoja santa*, the large, heart-shaped leaf with a black-peppery, anisey flavor. It's not available fresh in any grocery I frequent (such a pity!) and doesn't grow commonly in Chicago (except in my yard in the summer and my greenhouse in the winter), so here I've replaced it with the fresh flavor of fennel fronds, cut from the fennel bulb you'll already be roasting for the dish.

I've written this recipe using chicken broth because its body and natural sweetness make the best yellow *mole*. Replacing it with vegetable broth will give you a completely vegetarian (yes, vegan) dish that satisfies on all levels. And I've chosen three vegetables to spoon the *mole* over: fennel bulb, potato and portobello mushrooms. Each brings out a different aspect of the yellow *mole*, though you could say that about many different vegetables. Grill what you find that's fresh, distinctive and catches your eye.

Serves 4

4 medium (1 ounce total) dried guajillo chiles, stemmed, seeded and torn into several pieces

Half of a 15-ounce can fire-roasted tomatoes, drained

½ small white onion, roughly chopped

2 garlic cloves, peeled and cut in half

¼ teaspoon EACH ground cumin, allspice and cinnamon (preferably Mexican *canela*)

1 teaspoon dried oregano, preferably Mexican

5 cups chicken broth (divided use)

¼ cup vegetable or olive oil (divided use)

3 tablespoons *masa harina* or a generous 2 tablespoons fresh *masa*

1 large (about 1 pound) fennel bulb, fronds cut from the bulb and roughly chopped (you need ⅔ cup)

Salt

4 medium (about ¾ pound total)
portobello mushroom caps (you can use
a spoon to scrape out the dark gills if
you want, but I don't mind them)

2 large (about 1 pound) russet potatoes,
cut lengthwise into ¼-inch slices

In a blender jar, combine the torn guajillo chiles, tomatoes, onion, garlic, spices, oregano and *1 cup* of the broth. Blend as smooth as possible. (A food processor will work, though it won't completely puree the chile.)

In a large (4-quart) saucepan, heat *2 tablespoons* of the oil over medium-high. Set a medium-mesh strainer over the top and pour in the chile mixture. Press the mixture through into the hot oil, then stir until it's noticeably thicker, about 5 minutes.

Scoop the *masa harina* (or fresh *masa*) into a blender and add ⅓ cup fennel fronds. Add *1 cup* of the broth and blend thoroughly. Add the herby broth to the cooked chile mixture along with another ⅓ cup fennel fronds. Whisk until the sauce comes to a boil. Add the remaining *3 cups* of the broth and simmer for 15 minutes to meld the flavors. Taste the *mole* and season with salt, usually a generous teaspoon, depending on the saltiness of the broth. Keep the *mole* warm while you grill the vegetables.

Cut the stalks from the fennel bulb and discard them. Slice the fennel bulb length-wise into ¼-inch slices (the root of the bulb should keep the slices intact) and set aside.

Heat a gas grill to medium, or light a charcoal fire and let it burn until the charcoal is covered with white ash and medium-hot. Brush or spray the fennel, mushrooms and potatoes on all sides with the remaining oil and sprinkle generously with salt. Lay the vegetables on the grill, cover and cook, turning every few minutes, until they are ten-der and richly striped with grill marks (but not charred), 15 to 20 minutes total. Slice the portobellos into ¼-inch-thick strips.

Divide the *mole* among 4 shallow bowls and arrange the vegetables on top. Sprinkle with a few chopped fennel fronds if you reserved any, and serve to vegetarians and meat-lovers alike.

Going Carnivore:

Simply grill some boneless, skinless chicken thighs or breasts or some fish fillets alongside the vegetables. You can cube the chicken or flake the fish, gently mix everything together, then serve the whole thing as a buffet dish or taco filling; or you can serve the chicken or fish in full pieces with the vegetables and a generous ladle of *mole*.

Fennel Without Fronds?

If you happen to lay your hands on *hoja santa*, you can use it in place of the fennel fronds: use 2 large leaves, torn into small pieces. For a very different flavor, you can replace the fronds with ⅔ cup roughly chopped cilantro (save some for garnish, too).

Yellow *Mole* with Grilled
Fennel and Portobello
Mushrooms (page 204)

Celery Root Pancakes with Chipotle Crema and Cilantro

Tortitas de Apionabo con Crema Enchipotlada y Cilantro

◇◇◇

The first time I made these, it was for one of those chef-challenge competitions: come up with a dish featuring celery root, something you can complete in 15 minutes using only six ingredients. First you have to understand that I don't really like celery root (or celery, for that matter). But I *really* like what I turned out: a variation on potato pancakes (or latkes), infused with cilantro and smoky-spicy chipotle, plus Mexican *crema* and *queso añejo* (those four ingredients can make practically anything taste delicious as far as I'm concerned). To tell the truth, I've made these at home a number of times (yes, I really do like them), and on occasion I've sprinkled them with chopped crispy bacon or layered some smoked salmon underneath the *crema*, making them even more like Mexican latkes.

Serves 4

2 medium-large (about 1½ pounds total) celery roots, peeled and trimmed at the root end

1 pound boiling potatoes (3 medium Yukon Golds or 4 red- or white-skin), peeled if you wish

2 eggs

4 to 6 canned chipotle chiles *en adobo*, stemmed, seeded and finely chopped (divided use)

About 2/3 cup chopped cilantro (divided use)

Salt

A few tablespoons vegetable or olive oil

½ cup Mexican *crema*, sour cream, *crème fraîche* or Greek-style yogurt

About ¼ cup grated Mexican *queso añejo* or other garnishing cheese such as Romano or Parmesan

Using a food processor or box grater (use the large holes), grate the celery root and potatoes; you should have a generous 3 cups of each. In a medium bowl, mix together the celery root, potato, eggs, *3 to 4* chopped chipotles, *⅓ cup* of the cilantro and 1 teaspoon salt.

Heat enough oil to lightly coat the bottom of a very large (12-inch) skillet (preferably nonstick or seasoned cast iron) over medium-high. When the oil is hot, scoop up about ½ cup of the celery root mixture and drop it into the skillet; you should be able to get 6 mounds into your large skillet at a time. Using a spatula, flatten them into pancakes about ⅜-inch thick. Let the pancakes sizzle until they are richly browned and crispy, 3 or 4 minutes, then flip and cook the other side. Remove them to a baking sheet and keep warm in a low oven while you cook the remaining pancakes.

While the pancakes are cooking, stir the remaining chipotles into the *crema* (or one of its stand-ins). Serve the pancakes topped with chipotle *crema*, a shower of the remaining cilantro and a generous sprinkling of *queso añejo*.

Riffs on Celery Root Pancakes:

You can easily replace the celery root with shredded parsnip, regular sweet potato, white sweet potato, taro or yuca. I'd leave the regular potato in, since it adds a lot of structure.

Tangy Sorrel *Salsa Verde* with Stir-Fried Shrimp

Salsa Verde de Vinagrera con Camarones Salteados

orrel is one of those always-exciting signs of spring. But it's also tricky, I think. When you as much as get it near heat, it wilts into a slippery grayish mass. When you use it raw, all but the smallest leaves can be on the wrong side of tender. Yet I keep coming back to sorrel: Its racy, fresh tang makes me happy just about anywhere I taste it. And classic Mexican roasted tomatillo salsa is one of the best places I've found to weave it in, adding its fresh green lemoniness to an already vibrant condiment—a condiment I find perfect for everything from vegetables to the stir-fried shrimp I'm describing here. I have the great chef and cookbook author Cindy Pawlcyn to thank for bringing this brilliant marriage of tomatillo and sorrel to light for me.

Serves 4

2 garlic cloves, peeled

Fresh hot green chile to taste (usually 1 jalapeño or 2 serranos), stemmed

12 ounces (4 to 6 medium) tomatillos, husked, rinsed and cut in half around the equator

1 cup roughly chopped, loosely packed fresh sorrel leaves (if sorrel is out of season, wild arugula and wild watercress also work)

Salt

2 to 3 tablespoons olive oil

1 medium white onion, sliced ¼-inch thick

1¼ to 1½ pounds (30 to 35) medium-large shrimp, peeled (leave the final tail segment on for appearance's sake) and deveined if you wish

Set a large (10-inch) nonstick skillet or a heavy skillet lined with foil over medium heat. Lay in the garlic, chile and tomatillos, cut side down. When the vegetables are browned and softened on one side, about 4 minutes, turn everything over and brown the other side, about 4 minutes more. Cool to room temperature, transfer to a blender jar (including any juices from the tomatillos), add the sorrel and pulse until you have a puree that's nearly smooth. Add a little water (usually about 2 tablespoons) to give the salsa an easily spoonable consistency. Taste and season with a little salt if it needs it (believe it or not, sometimes it doesn't need any).

In a wok or very large (12-inch) skillet set over medium-high, heat enough oil to coat the bottom (it takes less oil for wok cooking, and I like the texture of the shrimp better from a wok). Add the onion and stir-fry until richly browned but still crunchy, about 5 minutes. Sprinkle the shrimp with salt, add them to the onion and continue to stir-fry until the shrimp are just barely cooked, about 5 minutes more. If they're still a tiny bit translucent in the middle, they'll coast to perfect doneness as you divide them between warm serving plates. Spoon the salsa over the shrimp and you're ready to serve.

Riffs on Sorrel *Salsa Verde* with Shrimp:

This beautiful salsa, all by itself, is perfect on everything from grilled vegetables to steak tacos, and of course you can easily replace the shrimp with cubed boneless, skinless chicken breast. The salsa is also spectacular spooned on broiled tofu or roasted or steamed white-flesh sweet potatoes (the ones they call Japanese in my farmers' market, *camote morado* in my Mexican market). Or stirred into creamy poblano chile soup. Or mixed with mayonnaise for a dynamic dressing for sturdy greens or potato salad.

Salsa Verde with Young Turnip and Red Onion:

When you don't have sorrel (or even when you do), another interesting alternative is to stud your *salsa verde* with bits of those mild-tasting young turnips they call Japanese turnips in my farmers' market (they're 1 to 1½ inches across). Their bright, slightly spicy flavor combines well with the citrusy qualities of tomatillos and tangy-fresh notes of sorrel (you can replace the sorrel with a big handful of cilantro). Chop 3 or 4 peeled or unpeeled young turnips (or daikon radish or golden beet, but not large grocery-store turnips, which taste bitter here) into very small pieces (less than ¼ inch). Place in a sealable plastic bag and add a generous sprinkling of salt and a big squeeze of lime juice. Press out all the air and let stand about half an hour to soften. Stir into the finished salsa. If you're going to serve this simply as a salsa, chop some red onion and marinate it with the turnip and lime.

Banana Pepper–Leek Soup with White Beans and Crispy Chorizo

Crema de Chile Güero y Poros con Alubias y Chorizo

◇◇

There's a moment in the late summer or early fall at my farmers' market when huge mounds of banana peppers show up near huge mounds of leeks. That's not a sight I've seen in Oaxaca, say, at the Central de Abastos, or in Mexico City's La Merced. But this is Chicago, and different synergies emerge.

My guess is that you share my attraction to leeks that are cooked slowly, until they melt into an aromatic creaminess. They're different from slow-cooked onions—a little brighter in flavor, more distinctive in texture. And because of my farmers' market's serendipitous vegetable display, I've come to appreciate the leeks' flavors even more fully when I've paired them with those bright-flavored, light green chiles we call banana peppers (versions in Mexico are called *chile güero* or *xcatic*).

When you make the classic leek and potato soup, flavoring and richness often come from bacon. This soup follows that same path, though it features chorizo (it's good with bacon, too) for flavor, while white beans (not potatoes) provide the creamy texture.

Makes about 6 cups, serving 4 as a light meal

6 ounces fresh Mexican chorizo sausage, casing removed (about ¾ cup)

1½ pounds (about 6 medium) leeks, roots cut off, cut in half lengthwise, thoroughly washed through all the layers, each half sliced crosswise into ¼-inch pieces

1 pound (about 6) fresh hot or mild banana peppers (aka güero chiles), stemmed, seeded and sliced crosswise ¼-inch thick

Two 15-ounce cans white beans, drained (divided use)

OR 3½ cups home-cooked white beans, drained (divided use)

1 quart chicken broth

Salt

A handful of cilantro or flat-leaf parsley leaves, for serving

OR a few tablespoons grated Mexican *queso añejo* or other garnishing cheese such as Romano or Parmesan, for serving

OR a few tablespoons Mexican *crema*, sour cream, *crème fraîche* or Greek-style yogurt, for serving

In a large (5- to 6-quart) soup pot, cook the chorizo over medium heat, stirring to break up any clumps, until it's crispy, about 10 minutes. With a slotted spoon, scoop the chorizo onto a paper towel to drain, leaving behind as much fat as possible.

Scoop the leeks and banana peppers into the pot, cover and return to medium heat. Let cook, uncovering to stir from time to time, until the vegetables are very soft, about 10 minutes. Uncover and continue to cook, stirring frequently, until the leeks and banana peppers look thoroughly melted and are just beginning to brown, about 10 minutes more. Scrape the mixture into a blender jar, add *1 can* (or *1¾ cups*) of the beans and the chicken broth. Cover loosely, blend until smooth and return to the pan. (Depending on the size of your blender, you may need to blend in batches.)

Add the remaining can of beans (or the remaining home-cooked beans) to the soup and bring to a simmer over medium heat. Taste and season with salt, usually a scant teaspoon, depending on the saltiness of your broth and beans. Let simmer for a few more minutes to blend the flavors, then ladle into warm soup bowls, sprinkle with the crispy chorizo and garnish with the herb leaves, cheese or *crema*—whatever you have. Soup's on.

Spicy Chipotle Eggplant with Black Beans (page 215)

Spicy Chipotle Eggplant with Black Beans

Berengena al Chipotle con Frijoles Negros

U ntil you taste this remarkable combination, you probably won't be able to imagine it. First the eggplant is roasted at a high temperature, meaning that it browns to a caramely deliciousness on the outside while staying creamy inside. But before you slide it into the oven, you coat it with the smoky dark richness of chipotle-spiked *salsa negra*. I like eggplant pretty much every way I've had it, but this rendition is one I dream of. Especially when it's served with a black bean sauce rich in flavor from the addition of a little more *salsa negra*. If I add a simple salad to the mix, I've got a great light dinner.

Serves 4

2 pounds eggplant (I like the smaller ones, such as Chinese, Japanese, graffiti or white, because their flesh is less bitter and more compact)

2 tablespoons olive oil, plus a little more for the baking sheet

9 tablespoons Sweet-Sour Dark Chipotle Seasoning (recipe follows; divided use)

2 cups seasoned black beans with enough broth to cover (if you're using canned beans, you'll need two 15-ounce cans, though you'll have some left over to, say, scramble into some eggs; use all the liquid in the cans, but be aware that bean sauce made from canned beans won't be as dark as one from home-cooked beans)

Salt

A few tablespoons of crumbled Mexican *queso fresco* or other fresh cheese such as feta or goat cheese

A handful of cilantro leaves, for serving

½ cup Mexican *crema* or *crème fraîche* (or sour cream or Greek-style yogurt that's been thinned with a little milk), for serving

Turn on the oven to 425 degrees and adjust the shelf to the middle level. Trim the stem end from the eggplants and cut them into rounds about ½-inch thick. (If any are larger than a couple of inches in diameter, cut them into half-moons.) Scoop them into a bowl, drizzle them with the oil and about *6 tablespoons* of the seasoning, toss to coat evenly, then spread onto a rimmed, lightly oiled baking sheet. Slide into the oven and roast, turning periodically with a metal spatula, until the slices are beginning to brown and are soft throughout, about 20 minutes.

While the eggplant is roasting, measure the beans (including their liquid) into a blender or food processor. Blend until smooth, adding a little more bean broth (or water) if necessary to get them to move through the blades. Scrape into a small (1- to 2-quart) saucepan and stir in enough bean broth or water to give the puree the consistency of a cream soup, usually about ¼ cup. Stir in the remaining *3 tablespoons* of the seasoning and warm over medium-low heat. Taste and season with salt if you think it needs it (depending on the saltiness of the beans, it may not).

When the eggplant is ready, spoon some of the warm sauce on each dinner plate and top with a portion of eggplant. Sprinkle with the *queso fresco* (or one of its stand-ins), some cilantro and a drizzle of *crema* (or one of its stand-ins), and you're ready to eat.

SWEET-SOUR DARK CHIPOTLE SEASONING

Place **2 cans chipotle chiles *en adobo* (canning liquid and all), 2 tablespoons molasses, ¼ cup balsamic or sweet sherry vinegar, ¼ cup (packed) brown sugar** and ½ cup water in a blender and process until smooth. Scrape into a small saucepan set over medium heat and bring to a brisk simmer, then turn the heat to medium-low and continue simmering, stirring regularly, until the mixture is the consistency of tomato paste, about 30 minutes. Remove from the heat and stir in **¼ cup soy sauce**. If necessary, add some water, a splash at a time, until the salsa is the consistency of runny ketchup. Cool, taste and season with salt; it may not need any, depending on the saltiness of your soy sauce.

Roasted chipotle eggplant

Braised Artichokes with Tomatoes, Jalapeños, Olives and Capers

Alcachofas Guisadas con Jitomates, Jalapeños, Aceitunas y Alcaparras

◇◇

This dish is easy to taste with your mind's tongue. It echoes the Mediterranean tomato-olive-caper trope as a flavoring for artichokes. So why is it here, amid recipes that show another side of flavor? The easy answer focuses on the pickled jalapeños. The more complex one has to do with the centuries-long interchange between Mexico and the Mediterranean, an interchange that enriched the Mediterranean with native Mexican tomatoes and chiles and Mexico with Mediterranean olives and garlic. What emerged, at least on the west side of the Atlantic, was a sauce we call "Veracruz style." And, of course, it's perfect with artichokes.

For a light dinner, I simply serve this flavorful vegetable braise with warm corn tortillas and a spoonful of *frijoles refritos*. To make it more substantial, I serve it with poached eggs. Or, for a hearty soft taco filling, I add cubed boneless, skinless chicken thigh or breast to the mixture as it simmers. If I have time, panko breadcrumbs, drizzled evenly with olive oil and toasted in a skillet over medium heat, make a wonderful garnish.

I've given you a range of quantity for the briny elements. Add them according to your own liking for that salty-tangy side of flavor.

Serves 4 as a light dinner

1 pound baby artichokes (about 8 artichokes total)
   OR one 14-ounce can artichoke hearts
2 tablespoons olive oil
1 medium white onion, cut into ¼-inch pieces
3 garlic cloves, peeled and finely chopped
One 28-ounce can diced fire-roasted tomatoes, undrained
3 or 4 tablespoons chopped green olives (manzanillas are common in Mexico)

2 or 3 canned pickled jalapeños, stemmed, seeded and thinly sliced
1 or 2 tablespoons capers
¼ cup chopped flat-leaf parsley leaves (optional)
Chicken broth or water
Salt
½ cup grated Mexican *queso añejo* or other garnishing cheese such as Romano or Parmesan

If you're working with baby artichokes, trim them for braising according to the instructions on page 201. Now cut the artichokes into quarters and drop them into a bowl of water to which you've added a couple of tablespoons of vinegar or lemon or lime juice. Carbon knives react with artichokes, so use stainless steel.

When all the artichokes are prepped, pour off the water, cover the bowl tightly with plastic wrap, poke a few holes in the top and microwave at 100% until tender, about 5 minutes, stopping halfway through to shake everything around to ensure even cooking. (If you're using canned artichoke hearts, simply drain and cut into quarters.)

Heat the oil in a large (10-inch) skillet over medium heat, add the onion and cook until golden but still crunchy, about 5 minutes. Add the garlic and stir for about a minute until fragrant, then add the tomatoes, olives, jalapeños, capers and parsley (if you're using it). Cook, stirring frequently, until the mixture is thicker than spaghetti sauce, about 10 minutes. Stir in enough chicken broth or water to give the mixture a saucy consistency (usually about ¼ cup), then taste and season with salt if necessary (if you added the larger quantities of briny elements, salt probably won't be needed).

Add the artichokes, adjust the heat to medium-low and let the mixture simmer gently for 15 minutes or so, for the flavors to mingle. Stir in the cheese and you're ready to serve.

3

DAILY
INSPIRATIONS
FOR BUSY COOKS

BREAKFAST ANYTIME

Spring Green *Licuado* **224**

Stone Fruit (or Mango) *Licuado* **226**

Carrot, Beet and Orange *Licuado* **227**

Xoco's Granola **228**

Open-Face Red Chile–Chard Omelet **230**

Open-Face Squash Blossom Omelet with Charred Tomato, Chile and Goat Cheese **232**

Open-Face Egg-Chorizo Tortas **234**

Cornmeal Pancakes **237**

Butternut-Pecan Muffins with Brown Sugar Crumble **240**

Horchata French Toast **243**

Spring Green *Licuado*

Licuado Verde

◇◇

This *licuado* walks that tightrope between fruity-sweet and herby-savory. If you want it to tip more savory, replace the pineapple with cucumber (peeled or not). An equivalent amount of green apple can replace the pineapple, too. If you want it to be a little spicy, add a small piece of health-promoting ginger. And speaking of health, it's very popular in Mexico to add the common *nopales* (prickly pear cactus paddles) to this kind of *licuado*, *nopal* being one of the most effective natural ways to regulate blood sugar levels. One substitution *not* to make: red chard for the green stuff—it turns the *licuado* a murky gray color.

Serves 4

2 cups cored, peeled, cubed (½-inch cubes) pineapple (you'll need about ½ of a sweet, ripe pineapple)

4 cups loosely packed sliced greens (in Mexico cooks typically use fresh alfalfa, but the drink is great with green kale, spinach or green chard; you'll want to cut off stems and thick central stalks)

2 tablespoons loosely packed roughly chopped herb leaves (I like mint the best, but some people prefer cilantro or parsley, or a combination of all of them)

2 tablespoons fresh lime juice

2 tablespoons sugar or agave nectar

In a blender combine the pineapple, greens, herb leaves, lime juice and sugar (or agave nectar) with 1½ cups water. Blend on high until the greens are pureed, about 1 minute. Taste for sugar; if your pineapple isn't very sweet, you may want to add a tablespoon or two more. Re-blend the mixture to dissolve the additional sugar, then strain the *licuado* into glasses filled with ice and serve right away. (This *licuado* starts to separate shortly after blending; a brisk stir will bring it back together.)

(From left) Carrot, Beet and Orange *Licuado* (page 227), Spring
Green *Licuado* (page 224), Stone Fruit (or Mango) *Licuado* (page 226)

Stone Fruit (or Mango) *Licuado*

Licuado de Drupas

◇◇◇

Though cherries, lychees, longans, rambutans, even olives and walnuts are technically part of the stone fruit family, this recipe is best prepared with peaches, mangos and the like. Very ripe apricots are good, too, though you'll want to use fewer (or more water). The basic proportions of this recipe work with melon as well.

If you like spiciness, you can embroider these flavors with freshly ground black pepper, chipotle or guajillo powder or a little serrano or jalapeño blended with the fruit. To add a bit more complexity, replace half the water with orange juice.

This (or any of the *licuados*) can be fortified, in traditional Mexican (and Rocky) style, with the original protein add-in: raw egg. If you're not convinced that the source of your eggs is completely trustworthy, you can use pasteurized eggs when you want that protein punch. Nutrition aside, I think it makes the *licuado* wonderfully creamy-frothy.

Serves 4

1½ cups peeled, pitted and chopped (1-inch pieces) stone fruit such as peaches, nectarines, plums, pluots or mangos

2 teaspoons finely grated lime zest (colored part only)

¼ cup fresh lime juice

¼ cup sugar

Combine the fruit, lime zest, lime juice and sugar in a blender with 2 cups water. Blend until the mixture is completely smooth. It should have a little more body than regular juice but be less thick than a traditional smoothie. Taste and season with a little more sugar (you may need it to bump up the fruit flavor) or a little more lime juice (if you think the brightness is needed). If it appeals, add a dash of vanilla or ground cinnamon, then cover and give the mixture a few pulses to incorporate the additions. Strain if you want to (I don't), then pour the *licuado* over ice and serve right away.

A Simple, Milky Riff on Stone Fruit *Licuado*:

You'll think of this *licuado* more as a smoothie when you make it with milk. Simply leave out the lime juice (you can still add the zest if you want) and replace the water with milk (or even a combination of milk and yogurt).

Carrot, Beet and Orange *Licuado*

Vampiro

I t's the blood-red beet, obviously, that evoked the Spanish name for this Mexican juice-bar classic of beet, carrot and orange. Though I never predicted it could be one of my favorites, just the right addition of sweetness (sugar) and tanginess (lime) throws it to the top of my *licuado* list.

Serves 4

2 cups fresh orange juice

1 cup carrot juice

1 generous tablespoon fresh lime juice

½ cup unpeeled chopped (½-inch pieces) beet (you'll need only 1 medium beet)

2 to 3 tablespoons sugar (optional)

In a blender combine the orange juice, carrot juice, lime juice and beet. Blend on high until the beet is pureed and has turned the juices a deep crimson color, about 1 minute. Taste the mixture. Some people, like me, will add the sugar at this point to take the edge off the beet's earthiness. Re-blend the mixture to dissolve the sugar (30 seconds or so). Strain the *licuado* into glasses filled with ice and serve right away.

Xoco's Granola

Granola Estilo Xoco

◇◇◇

Most folks think of granola as having an American, sixties-ish, hippieish origin, but for whatever reason, years ago it found a happy home in Mexico, establishing itself as a very popular resident of juice bars and other food spots that tout natural products. The Mexican version emphasizes nuts and seeds (easy to find) as well as ancient Mexican, high-protein amaranth (a little more difficult to procure). I love this granola so much that we offer it every day for breakfast at our quick-service spot, Xoco. Don't get caught up in equal quantities of each nut and seed; you need 2 cups total of whatever combination you use.

Makes 2 quarts

1½ cups old-fashioned rolled oats (quick-cooking oats will work here, but the texture isn't as attractive)

½ cup (about 2 ounces) raw almonds

½ cup (about 2 ounces) raw peanuts

½ cup (about 2 ounces) raw cashews

½ cup (about 2 ounces) hulled raw pumpkin seeds

1¼ cups puffed amaranth (classic in Mexico, but if you can't find it, replace it with puffed millet)

¼ cup all-purpose flour

¼ cup vegetable oil

⅓ cup honey

¼ cup sugar

1 teaspoon salt

Turn on the oven to 300 degrees. On a rimmed baking sheet lined with parchment paper, spread out the oats, nuts, pumpkin seeds and amaranth. Bake, stirring halfway through, until the nuts are just beginning to color and the oats are crispy, about 20 minutes. Scrape it all into a large bowl, sprinkle on the flour and toss to coat. In a medium bowl, whisk together the oil, honey, sugar and salt. Pour this mixture over the oats and mix until everything is evenly coated. Spread the mixture in an even layer on that same parchment-lined baking sheet and return it to the oven. Bake, stirring with a spatula every 10 minutes, until the oats are a rich caramel color, the nuts are browned and shiny and the granola is fragrant, about 40 minutes. (The baked mixture may feel dampish when you stir it, but it will crisp as it cools.) Transfer the sheet to a cooling rack and let the granola cool completely. With your hands, break it into bite-size clusters and transfer it to an airtight container; it will keep for 2 weeks or so.

Open-Face Red Chile–Chard Omelet (page 230)

Open-Face Red Chile–Chard Omelet

Omelet Abierto de Chile Rojo y Acelgas

◆◇

Rather than make omelets individually, each rolled around some delicious filling, I make a single big open-face one, distribute the "filling" ingredients over the top and cut it into wedges. That way, no one has to sit at the table watching their brunch or supper get cold while the rest of the omelets are made.

This version has bits of smoky-sweet-toasty ancho chile mixed into the eggs, lightly wilted chard over the top, and a sprinkling of cheese—you choose how pungent—to bring it all together. If ancho chiles aren't at hand, you can use a little chopped canned chipotle or even about ½ teaspoon powdered ancho, guajillo, or chipotle chile or smoked paprika.

And chard isn't your only option here. I've made this omelet with everything from spinach and amaranth greens to lamb's quarters, Sylvetta arugula and succulent New Zealand spinach. Practically any green can be worked in.

Serves 4

1 dried ancho chile, stemmed, seeded and torn into several flat pieces

2 ounces green or rainbow chard, cut crosswise into ½-inch strips (stems included) (about 2 cups)

3 tablespoons vegetable oil (divided use)

Salt

8 eggs

1 garlic clove, finely chopped
  OR 1 tablespoon finely chopped garlic chives or red onion

¼ cup crumbled Mexican *queso fresco* or other fresh cheese such as feta or goat cheese
  OR 2 tablespoons grated Mexican *queso añejo* or other garnishing cheese such as Romano or Parmesan

About 1 tablespoon chopped fresh cilantro, mint or other herb that appeals

Set a large (10-inch) nonstick skillet over medium heat. When hot, lay the chile pieces in the skillet, flatten with a spatula for a few seconds until aromatic, then flip and toast the other side. Cool slightly, then chop or break into roughly ¼-inch pieces.

In a microwave-safe bowl, toss the chard with *1 tablespoon* of the oil, 1 tablespoon water and ¼ teaspoon salt. Cover with plastic wrap, poke a few holes into the top and microwave at 100% for 1 minute. Uncover and toss the chard again. In a large bowl, whisk the eggs with the chile pieces and ½ teaspoon salt until they are broken up but not completely homogenous.

Return the skillet to medium heat. Add the remaining *2 tablespoons* oil, then add the garlic (or one of its stand-ins) and cook, stirring, for a few seconds, just until it's fragrant. Add the egg mixture and let it cook without stirring for about 30 seconds. Using a rubber or silicone spatula, start drawing the cooked egg on the bottom of the pan from the edge into the center, letting the uncooked egg flow around to take its place. Repeat every 15 seconds or so until most of the omelet has cooked but the top is still moist, about 2 minutes. Scatter the chard evenly across the top of the omelet and press it gently into the moist egg. Immediately cover the pan, remove it from the heat and let it sit for a minute or two until the top of the omelet has set. Run your spatula along the underside of the omelet, give the pan a good shake to ensure it's completely loosened, then slide the omelet onto a platter. Sprinkle the cheese and herb over the omelet, cut it into 4 wedges and serve immediately.

Green Chile Riff on the Red Chile–Chard Omelet:

Instead of ancho chile, use a small fresh poblano chile (roasted, peeled, seeded and chopped). Dollops of avocado-tomatillo salsa instead of the herb would put this green chile version over the top.

Open-Face Squash Blossom Omelet with Charred Tomato, Chile and Goat Cheese

Omelet Abierto de Flores, Jitomate Tatemado, Chile y Queso de Cabra

◇◇

Think of this omelet as a soft-cooked, four-person frittata with classic Mexican flavors scattered on top. And don't get derailed when you encounter squash blossoms in the ingredients list. I can lay my hands on them for only two or three months a year. Even without them, you'll still have a memorable omelet (the classic flavor of dry-roasted tomato, chile and onion embroidered with the tangy creaminess of good goat cheese is always appealing). Or you can replace squash blossoms with lilly blossoms, nasturtium blossoms or a little sliced spinach.

Serves 4

2 small (about 6 ounces total) plum tomatoes, chopped into ½-inch pieces (about 1 cup)

¼ to ½ cup chopped (½-inch pieces) medium-spicy fresh chile (anything from shishitos or mild jalapeños to roasted and peeled poblanos or banana peppers)

1 small red onion (fresh-dug tropeas from the farmers' market are my favorite), cut into ½-inch pieces

Salt

8 eggs

12 squash blossoms, stamens and sepals removed, flowers sliced crosswise into ¼-inch strips

1 tablespoon chopped fresh cilantro, mint or other herb

Ground black pepper

2 tablespoons butter

About ¼ cup crumbled goat cheese, Mexican *queso fresco* or other fresh cheese such as feta

Heat a large (10-inch) nonstick skillet over medium. Scoop in the chopped tomatoes, chiles and onion, spreading them into an even layer in the dry pan. Cook, stirring occasionally, until they're softened and darkened in spots, about 7 minutes. Sprinkle with a generous ¼ teaspoon salt and scrape into a shallow bowl. Wash and dry the skillet and put it back over medium heat.

In a medium bowl, beat the eggs until broken up but not completely homogenous. Stir in the squash blossoms, herb, ½ teaspoon salt and about ¼ teaspoon pepper. Slide the butter to the hot skillet and swirl it around, letting it bubble and foam. When the butter begins to brown, add the egg mixture and let it cook without stirring for about 30 seconds. Using a rubber or silicone spatula, start drawing the cooked egg on the bottom of the pan from the edge into the center, letting the uncooked egg flow around to take its place. Repeat every 15 seconds or so until most of the omelet has cooked but the top is still moist, about 2 minutes. Scatter the charred tomato mixture evenly across the top of the omelet and press it gently into the moist egg. Immediately cover the pan, remove it from the heat and let it sit for a minute or two until the top of the omelet has set. Run your spatula along the underside of the omelet, give the pan a good shake to ensure it's completely loosened, then slide the omelet onto a platter. Sprinkle the cheese over the top, cut it into 4 wedges and serve immediately.

Open-Face Egg-Chorizo Tortas

Molletes de Chorizo y Huevo

◇◇◇

I'm kind of on a crusade for *molletes*, those open-face sandwiches I used to eat most evenings during my early days in Mexico City. They were cheap (a primary motivation on my student's budget): half a *telera* roll that's smeared with a satisfying layer of beans, topped with melted cheese and served with salsa—a sandwich version of my favorite ready-at-a-moment's-notice bean and cheese taco. I've made them with dozens of different add-ons, and every one comes out satisfying, easy and delicious. Especially at breakfast, with chorizo and eggs piled on.

Serves 6

8 ounces fresh Mexican chorizo sausage, casing removed (about 1 cup)

One 15-ounce can black beans, most of the liquid drained off
OR about 2 cups home-cooked black beans

Salt

1 tablespoon vegetable oil

1 large red or white onion, chopped into ¼-inch pieces

4 eggs

3 good-quality *telera* rolls, cut in half as you would for a sandwich
OR 1 good-quality baguette, cut into three 5-inch-long portions and sliced in half as for a sandwich

1½ cups (about 6 ounces) shredded Mexican melting cheese (such as Chihuahua, quesadilla or asadero) or Monterey Jack, brick or mild cheddar

About 2 tablespoons chopped cilantro

About ¾ cup of your favorite salsa, for serving

Heat a medium (8-inch) nonstick skillet over medium and add the chorizo. Cook, stirring to break up the clumps, until it just starts to brown, about 4 minutes. Use a slotted spoon to transfer the chorizo to a plate, leaving the rendered fat behind. Add the beans to the skillet and cook, mashing them with the back of a large spoon, an old-fashioned potato masher or a Mexican bean masher until you have a coarse puree. (If the beans are stiffer than very soft mashed potatoes, stir in a little water.) Taste and season with salt (home-cooked beans usually take about ¼ teaspoon; canned beans may not need any). Scrape into a bowl and clean the skillet.

Return the skillet to medium heat and add the oil. When hot, scoop in the onion and cook, stirring regularly, until it is soft and beginning to caramelize, about 7 minutes. Beat the eggs in a small bowl and add them to the skillet, along with the chorizo. Cook, stirring nearly constantly, until the eggs have scrambled to a soft mass, about 3 minutes. (They will cook more later, so don't overcook them.) Immediately remove from the heat.

Turn on the broiler and adjust the rack to its highest setting. Slide a heavy-duty baking sheet onto the rack to preheat. Lay the six slices of bread cut side up on a cutting board. Use your fingers or a spoon to scrape out a good amount of the soft bread in the center of each slice, making a hollow. Smear each slice with about ¼ cup of beans, then spread on ½ cup of the egg-chorizo mixture and sprinkle with ¼ cup of cheese. Lay the *molletes* on the hot baking sheet and broil until the cheese has melted and is starting to brown, about 5 minutes. Sprinkle each with a teaspoon or so of chopped cilantro and serve immediately with the salsa on the side.

A Few *Mollete* Riffs:

Honestly, a bean and cheese *mollete* will welcome pretty much any additional topping that you can dream up. Here are three of my favorites: Replace the chorizo scramble with (1) caramelized onions mixed with chopped canned chipotle chiles and crumbled crisp bacon, (2) caramelized onions mixed with roasted poblano and crumbled goat cheese, or (3) sliced farmers' market tomatoes and a sprinkling of fresh herbs (I actually like them on top, after melting the cheese). Any of these (as well as the chorizo scramble) can benefit from sprinkling of grated *añejo* cheese, Romano or Parmesan.

Open-Face Egg-Chorizo Tortas (page 234)

Cornmeal Pancakes

Hotcakes de Harina de Maiz

◇◇◇

These aren't a little-known Mexican specialty I sussed out from the pages of some obscure cookbook. No, we created them at Frontera to celebrate an amazing, flinty cornmeal made from heirloom corn that had been raised by the Iroquois Nation since time immemorial. It can be made with a special yellow or white or blue cornmeal you discover, too, or with cornmeal from the grocery store—you have lots of choices. First choose the texture of the pancake: a coarser grind of cornmeal gives the pancake a bit of crunch. Then choose its thickness: less buttermilk gives you a thicker, heftier pancake, while more gives you one that's lacier and lighter, with a creamy texture. Finally, choose the adornment: for that, I think the cinnamon-infused agave syrup is delicious.

Serves 4 or 5

1½ cups coarsely ground cornmeal, finely ground cornmeal or a combination of the two

¾ cup all-purpose flour

2 tablespoons sugar

2 teaspoons baking soda

Salt

2 to 3 cups buttermilk

3 eggs

¾ cup vegetable oil

4 to 8 tablespoons (2 to 4 ounces) butter

About 1 cup warm Cinnamon Agave Syrup (recipe follows), *Piloncillo* Syrup (page 244) or maple syrup, for serving

In a large bowl, whisk together the cornmeal, flour, sugar, baking soda and 2 teaspoons salt. In a medium bowl, whisk together the buttermilk, eggs and vegetable oil. Pour the wet mixture into the dry and whisk until a smooth batter forms. (If you used the full amount of buttermilk, the batter will be thin.)

Heat a heavy (preferably nonstick or seasoned cast iron) griddle or very large (12-inch) skillet over medium until it's hot enough for a drop of water to skip across the surface and evaporate almost immediately. Use 1 tablespoon butter to film the surface, then pour the batter onto the hot griddle, using about ¼ cup per pancake. Leave 1 inch of space between them. Cook until bubbles form and pop on the surface, about

2 minutes, then flip the pancakes and cook until golden brown on the other side. Transfer to a baking sheet and keep warm in a low oven. Repeat with the remaining batter, regreasing the griddle between batches, until all has been used. Serve the pancakes immediately with the warm syrup.

A Savory Riff on Cornmeal Pancakes:

There's nothing inherently sweet in the pancakes themselves, so sometimes I like to make them small and serve them as a savory light dinner with dollops of Greek-style yogurt, crumbled crispy bacon and a spoonful of salsa. Scrambled eggs can work themselves onto the top, too, if you want. And some crumbled hot-smoked salmon (or practically any smoked pork product) is a delicious replacement for the bacon.

CINNAMON AGAVE SYRUP • *Miel de Agave y Canela*

Makes about 1 cup

1 cup agave nectar (light organic nectar gives the best flavor)

A 2- or 3-inch piece of cinnamon stick,
   preferably Mexican *canela*

In a small saucepan combine the agave nectar and cinnamon over medium heat. Bring the syrup to a simmer, turn off the heat, cover the pan and let the cinnamon infuse until the syrup has cooled. Discard the cinnamon stick. This syrup is best served warm.

Butternut-Pecan Muffin with Brown Sugar Crumble (page 240)

Butternut-Pecan Muffins with Brown Sugar Crumble

Muffins de Calabaza y Nuez

◇◇

You shouldn't trust me when I say this (I'm prone to enthusiastic proclamations), but these are my favorite muffins in the world. At least right here, right now. It's fall as I'm writing these words, we've just picked the butternut from our garden, and with these muffins in the oven, the house smells so amazing I can't imagine ever leaving. Their texture is so moist, tender and surprisingly light (they stay moist for several days after baking). And the nutty crunch of pecan is the perfect foil to their gentle sweetness.

Makes 12 muffins

½ small (2-pound) butternut squash, peeled, seeded and cut into 1-inch chunks (about 3 cups)

⅓ cup brown sugar

¾ cup toasted pecan pieces (divided use)

2 tablespoons sour cream

1½ teaspoons pure vanilla extract, preferably Mexican

2 eggs

1½ cups cake flour

¾ cup granulated sugar

1 teaspoon ground cinnamon, preferably Mexican *canela*

1 teaspoon baking soda

¾ teaspoon baking powder

Salt

10 tablespoons (5 ounces) unsalted butter, cut into pieces and softened

Turn on the oven to 300 degrees. Spray a standard-size (not jumbo) 12-cup muffin tin with nonstick spray or line each cup with a paper cupcake liner.

Scoop the butternut pieces into a microwave-safe bowl, cover with plastic wrap, poke a few holes in the top, and microwave at 100% for 10 minutes. Uncover the bowl and mash with the back of a large spoon until the squash is the consistency of loose mashed potatoes. Let cool completely.

In a small bowl, mix the brown sugar with ¼ *cup* of the pecans and set aside. Stir the sour cream and vanilla into the now-cool butternut, then whisk in the eggs, one at a time, until the mixture is smooth (though if you have a few lumps you can't get rid of, that's okay).

Scoop the flour, granulated sugar, cinnamon, baking soda, baking powder and ½ teaspoon salt into the bowl of a stand mixer fitted with the paddle attachment (or, if you're using a hand mixer, into a large bowl) and mix on low speed for 30 seconds. Add the butter and mix until well blended, about 1 minute. Stop the mixer, add half of the squash mixture and beat on medium speed for 30 seconds. Stop the mixer, scrape down the sides of the bowl with a rubber spatula, add the rest of the squash and beat on medium until you have a smooth batter, about 30 seconds more. Add the remaining ½ cup of the pecans and mix until just incorporated.

Divide the batter among the muffin cups (you'll use about 3 tablespoons per muffin) and top each with a rounded teaspoon of the brown sugar mixture. Bake, rotating the pan halfway through, for about 25 minutes, until the muffins spring back when gently pressed and a skewer inserted into their middle comes out *almost* clean (a few crumbs attached is fine). Cool in the pan on a cooling rack for 20 minutes before unmolding.

Horchata French Toast (page 243)

Horchata French Toast

Torrejas Sabor a Horchata

◇◇

Torrejas in Mexico are made like French toast but don't show up at breakfast. They're a dessert, typically, which makes sense when you recognize that French toast has basically the same ingredients as bread pudding, just in a different form. For this one I've gone out on a limb, though. I've made the soaking custard out of eggs and *horchata*, that cinnamony rice (and sometimes almond) drink that's popular among the street vendors and *taquerias*, which makes it great for those who can't have dairy. But it works well, too, with regular milk replacing the almond milk I've called for. However you make it, this is a luscious, special-occasion breakfast.

Our Xoco version of *torrejas* is made with day-old artisan Mexican *bolillos* that are sturdy enough to soak overnight but light enough to cook in our wood-burning oven to a custardy succulence. Most of the commercial *bolillos* that I've tried from Mexican bakeries are too spongy and fluffy to work here, so I've suggested a good baguette or ciabatta as an alternative to an artisan *bolillo*.

Serves 4

1 good-quality French baguette (about 15 inches long by 4 inches wide), preferably day-old
  OR 1 good-quality loaf of ciabatta (about 12 inches long by 4 inches wide), preferably day-old
8 to 12 tablespoons (4 to 6 ounces) butter (divided use)
1½ cups almond milk
3 tablespoons uncooked white rice
A 2-inch piece of cinnamon stick, preferably Mexican *canela*, broken up

  OR 1 to 2 teaspoons ground cinnamon, preferably Mexican *canela*
3 egg yolks
¼ cup sugar
1 tablespoon pure vanilla extract, preferably Mexican
Salt
Toasted slivered almonds (optional)
About 1 cup warm *Piloncillo* Syrup (recipe follows), Cinnamon Agave Syrup (page 238) or maple syrup, for serving

If using a baguette, slice off and discard the end pieces. Holding your bread knife at a 45-degree angle to the loaf, cut off one 1-inch-thick slice (it should be roughly 4 inches long). Repeat until you have 8 similar slices. If you're using ciabatta, no need to slice on the diagonal; simply discard the end pieces and cut eight 1-inch slices. If the bread is very fresh, arrange the slices on a baking sheet and place in a 300-degree oven until they feel slightly hard and stale, about 30 minutes.

Place *4 tablespoons* of the butter in a microwave-safe bowl and melt it in the microwave at 50% power for 30 seconds. Combine the almond milk, rice and cinnamon in a blender and process for several minutes, until the rice no longer feels very gritty when the liquid is rubbed between your fingers. Add the egg yolks, sugar, vanilla, melted butter and ½ teaspoon salt to the rice mixture and blend again, covered, until everything is well combined. Pour the mixture through a fine-mesh strainer into a 9x13-inch baking pan. Lay in the bread and let it soak until the bottom of the bread feels heavy with liquid but isn't disintegrating, 10 to 15 minutes. Flip the bread and soak the other side. (If it's more convenient, cover the pan with plastic wrap and refrigerate overnight.)

Heat a very large (12-inch) heavy skillet (cast iron is perfect for this) over medium. Add *2 tablespoons* of butter and swirl it around the pan a few times until it has completely melted and the foaming has subsided. Use a spatula to transfer 3 slices of bread to the hot skillet. When they are richly browned underneath (about 5 minutes), flip the slices and cook until browned and crispy but custardy on the inside (about another 5 minutes). Transfer to a baking sheet and keep warm in a low oven. Add more butter to the pan (you'll usually need another 2 tablespoons per batch) and cook the remaining slices the same way. Top your French toast with slivered almonds if you like, and serve right away with warm syrup.

PILONCILLO SYRUP • *Miel de Piloncillo*

Make friends with *piloncillo*. It's unrefined cane sugar that comes in sturdy cones, the solidity of which may seem like a deterrent . . . until you give the *piloncillo* a taste. *Piloncillo* offers a rich complexity that sugar could only hope for, even organic evaporated cane juice. It's not brown sugar either; that has a one-note flavor by comparison. *Piloncillo* is the full expression of what sugar cane has to offer. It is typically sold in small, medium or large cones, from golden amber to near-chocolate brown, reflecting the progression toward molasses-like pungency. Choose your flavor, then chop or shave the hard cone with a large knife and measure. Or put the cone into a microwave for 30 seconds or so, to heat the residual moisture, at which point the hot cone will just kind of fall apart and make it easy to measure.

Makes about 1 cup

2 cups (8 ounces) chopped *piloncillo* (Mexican raw sugar)

½ teaspoon pure vanilla extract, preferably Mexican

In a medium saucepan, combine the *piloncillo* and 1 cup water over medium heat. Cook, stirring regularly, until the sugar has completely dissolved and the mixture has thickened to the consistency of real maple syrup, about 5 minutes. Remove from the heat, let cool to room temperature, then stir in the vanilla. Serve warm.

RICE-COOKER SIMPLICITY

Creamy Rice and Beans in Three Classic Flavors **250**

Black Bean Rice with Plantains and Smoky Pork **254**

Chorizo Rice with Lentils **256**

Herb Green Chicken and Rice **258**

Chipotle Rice with Shrimp **260**

Mexican Red Rice and Three Delicious Dishes to Make from It **262**

♦ Creamy Rice Soup with Poblano and Spinach **264**

♦ Crispy Rice Cakes with White Beans, Roasted Garlic, Aged Cheese and Smoky Chile **265**

♦ Spicy Bacon-and-Egg Fried Rice with Pickled Jalapeños and Cilantro **266**

RICE COOKERS (OR LACK THEREOF)

Why You Need a Rice Cooker: I have written this chapter because I find a rice cooker very useful. It cooks at the perfect gentle temperature to turn out great rice every time and it keeps that rice warm for a long time, meaning it's waiting when you're ready. Great for busy families.

Choosing a Rice Cooker and What You Should Know About How They Work: We have tested (and tested and tested) these recipes using a variety of simple 6-cup rice cookers (Zojirushi, Sanyo, Aroma), not the fancy, bulkier, computerized "fuzzy logic" ones. These simple rice cookers use an internal thermometer to determine when regular white rice is cooked; that's when the cooker switches to the "keep warm" mode. They all operate slightly differently, but all turn out good results.

Since the recipes in this chapter use the rice cooker for a few preparations beyond basic white rice (I even use it to sauté vegetables), I sometimes confuse my trusty appliance. Every once in a while, it turns to "keep warm" before I'm ready for that to happen. That just means I have to be a little flexible as I proceed. Should your rice cooker switch to "keep warm" earlier than I've said it will, wait a minute or so for it to cool down, click it back on and continue. At the end of most recipes, I ask you to taste the rice to make sure it is done; if it's not quite there, you'll sprinkle in a little water, click the cooker back on "cook" and let the rice cook for a few more minutes. Each rice cooker make and model is bound to be a little different. Take the times I've provided as a general guide.

Though I really like the meatier texture of medium-grain rice, I rarely use it for Mexican dishes in the rice cooker. Sure, it can provide creaminess (as in the Creamy Rice and Beans recipe), but to utilize it for fluffy rice dishes you have to sauté it first, pilaf style. And sautéing in the rice cooker occasionally stresses the appliance beyond its abilities, turning rice-cooker simplicity into rice-cooker frustration. So the easier-to-work-with long-grain rice it is: just mix everything together, turn on the appliance and get ready to eat.

How to Cook These Recipes Without a Rice Cooker: You can cook these recipes in a covered pot on the stovetop: Use medium heat for any "first steps" cooking, then turn the heat down to medium-low and cover the pot once the rice and liquid have been added and have come to a simmer. The liquid quantities in these recipes may not translate precisely to stovetop cooking (there may be more or less evaporation when you're cooking on the stovetop) and the times may be a little shorter, depending on your exact heat. Just know that there's no "keep warm" function on your stovetop, so you'll want to serve the rice within 10 or 15 minutes of finishing it.

Creamy Rice and Beans (Herby
Green Chile version) (page 250)

Creamy Rice and Beans in Three Classic Flavors

Arroz Cremoso y Frijoles en Tres Sabores Clásicos

◇◇

It's fascinating to me how cuisines develop different approaches to the same ingredients. Rice is the perfect example: the shorter-grain varieties of rice get cooked clumpy in Asia, creamy in Italy, separate in Mexico. Well, *mostly* separate, except when Mexico adopts the creamy style for making rice pudding. Sweet, never savory. That is, until some of the more modern chefs traveled to distant (mostly European) lands for training and returned with a newfound appreciation for savory, creamy rice, what the Italians call risotto. Now creamy rice—*arroz cremoso*—has become very popular among a certain crowd, and with good reason. It's a wonderful way to create a main dish that's satisfying, simple to put together and welcoming to many flavors. Here I'm offering you three such flavors: smoky red chile and white beans, roasted garlic with tomato and black beans, and herbs with green chile and white beans.

Most folks in Mexico will tell you that the country's most famous rice is from Morelos (it even has a specified denomination of origin), just south of Mexico City. In its traditional form, the rice loved in Mexico is a medium grain, the type that you have to fry in its raw state to solidify the exterior starch enough to cook it up into separate grains; eliminating the dry-frying step yields clumpy (or, if cooked with extra broth and stirred, creamy) rice. The rice's exterior starch literally melts away, creating that clumpy or creamy texture—what most Mexican cooks are looking for in their rice pudding, and some cooks, nowadays, in savory rice dishes as well.

Traditional Italian cooks create the most brilliant creaminess by painstakingly adding doses of broth to the pan and stirring ceaselessly. A rice cooker turns out a very respectable creamy rice with little effort. A pressure cooker does the same and in less time; you'll need a 4- to 6-quart pressure cooker for these quantities.

I've left this recipe a meatless one. It's easy to add coarsely shredded leftover roast chicken or pork, flaked fish (I always keep some smoked fish in my freezer for just these occasions), maybe some crab. Extra roasted, grilled, or blanched vegetables can always be stirred in just before serving.

Serves 4

2 medium fresh poblano peppers (for the
 red chile version, choose red poblanos,
 red Anaheim/New Mexicos, red
 pimientos or red bell peppers)

3 tablespoons olive oil

1 medium white onion, cut into ¼-inch
 pieces

1 cup medium-grain rice (you can use
 Arborio or any other risotto-appropriate
 rice here)

3 cups chicken or vegetable broth (2 cups
 if using a pressure cooker)

Salt

*For **smoky red chile rice**:*

1 to 2 canned chipotle chiles *en adobo*,
 stemmed, seeded and finely chopped

2 tablespoons chipotle canning sauce

1 tablespoon paprika, preferably smoked
 Spanish paprika

Half a 15-ounce can white beans
 (cannellini, navy or Great Northern),
 drained

*For **garlicky tomato rice**:*

¼ cup chopped sundried tomatoes,
 rehydrated for 15 minutes in about ¼
 cup white wine, beer or water

4 unpeeled garlic cloves, roasted in a dry
 skillet over medium heat for about 15

minutes until soft, peeled and finely
 chopped

Half a 15-ounce can black beans,
 drained

*For **herby green chile rice**:*

¾ cup chopped fresh herbs (I usually use
 half cilantro, half flat-leaf parsley)
 OR ¼ cup Green Chile *Adobo* (recipe
 follows)

⅓ cup grated Mexican *queso añejo*
 or other garnishing cheese such as
 Romano or Parmesan

Half a 15-ounce can white beans
 (cannellini, navy or Great Northern),
 drained

Roast the poblanos over an open flame or close up under a preheated broiler, turning
them regularly, until evenly blackened and blistered, about 5 minutes for an open flame,

10 minutes for the broiler. Place in a bowl, cover with a kitchen towel and cool until handleable. Rub off the blackened skin, pull out the seedpods and scrape out the seeds. Rinse briefly to remove any stray seeds and bits of blackened skin. Cut into ¼-inch pieces.

Measure the olive oil into a rice cooker and add the onion. Turn on the cooker, set the lid in place and cook, stirring from time to time, for about 10 minutes or until the rice cooker turns to "keep warm" mode. The onions should be translucent and beginning to brown. (If using a pressure cooker, cook the onion in it.)

Add the rice to the rice cooker and stir it with the onion for a minute. Stir in the broth, roasted poblanos and salt (½ teaspoon if using salted broth, 1 teaspoon if using unsalted broth). If making the **smoky red chile rice**, stir in the chipotles, canning sauce and paprika. If making the **garlicky tomato rice**, stir in the drained, rehydrated tomatoes and roasted garlic.

For all versions, cover the rice cooker, turn it to "cook" and let the rice cook for 10 minutes. Stir the mixture thoroughly, re-cover and cook for 10 minutes more. (For the pressure cooker, set over medium heat, time 7 minutes once full pressure is reached, then do a quick release.) Turn off the rice cooker. The rice will look soupy, but the grains should be cooked through; the creamy rice will thicken considerably over the next few minutes. (If you're craving a bit more richness, stir in a couple tablespoons melted butter or olive oil.)

If making the **herby green chile rice**, stir in the herbs (or Green Chile *Adobo*) and cheese.

For all versions, stir in the beans, then taste and add a little more salt if it needs it. Serve right away in warm, shallow bowls or pasta bowls, sprinkled with a little extra cheese.

GREEN CHILE *ADOBO*

Set a large (10-inch) skillet over medium heat and lay in ½ **head of garlic,** separated into cloves but not peeled, and **4 to 5 fresh serrano chiles,** stems removed. Roast, turning regularly, until soft and browned in spots, about 10 minutes for the chiles and 15 for the garlic. Cool, slip off the garlic's husks and give it all a rough chop (no need to remove the chile seeds). In a blender or food processor, combine the garlic and chiles with **1 large bunch cilantro, 1 large bunch flat-leaf parsley, 1 cup olive oil** and **2 generous teaspoons salt**. Process, stopping to scrape down the sides if necessary, until nearly smooth (it should look a little like pesto).

Black Bean Rice with Plantains
and Smoky Pork (page 254)

Black Bean Rice with Plantains and Smoky Pork

Arroz de Frijol Negro con Plátanos y Puerco Ahumado

◇◇◇

I'll say it right off the bat: There are a couple of hurdles to this recipe, which means it falls into the category of an everyday, easy recipe that you may not be able to throw together on the spur of the moment. First, it requires very ripe plantain, the kind you rarely find in a regular grocery—the kind that's soft, black and ripe enough to sauté to a beautiful caramely flavor. From green to the necessary black-ripe state requires about a week, meaning you have to either stop by a Mexican grocery to look for a ripe one or plan way ahead.

Second, to get the darkest broth from the black beans, I strain the beans from the broth and let it sit in the refrigerator for several hours or overnight for the clearish liquid to rise to the top. I carefully remove that liquid, then use the darker broth that has settled. You can use canned black beans in this recipe, but don't use their canning liquid; rinse the beans and replace the bean liquid with an additional cup of chicken broth instead. The result will be good but not as black.

Nonetheless, this is one of my favorite rice dishes of all time. It's elementally satisfying, the kind of dish that evokes low moans from almost everyone to whom I've offered a spoon-ful. Beans and rice have nourished countless generations in countless cultures for millennia, so perhaps our reaction to a dish like this one is a primal one. I can't imagine that our primal reaction isn't further enhanced, however, by the earthy sweetness of black beans, the cara-mel-tinged sweet tang of ripe plantain and the captivating charms of all smoked pork products.

Serves 4

3 tablespoons vegetable or olive oil (divided use)

1 large black-ripe plantain, peeled and cut into ½-inch cubes

1 cup long-grain rice

2 green onions, trimmed of roots and withered outer leaves, cut crosswise into ¼-inch pieces

1 cup darkest broth from home-cooked, seasoned black beans (or additional chicken broth)

¾ cup chicken broth or water

Salt

A generous ½ cup (about 4 ounces) coarsely shredded meat from smoked pork shanks or pork hocks

OR a generous ½ cup (about 4 ounces) cubed ham

OR 4 to 6 thick slices (4 to 6 ounces) bacon, cut crosswise into ½-inch pieces, cooked over medium heat until crisp, then drained (you can use the rendered fat in place of the vegetable or olive oil listed above)

1 cup drained, cooked, seasoned black beans

About ¼ cup cilantro leaves, for serving

Though it's possible to sauté the plantains in the rice cooker, the stovetop is more reliable. Heat 2 *tablespoons* of the oil in a large (10-inch) skillet (preferably nonstick) over medium. When it's hot, add the plantain in an uncrowded single layer and cook, turning the pieces occasionally but keeping them spread out, for about 8 minutes, until browned on all sides. Remove the plantain to drain on paper towels. Pour the remaining *1 tablespoon* oil into the rice cooker and add the rice, green onions, bean broth and chicken broth (or water). Taste the broth: it should taste slightly salty; if it doesn't, season it to that level (quantities will vary depending on the saltiness of your broths).

Cover the rice cooker, turn it to "cook" and let the rice cook until the appliance switches to "keep warm" mode, 15 to 20 minutes. Taste a grain of rice: it should be very close to done at the core. If not, sprinkle in a little water, re-cover and cook 5 minutes more. Uncover the rice cooker and sprinkle the plantain, smoked pork (or one of its stand-ins) and beans over the top. Carefully fluff the rice with a fork, reaching all the way to the edges of the bottom, to release steam, slow the cooking and mix in the plantain and beans. Re-cover and keep warm for at least 5 minutes—preferably 15 to 20 minutes—to finish the cooking. Of course it can hold for up to an hour or so in "keep warm" mode. The dish is ready to spoon into warm bowls and top with the cilantro.

Chorizo Rice with Lentils

Arroz con Chorizo y Lentejas

◇◇◇

There's almost nothing as perfect for those nights when it's just you, the couch and a good movie as this comforting one-pot meal. There'll be leftovers for lunch, which is good because this rice dish is great reheated in the microwave. If the chorizo that is used to flavor the rice doesn't offer enough substance, cook double the quantity, add half to the rice and sprinkle the other half on top. Or use the rice as a bed for grilled or sautéed chicken or fish. That version makes a great main dish for company.

Each variety of lentil cooks differently: some hold their shape (like the black belugas and French greens); others soften and blend into the rice (like the common browns and reds). For this dish I prefer the former, but either is good. Try as I might, I can't get the lentils to cook in the same amount of time as the rice in the rice cooker. So I start them earlier to ensure they're not crunchy.

Serves 4 as a main course, 6 as a side dish

⅓ cup lentils, preferably the black beluga or green French lentils

4 ounces fresh Mexican chorizo, casing removed (about ½ cup)

1 cup long-grain rice

½ cup chopped green or knob onions (about 2 onions)

OR about 1/3 cup chopped garlic chives or regular chives

Salt

Place the lentils and ¾ cup water in a rice cooker and cook for about 20 minutes or until the rice cooker turns to "keep warm" mode; the lentils should taste about half done. Meanwhile, in a large (10-inch) nonstick skillet set over medium heat, cook the chorizo, breaking up any clumps, until it has begun to brown, about 7 minutes. Stir the rice into the chorizo and cook, stirring nearly constantly, until it has turned from translucent to milky white, about 3 minutes more.

When the lentils are ready, scrape the chorizo and rice mixture into the rice cooker along with the onion (or chives), 1 teaspoon salt and 1¾ cups water. Cover the rice cooker, once again turn it to "cook" and let the rice cook until the appliance switches to "keep warm" mode, 15 to 20 minutes. Taste a grain of rice: it should be very close to done at the core. If not, sprinkle in a little water, re-cover and cook 5 minutes more. Gently fluff the mixture with a fork, reaching all the way to the edges of the bottom, to release steam and slow the cooking. Re-cover and keep warm for at least 5 minutes—preferably 15 to 20 minutes—to finish the cooking. Of course it can hold for up to an hour or so in "keep warm" mode. You're ready to serve.

Herb Green Chicken and Rice

Arroz Verde con Pollo

◇◇

Since I first tasted the Peruvian version of *arroz con pollo* a dozen years ago, that has been the version of this homey dish I've turned to more than any other. I like the beautiful green herbiness and the glow of chile, though I've morphed the not-so-easy-to-find Peruvian *aji amarillo* into the now-common-in-the-United States poblano. This is a super-easy, very tasty dish you can prep in just a little longer than it takes to make a pot of rice.

I like to make this dish with medium-grain rice because I like its meaty texture; the dish turns out moister, though. You can make it, as they do in Peru, with the fluffier, drier-textured long-grain rice. You may find that you need slightly more or less liquid than I've called for here, depending on the length of the rice grains and their freshness. Likewise, feel free to stir in chopped blanched green beans, long beans, broccoli or broccolini (I blanch them in the microwave with a splash of water, covered with plastic wrap). Blanched peeled fresh fava beans are delicious here, too.

Serves 4

½ cup chopped (½-inch pieces) fresh poblano chile (you'll need 1 small poblano)

2 garlic cloves, peeled and cut in half

¼ teaspoon ground cumin

¼ teaspoon ground black pepper

1¾ cups chicken broth or water

Salt

½ cup loosely packed, roughly chopped cilantro

1 cup white rice

8 ounces (about 1½ cups) coarsely shredded cooked chicken

1 cup frozen or blanched fresh peas

In a medium (3-quart) saucepan, combine the poblano, garlic, spices and chicken broth (or water). Measure in ½ teaspoon salt for salted broth, 1 teaspoon for unsalted broth or water. Bring to a simmer over medium-high heat, cook for a couple of minutes, then pour into a blender jar and add the cilantro. *Cover the blender loosely*, then blend to a smooth puree.

Pour the herby green mixture into your rice cooker and stir in the rice. Cover, turn it to "cook" and let the rice cook for 10 minutes. Stir the mixture thoroughly, re-cover and continue to cook until the appliance switches to "keep warm" mode, about 15 minutes. Taste a grain of rice: it should be very close to done at the core. If not, sprinkle in a little water, re-cover and cook 5 minutes more. Scatter the chicken and peas on top of the rice. Very gently fluff the rice, reaching all the way to the edges of the bottom, to release steam, slow the cooking and mix in the chicken and peas. Re-cover and keep warm for at least 5 minutes—preferably 15 to 20 minutes—to finish the cooking. Of course it can hold for another 30 minutes on "keep warm" mode. Dinner's ready.

Chipotle Rice with Shrimp

Arroz al Chipotle con Camarones

◇◇◇

Straight-ahead delicious, this is Mexican-style rice infused with smoky chipotles, garlic and cilantro. And studded with shrimp, which may seem pretty special-occasion for everyday eating. Chicken is more available and affordable, so feel free to replace the shrimp with an equal amount of boneless, skinless chicken thigh or breast cut into ½-inch cubes. Add them along with the broth rather than halfway through the rice cooking.

If you have Quick Red Chile *Adobo* (page 37) in your refrigerator, replace the chipotle, canning liquid and garlic with 3 tablespoons of your prepared seasoning, cooking it in the oil until the oil separates out. The finished dish won't be as smoky or as spicy, but the flavor will be enticing and the preparation very easy. Shrimp overcooks quickly, so this is one rice-cooker dish you don't want to let sit around; prepare it shortly before serving.

Serves 4

2 tablespoons vegetable or olive oil

3 garlic cloves, peeled and finely chopped

2 canned chipotle chiles *en adobo*, stemmed, seeded and finely chopped

2 tablespoons chipotle canning sauce (if you like it really spicy)

1 cup long-grain rice

1⅔ cups chicken broth

Salt

1 pound (about 30) medium shrimp, peeled and deveined if you wish

1 cup loosely packed cilantro leaves

Turn your rice cooker to "cook" and pour in the oil. When it's hot, add the garlic, stir a minute, then add the chipotles, their canning sauce (if using), the broth and salt (a scant 1 teaspoon if you're using salted broth, 1½ teaspoons if your broth is unsalted). Cover the rice cooker and let the rice cook for 10 minutes. Uncover, lay the shrimp on top of the rice, then re-cover and continue to cook until the appliance switches to "keep warm" mode, usually about 15 minutes more. Taste a grain of rice: it should be very close to done at the core. If not, sprinkle in a little water, re-cover and cook 5 minutes more. Very gently fluff the rice, reaching all the way to the edges of the bottom, to release steam, slow the cooking and mix in the shrimp. Re-cover and keep warm for 5 to 10 minutes to finish the cooking. The dish is ready to spoon into warm bowls and top with the cilantro.

Chipotle Rice with Shrimp (page 260)

Mexican Red Rice and Three Delicious Dishes to Make from It

Arroz Rojo Mexicano y Tres Comidas que Lo Utiliza

◇◇◇

H ere's the idea: make a big pot of classic Mexican red-tomato rice to have on hand as the starting point for three different meals. I know it's appealing simply as is, as the just-right accompaniment to Chipotle Meatballs (page 117), Roasted Tomatillo Enchiladas (page 73) or perhaps Red Peanut *Mole* (page 105). But this is different: Once you've made your pot of rice and, let's say, served some of it for tonight's dinner, the leftovers can be turned into truly irresistible crispy rice cakes, or a Mexican-infused take on fried rice or a creamy, vegetable-rich soup.

Typically I'd have you start this big pot of rice on the stovetop, then finish it in the oven to ensure even cooking. To tell the truth, it's easier to do it in a rice cooker: it'll be hot and ready when you are, and the results are excellent. You just need to have an 8-cup rice cooker, which is bigger than the 6-cup version many folks have. If you have a 6-cup rice cooker, make a half batch following the directions on page 264.

And here's a tip for ensuring great-textured leftover rice: once you've served as much of the warm rice as you need, immediately scoop what's left into a baking dish (or something similar) to cool quickly at room temperature, then cover it with plastic wrap and refrigerate (for up to 5 days) or freeze (for up to 3 months) until you're ready to use it for one of the dishes that follows.

MEXICAN RED RICE • *Arroz Rojo Mexicano*

Except during that part of the summer when we have local vine-ripe tomatoes, I make this rice with canned fire-roasted tomatoes, as I find that the fire-roasted flavor adds depth that tastes like that of the best red rice I've had in Mexico. When I have good fresh tomatoes, I use 1 scant pound, cut them into pieces and puree them raw in a blender or food processor. (You can roast them under a broiler if you like, though really ripe fresh raw tomatoes are wonderful in Mexican rice.)

When I want that traditional Mexican toasty rice flavor, which comes from sautéing the raw rice in oil until it browns lightly, I do that in a pot on the stovetop over medium heat, then scrape the browned rice into the rice cooker and continue.

Makes about 10 cups

4 garlic cloves, peeled

One 15-ounce can diced fire-roasted
 tomatoes, undrained

3 tablespoons vegetable oil

3 cups long-grain white rice (I typically
 like the meatier texture of medium-
 grain rice, but since I don't fry the rice
 in this version, medium-grain turns out
 too sticky)

3 cups chicken broth or water

Salt

Hot green chiles to taste (roughly 3
 or 4 serranos or 2 large jalapeños),
 stemmed, a slit cut down the side of
 each one

4 medium carrots, peeled and chopped
 into ¼-inch cubes (optional)

About 1 cup defrosted frozen or fresh
 peas (optional)

About ½ cup chopped flat-leaf parsley or
 cilantro

Put the garlic in a small microwave-safe bowl, cover with water and microwave at 100% for 1 minute. Drain, scoop into a blender or food processor and add the canned tomatoes. Process to a smooth puree.

In an 8-cup rice cooker, stir together the oil and rice. When the rice is thoroughly coated, stir in the tomato puree, broth (or water) and 1 tablespoon salt if using unsalted broth or water, 2 teaspoons if using salted broth. Nestle in the chiles (the slit in the side lets out flavor with little heat). Cover the rice cooker, turn it to "cook" and set a timer for 15 minutes. When the timer goes off, gently stir the rice to incorporate the tomato mixture. Re-cover and let the rice cook until the appliance switches to "keep warm" mode, about 20 minutes. Taste a grain of rice: It should be very close to done at the core. If not, sprinkle in a little water, re-cover and cook 5 minutes more.

If you're using carrots, scoop them into a microwave-safe bowl, splash with a couple of tablespoons water, cover with plastic wrap, poke a few holes in the top and micro-wave at 100% for 2 minutes. Carefully uncover (it's steamy and hot) and tip off the water. If you're using *fresh* peas, microwave them in the same way for 2 to 5 minutes, depending on how small and tender they are.

When the rice is done, uncover it and sprinkle in the parsley (or cilantro) plus any vegetables you've chosen. Use a fork to gently fluff the rice, reaching all the way to the edges of the bottom, to release steam and slow the cooking. Re-cover, let stand 5 to 15 minutes and the rice is ready to serve. In my rice cooker, I can hold this warm for about 30 minutes without having the peas turn gray.

Half Batch for a 6-Cup Rice Cooker:

Follow the directions above, using half of each ingredient EXCEPT for the broth or water: use 1¾ cups. The total cooking time will be shorter.

CREAMY RICE SOUP WITH POBLANO AND SPINACH • *Crema de Arroz con Chile Poblano y Espinacas*

When rice is blended with broth, as it is here, the result is beautifully creamy but not rich. I've called for baby spinach in this recipe because so many of us have it on hand for salads. It's also really easy, because it comes cleaned and needs no trimming or chopping. If you want to use large spinach, stem it and cut it into roughly 1-inch pieces. This soup is also good with shredded chicken, crushed tortilla chips, cooked shrimp or just about anything else you want to throw in.

Makes about 5 cups of soup, enough for 4

2 large fresh poblano chiles

2 cups cooked Mexican Red Rice

1 quart chicken or vegetable broth

2½ ounces (about 5 loosely packed cups) baby spinach

¼ cup Mexican *crema*, *crème fraîche*, heavy cream or Greek-style yogurt

Salt

About ¼ cup crumbled Mexican *queso fresco* or other fresh cheese such as feta or goat cheese, or firm tofu, cut into cubes

Roast the chiles over an open flame or close up under a preheated broiler, turning them regularly, until evenly blackened and blistered, about 5 minutes for an open flame, 10 minutes for the broiler. Place in a bowl, cover with a kitchen towel and cool until handleable. Rub off the blackened skin, pull out the seedpods and scrape out the seeds. Rinse briefly to remove any stray seeds and bits of blackened skin. Chop into ¼-inch pieces.

In a blender, combine the rice and broth and process until smooth. Pour into a large (4-quart) saucepan and set over medium heat. When the soup comes to a simmer, add the poblano and spinach, then let the soup return to a simmer and cook for a couple of minutes, until the spinach is wilted. Turn off the heat, stir in the *crema* (or one of its stand-ins), taste and season the soup with salt (it may not need any if you're using salted broth). Ladle the soup into warm bowls, scatter on the cheese or tofu and you're ready to serve.

CRISPY RICE CAKES WITH WHITE BEANS, ROASTED GARLIC, AGED CHEESE AND SMOKY CHILE • *Tortitas Doradas de Arroz con Alubias, Ajo Asado, Queso Añejo y Chile Ahumado*

Like the Crispy Cakes of Greens, Potato and Green Chile earlier in this book (page 132), these crispy patties come out of a long Mexican tradition of repurposing leftovers. If you're planning ahead, form the cakes and store them, wrapped in plastic and in a resealable bag, in the freezer. One makes a great snack; three (plus a salad) make dinner.

Serves 4

6 unpeeled garlic cloves

One 15-ounce can cooked, seasoned white beans, drained OR 1½ cups home-cooked, seasoned white beans

⅔ cup grated Mexican *queso añejo* or other garnishing cheese such as Romano or Parmesan, plus a little more for serving

½ cup loosely packed, roughly chopped cilantro or flat-leaf parsley, plus a little more for serving

3 cups cooked Mexican Red Rice

About 2 tablespoons vegetable or olive oil

About 1½ cups of any salsa you love (one made with roasted tomatoes is great here), for serving

Roast the unpeeled garlic in a dry skillet over medium heat, turning it regularly, until it's soft and blotchy black, about 15 minutes. Cool until handleable, then peel. (If you're in a real hurry, peel the garlic, collect it in a microwave-safe bowl, cover with water, microwave at 100% for 1 minute, drain and cool.)

In a food processor, combine the garlic, beans, *queso añejo* (or one of its stand-ins) and cilantro (or parsley). Pulse until everything is chopped, then run the processor until you have a coarse puree. Scrape into a large bowl, add the rice and smoosh the two together until thoroughly blended. Divide into 12 portions and use your hands to form them into 3-inch patties about 1½ inches thick. They should look a little like hockey pucks.

Set a very large (12-inch) nonstick or seasoned cast-iron skillet over medium heat and film the bottom with oil. When quite hot (the cakes may stick to the pan if the skillet isn't hot enough), lay in the cakes. (If you don't have a very large skillet, you'll need to fry the cakes in 2 batches.) When they are crusty and richly browned underneath, about 5 minutes, use a spatula to turn them over and brown the other side, about 5 minutes more.

Serve the crispy cakes on warm plates with a sprinkling of cheese and herbs. Pass the salsa for everyone to spoon *al gusto*.

SPICY BACON-AND-EGG FRIED RICE WITH PICKLED JALAPEÑOS AND CILANTRO • *Arroz Frito Picante con Huevo, Tocino, Jalapeños en Escabeche y Cilantro*

I'm guessing you didn't expect to find a fried-rice recipe in this book, but it's a great way to use leftover rice. In fact, I nearly always have rice in my freezer that I can defrost at a moment's notice to put together a quick fried-rice dinner. I always have bacon and eggs on hand, too. And Mexican hot sauce and cilantro. Basically, this is an always-doable pantry recipe at my house. Its style is based on the fried rice I learned to make in Thailand; there it's finished with a drizzle of fish sauce and Thai basil rather than Worcestershire sauce and cilantro. If you have white rice in your freezer, feel free to use it for this recipe.

Serves 4

3 tablespoons Worcestershire sauce

2 tablespoons Mexican hot sauce (like Tamazula or Valentina, or choose your favorite hot sauce)

2 teaspoons sugar

4 thick slices (4 ounces) bacon, cut crosswise into ½-inch pieces

2 green onions, trimmed of roots and withered outer leaves, cut crosswise into ¼-inch pieces

4 cups Mexican Red Rice (for best results, the rice needs to have cooled completely; it's even better if it's been refrigerated)

4 eggs, beaten just enough to mix the yolks and whites

3 or 4 pickled jalapeños, stemmed, seeded if you wish and chopped

About 1 cup loosely packed chopped cilantro

In a small bowl, mix together the Worcestershire sauce, hot sauce and sugar.

Set a wok or very large (12-inch) skillet (preferably nonstick or seasoned cast iron) over medium heat and add the bacon. Cook, stirring frequently, until the bacon is browned and crispy, about 10 minutes. With a slotted spoon, remove the bacon to a paper towel–lined plate.

Raise the heat under the wok or skillet to medium-high. You need about 3 tablespoons of rendered fat in the pan to fry the rice; if you need to, add vegetable oil to bring it to about that much. When the fat is really hot, add the green onions and stir-fry for 30 seconds or so, until wilted, then add the rice. Let the rice cook without stirring for a minute or so, then stir, scraping the bottom of the pan, and let it rest for another minute before stirring again. Continue like this until the rice is browned, 6 to 8 minutes. (If the rice starts to stick, pour in a little more oil.) Pour the beaten eggs around the sides of the wok or skillet and stir-fry with the rice until the egg is barely set. Drizzle the Worcestershire mixture over the rice, stir a couple of times to distribute it evenly, then remove the rice from the heat. Stir in the jalapeños, cilantro and bacon, and dinner's ready.

SLOW-COOKER SATISFACTION

Mexican Chicken Soup **270**

Red Chile Short Rib Soup **272**

Weekend Dish: Red Chile Pozole with Pork **276**

Weekend Dish: Pork Carnitas Dinner **280**

Five Simple Meals from a Pot of Beans **284**

◆ Silky Tortilla Soup **285**

◆ Scrambled Eggs with Beans, Green Onions and Avocado **286**

◆ Plantain-Bacon *Enfrijoladas* **287**

◆ Beans and Greens with Clams and Chorizo **289**

◆ Cheesy Open-Face *Mollete* **289**

Green Chile–Braised Beef with Potatoes and Caramelized Onions **291**

Lamb or Beef *Barbacoa* **294**

Roasted Garlic Chicken with Mushrooms, Potatoes and Spinach **296**

Mexican Chicken Soup

Caldo de Pollo

◇◇◇

This is the purest form of comfort food, no matter where in the world you were raised. Seasonings may change, of course, as will the garnishes. Which is exactly why this recipe belongs here. In Mexico, the ancient satisfaction of long-simmered chicken and roots gets gilded with sizzling green chile and soothing avocado, with fragrant cilantro and vibrant white onion. And, of course, Mexico's answer to most culinary quandaries: a big squeeze of fresh lime juice.

The chicken makes a difference here. Factory chicken will contribute little but a simple, anemic taste. Free-range chicken, in contrast, will give depth and character to the broth, convincing you at the most fundamental level that you've truly nourished yourself.

Makes about 10 cups, serving 6 heartily

2 medium-large carrots, peeled if you wish and cut into 1-inch pieces

4 garlic cloves, peeled and halved

1 medium white onion, half sliced ¼-inch thick, the other half chopped into ¼-inch pieces (divided use)

A small handful of cilantro (divided use)

Fresh hierbas de olor (aromatic herbs such as a few bay leaves plus a few sprigs of thyme and marjoram, if you have them; otherwise a sprinkling of the same dried herbs will work)

4 large (about 1¾ pounds total) bone-in, skin-on chicken thighs

1 tablespoon Worcestershire sauce

Salt

⅔ cup rice (I like medium-grain here)

3 fresh serrano chiles or 2 fresh jalapeños, stemmed, seeded if you wish and finely chopped, for serving

1 ripe avocado, pit removed, flesh scooped from the skin and cut into ½-inch pieces, for serving

1 lime, cut into wedges, for serving

In a 6-quart slow cooker, layer the carrot, the garlic, the sliced *half* of the onion, and *half* of the cilantro. Strew with the herbs. Top with the chicken in a single layer. Pour the Worcestershire sauce and 2 quarts water over the top, sprinkle with 1 teaspoon salt, cover and turn on to high. Your soup will be done in 4 to 6 hours, though you can hold it for longer. (My slow cooker can be programmed to switch from high to a "keep warm" temperature for up to another 6 hours. Some slow cookers click to "keep warm" automatically; others need to be switched manually.)

About an hour and a half before you want to serve dinner, add the rice, turn the slow cooker to high, cover and cook until the rice is cooked through, about an hour. Remove the chicken pieces, pull off the skin and discard, then pull the meat from the bones in coarse shreds. Keep warm, covered with foil, in a low oven; or microwave to warm just before serving. Taste the soup and season with salt if necessary (it sometimes needs about ½ teaspoon). One of the hallmarks of this soup is little beads of golden chicken fat floating on the broth; if that's not to your taste, spoon them off.

Pull out and discard the cooked cilantro. Chop the remaining fresh cilantro and rinse the chopped onion under cool running water. Set them out on a serving plate with the chopped green chile, avocado and lime.

Divide the chicken among warm bowls and ladle the soup over it. Pass the garnishes for each person at the table to add *al gusto*.

No Slow Cooker?

In a large (4-quart) saucepan, layer the ingredients as described. Bring to a gentle simmer over medium, then reduce the heat to medium-low, partially cover and cook at a bare simmer for 2 to 3 hours, adding water occasionally to ensure that the liquid stays at about the same level. Add the rice during the last 30 minutes of cooking, then proceed with cleaning the cooked chicken, seasoning and serving the soup as described above with all its fresh garnishes.

Riffs on Mexican Chicken Soup:

Though I feel silly messing with such a classic, there are some legitimate options. The onion that's cooked in the broth can be replaced by leeks (Mexico City friends do that regularly). Sometimes I add garlic chives from my garden (or farmers' market), because I always have a lot of them. When I add the rice, I occasionally add cubed zucchini (or other summer squash) or an ear of corn cut into 4 pieces, both of which Mexican moms do pretty regularly. Though it's typical to serve the soup with chopped raw chile, roasted poblano (added with the rice) instead can be really, really scrumptious, though admittedly more modern. When I'm looking for the richest flavor (which is most of the time), I brown the chicken before starting the soup (some slow cookers have a special setting that allows for browning right in the cooker, while others have a removable insert that can be set directly on the stovetop). I've even grilled it, which adds an amazing flavor, though no one would call it traditional.

Red Chile Short Rib Soup

Mole de Olla

◇◇

First, know that this "soup pot *mole*," as the name translates directly from Spanish, isn't a *mole* in the way we typically think of *moles*. It's a brothy soup, not a sauce, but one that celebrates dried chile, as do Mexico's most famous *moles*. Many Mexican cooks will tell you to make your *mole de olla* with *espinazo*, the meaty backbone, plus some stewing beef or beef shank. But I suggest using short ribs, knocking off two birds with one stone: the bones provide the richness you'd get from backbone, while the meat adds that incredible beefiness that's brought by beef shank.

I believe that every cook should think of this soup as a bowlful of satisfaction rather than the output of an exact list of ingredients. The short ribs provide soul, while the chiles provide spirit. Choose guajillos for lovely bright spiciness, anchos for sweet complexity and pasillas for a rustic depth of flavor that hints at bitter chocolate. (I've called for chile pods here because powder doesn't give enough texture to the broth.) Though I love the combination of chayote, green beans and potatoes in this soup, practically any vegetable is welcome: chayote can be replaced with any summer squash; potatoes can become winter squash or any color sweet potatoes; and the role of green beans can be played by long beans, snap peas, baby artichokes, even a handful of kale or chard.

There are two unusual ingredients that are classic in a traditional *mole de olla*. Folks will be wild about the soup even without them, but if you can find them in your grocery store, or search them out in a Mexican grocery, the experience you'll offer will be truly memorable. Epazote is the jagged-leaf herb that adds its distinctive—I'd say iconic—complexity to the broth as it simmers. And *xoconostle* is the sour prickly-pear cactus fruit, which is peeled, seeded and chopped into tangy bits to stir into the finished soup.

Makes about 14 cups, serving 6 to 8 heartily

1 medium white onion, sliced ¼-inch thick

1 pound small red- or white-skin boiling potatoes (I like ones that are about 1 inch across; if they're larger I cut them into halves or quarters)

1 large chayote, peeled if you wish, seed cut out, flesh cut into 1-inch pieces

4 pounds (about 6 pieces) bone-in English-cut (that is, cut parallel to the bone) short ribs

1½ ounces dried chiles (roughly 6
   guajillos, 4 to 5 pasillas or 3 anchos),
   stemmed, seeded and torn into 2-inch
   pieces
4 garlic cloves, peeled and halved
1 tablespoon Worcestershire sauce
Salt

A large sprig of epazote, if you have it
About 6 ounces green beans, stemmed
   and cut into 1-inch lengths
2 or 3 sour prickly-pear cactus fruits
   (xoconostles), if you have them
1 large lime, cut into wedges, for serving

In a 6-quart slow cooker, layer the onion, potatoes, chayote and short ribs in that order.
In a blender, combine the cleaned chiles, garlic, Worcestershire sauce, 1 teaspoon salt
and 5 cups water. Blend until smooth (which will take a couple of minutes unless you
have a high-speed blender). Pour through a medium-mesh strainer into the slow cooker.
The liquid should nearly cover the short ribs; if not, add more water. Nestle in the
epazote if you're using it. Cover and turn on to high. Your *mole de olla* will be done in
about 6 hours, though you can hold it for longer. (My slow cooker can be programmed to
switch from high after 6 hours to a "keep warm" temperature for up to another 6 hours.
Some slow cookers click to "keep warm" automatically; others need to be switched
manually.)

When you're ready to serve, place the green beans in a microwaveable bowl, sprinkle
with a little water, cover with plastic wrap, poke a few holes in the top and microwave
at 100% for 90 seconds, until just tender. If using the sour prickly-pear fruits, cut them
into small pieces: Holding each one with tongs or a towel, cut the ends off, make a slit
down the side from end to end, then peel back the thick skin, revealing the nugget of
fruit. Cut it in half and, using a small spoon, scoop out the reddish seedpod in the center and discard it. Cut the light-colored flesh into ¼-inch pieces.

Fish the short ribs out of the slow cooker. The meat will fall from the bones: discard
the bones and tear the meat into bite-size pieces. If a lot of fat has rendered and col-
lected on the top of the broth in the slow cooker, skim it off. Stir the meat, green beans
and prickly-pear cactus, if using, into the soup. Taste and season with salt (usually a
generous teaspoon).

Ladle into warm, deep bowls and carry to the table. Pass the lime wedges separately
for everyone to add *al gusto*.

No Slow Cooker?

In a large (6- to 8-quart, at least 12 inches in diameter) heavy pot (preferably a Dutch oven), layer the ingredients as described. Bring to a gentle simmer over medium heat, set the cover in place and braise in a 300-degree oven about 3 hours, adding water occasionally if necessary to ensure that the liquid stays at about the same level. Finish with the coarsely shredded meat, green beans and optional prickly-pear cactus as described in the recipe.

A Few More Riffs on *Mole de Olla*:

I've sketched out a lot of vegetable alternatives in the headnote. If English-cut short ribs aren't within easy reach, use about 2½ pounds of cubed boneless stew meat, beef chuck or boneless short ribs plus about 1½ pounds of soup bones. For the most memorably rich broth, brown the meat in an oil-filmed skillet before starting the soup (some slow cookers have a special setting that allows for browning right in the cooker, while others have a removable insert that can be set directly on the stovetop).

Red Chile Short Rib Soup (page 272)

Weekend Dish: Red Chile Pozole with Pork

Pozole Rojo de Puerco

◇◇◇

In Mexico, pozole traditionally spells festivity (or at least weekend relaxation), but it spells comfort and community, too. So here's a simple slow-cooker recipe for that moment when you need to fill the house with the appetizing aroma of anticipation, then proffer satisfaction in the form of steaming bowls filled with tender pork, toothsome pozole corn, rich red chile broth and fresh crunchy garnishes. *Pozole Rojo* is such a perfect dish that it's seen little evolution through the years.

This recipe is very easy if you have Quick Red Chile *Adobo* on hand. I'm not offering an alternative here, because to tell the truth, everything I came up with took longer than the 10 minutes necessary to make the *adobo*. If pigs' feet aren't on your horizon, replace them with an equal weight of meaty pork neck bones; the broth will be delicious but lack a little of the texture and flavor complexity provided by the trotters.

A Note about Nixtamal Corn: This is dried grain corn that's been blanched with mineral lime (calcium hydroxide, *cal* in Mexican Spanish). It is available freshly made at tortilla factories or in the refrigerated or frozen section of well-stocked Mexican groceries; you can also find it already processed and dried in those same Mexican groceries (sold near the dried beans) or order it online from several mail-order sources. All of these pozole corns take several hours of simmering in a slow cooker to soften into what we call hominy. Fully cooked canned hominy is your other option, though some of the canned options are mushy compared to freshly cooked hominy. I've had good luck with the Juanita's brand.

Makes 12 cups, serving 6 to 8 heartily

3 cups fresh or frozen (about 20 ounces) or dried (14 ounces) *nixtamal* (pozole) corn (see note above)

OR 6 cups (two 29-ounce cans) fully cooked hominy, drained

1½ pounds boneless pork for stew (preferably from the shoulder), cut into 1-inch chunks

2 medium (about 2 pounds) pigs' feet

1 cup Quick Red Chile *Adobo* (recipe follows)

Salt

Fresh garnishes for serving:

About 4 cups thinly sliced cabbage
(I like Napa or savoy cabbage here) or
iceberg lettuce

1 generous cup loosely packed, thinly
sliced radishes

About 1 cup finely chopped white onion,
rinsed under cold water to remove
sulfurous flavors

A few tablespoons Mexican oregano (for
tradition's sake, the whole leaf type you
find in Mexican groceries)

3 limes, cut into wedges

In a 6-quart slow cooker, spread out the fresh, frozen or dried *nixtamal* (pozole) corn.
(If you're using cooked hominy, hold off for now—you'll add it at the end.) Top with the
boneless pork chunks and feet, nestling everything together. Whisk the *adobo* into
2½ quarts water, then pour over the pork and corn. Cover and turn the slow cooker
on to high. Your pozole will be done in about 6 to 7 hours (meaning the broth will be
deliciously rich and the pozole corn fully tender), though you can hold it for longer. (My
slow cooker can be programmed to switch from high after 6 hours to a "keep warm"
temperature for up to another 6 hours. Some slow cookers click to "keep warm" automatically; others need to be switched manually.)

When you're ready to serve, carefully remove the pigs' feet from the pozole (I utilize a
flat skimmer to keep them from falling apart). Fish out all the bones and any hard car-
tilage from the feet, then chop what remains and return to the soup. (Though it's desir-
able to have some fat floating on the pozole, I typically find myself skimming the soup a
little, especially if the pork or feet rendered a lot.) Use a fork to break up the pork pieces
in the pozole if you think they're too big. If you're using cooked hominy, now is the time
to stir it in. Taste and season with salt, usually 2 teaspoons.

In serving bowls, set out the cabbage (or lettuce), radishes, onion, oregano and lime
wedges. Ladle the pozole into warm deep bowls and, if you like, season each bowl
with a little more salt. Pass the garnishes for each person to spoon on, sprinkle over
or squeeze in to their liking. Encourage them to crush a big pinch of oregano between
their palms and let the finely crumbled leaves fall over everything, adding their distinctive aroma to the experience.

No Slow Cooker?

You can do the whole preparation in a 6-quart soup pot (or Dutch oven), bringing the pozole to a gentle boil over medium heat, then simmering, partially covered, over medium-low until the broth is rich and the pozole corn is tender, usually 4 to 5 hours. You'll find it necessary to add water from time to time to ensure that the level of liquid remains about the same.

Riffs on Red Chile Pozole:

A lot of people are making chicken pozole in Mexico these days. Do it as described above with 2½ to 3 pounds bone-in, skin-on chicken thighs and omit the pigs' feet. You'll want really good chicken for the best-flavored broth. I've tasted lamb and goat pozoles, which were delicious, but the best one I've ever tasted, I still contend, is one that cooked overnight over a wood fire with a pig's head. I don't know when I'll get that chance again, so I'll rely on my slow cooker to bring pozole's elemental satisfaction regularly.

QUICK RED CHILE *ADOBO*

Scoop **a scant ½ cup powdered ancho chile** into a blender or small food processor. Bring 1¼ cups water to a boil, pour over the chile, *loosely cover* the blender or secure the top of the processor and pulse to blend thoroughly. In a small microwave-safe bowl, collect **8 peeled garlic cloves**, cover with water and microwave at 100% for 1 minute. Drain and add to the blender or processor, along with ½ **teaspoon ground cinnamon**, ¼ **teaspoon ground black pepper**, ⅛ **teaspoon ground cumin**, **1 teaspoon dried oregano**, **3 tablespoons apple cider vinegar** and 1½ **teaspoons salt**. Process until smooth.

Red Chile Pozole with Pork (page 276)

Weekend Dish: Pork Carnitas Dinner

Cena Completa de Carnitas de Puerco

◇◇◇

Carnitas are pure luxury, offering the kind of delectable mouthfuls that make a weekend meal seem like a celebration. In Mexico, people rarely tackle the classic version of carnitas on their own, unless, of course, they're the designated carnitas maker for big family parties or community events. You just don't heat a huge cauldron of pork fat and cook a cut-up pig in it for a little family meal. Instead, you go to a restaurant that's known for its carnitas and buy some to bring home. But this near-effortless version of the classic Mexican preparation allows you to make your own—good news for those of us who don't have a great carnitas restaurant nearby.

Cooking pork submerged in its own fat—what chefs have classically called confit—produces a lusciously tender and juicy result you can never achieve by roasting or simmering. In the traditional Mexican kitchen, carnitas are typically cooked first at a high temperature to promote browning, then simmered low and slow until they are richly tender. Here I'm doing the reverse, cooking the pork slowly in its own fat in a slow cooker (it requires much less fat and much less tending), then browning it when I'm ready to serve.

In my opinion, carnitas demand a big stack of warm tortillas for making tacos. And I never want to eat my carnitas tacos without some guacamole to spoon on them, plus a little salsa and maybe a spoonful of beans to smear on the tortilla before I build my masterpiece. That may spell a complete dinner for you, as it does for many. I always want a simple salad on the table, too.

Serves 6

2 pounds boneless pork shoulder

Salt

1½ to 2 cups freshly rendered pork lard (you can buy good-quality lard from a local butcher or Mexican market; I don't recommend the hydrogenated lard that's sold in bricks)

Hot fresh green chiles to taste (roughly 3 serranos or 2 jalapeños), stemmed, seeded if you wish

10 unpeeled garlic cloves

4½ cups seasoned, cooked beans (any kind you like), drained, cooking liquid reserved (this is the quantity you'll get from three 15-ounce cans)

One 15-ounce can diced fire-roasted
tomatoes, drained
About ½ cup chopped cilantro (divided
use)
3 or 4 limes (divided use)

3 ripe avocados, pitted, flesh scooped
from the skins
2 dozen tortillas, heated according to the
instructions on page 60

Cut the pork into 2½- to 3-inch pieces and sprinkle generously on all sides with salt. Scoop the lard into a 6-quart slow cooker and turn on to high. When the lard is melted, fit in the pork in a single layer (there should be few gaps between the pieces and they should be barely covered with the fat). Cover and cook until thoroughly tender, 3 to 4 hours. Turn off, uncover and let cool while you prepare the accompaniments.

In a very large (12-inch) nonstick or seasoned cast-iron skillet over medium heat, roast the chiles and garlic, turning regularly until they are softened and blackened in spots, about 10 minutes for the chiles, 15 minutes for the garlic. Cool, then slip the garlic cloves from their skins and put into a food processor. Pulse the garlic until it's finely chopped.

Set the skillet over medium heat and spoon in a few tablespoons of the pork fat from the carnitas. Add the beans and *one-third* of the chopped garlic. Mash with an old-fashioned potato masher or back of a large spoon until as smooth as you like (I like mine to retain a little texture)—adding the bean cooking liquid (or water) a few tablespoons at a time until the beans have a slightly soupy consistency. Scrape the beans into a serving bowl, cover with a piece of foil and keep warm in a very low oven.

Divide the remaining garlic between 2 medium serving bowls. Without cleaning the processor, pulse the chiles until finely chopped. Divide between the 2 bowls.

Again without washing the processor, pulse the drained tomatoes until they resemble salsa in texture. Scrape into one of the bowls with the chile and garlic. Stir *half* of the cilantro into the tomato salsa bowl and season with a tablespoon or two of juice from a lime. Thin the salsa with a little water if it needs it, then taste and season with salt, usually about ½ teaspoon.

Scoop the avocados into the other bowl and mash with the potato masher or back of a spoon until smooth or chunky, depending on your favorite guacamole texture. Stir in the remaining cilantro and squeeze in a little fresh lime juice; 1 tablespoon is usually enough to brighten the flavors. Taste and season with salt, usually about ½ teaspoon.

Cut the remaining limes into wedges and scoop into a serving bowl.

Remove the pork to a cutting board, leaving behind as much fat as possible. (You can refrigerate the lard to use for another round of carnitas, to season beans, to fry potatoes or the like.) Shred the carnitas into very large, coarse pieces. Set the cleaned bean-cooking skillet over medium heat. When the pan is very hot, spoon in enough carnitas-cooking fat to film the bottom generously. Scoop in the pork, spreading it out evenly over the bottom of the pan. Cook undisturbed for a couple of minutes, until it is richly browned and releases itself from the bottom of the pan. Gently turn the pieces to brown the other side. Remove to a plate lined with paper towels. Sprinkle with salt (coarse salt is welcome here, if you have it). Serve on a warm platter with the beans, salsa, guacamole, lime wedges and warm tortillas.

Pork Carnitas Dinner (page 280)

Five Simple Meals from a Pot of Beans

Cinco Comidas de Una Sola Olla de Frijoles

◇◇

After lots of years in the kitchen, this is the way my mind works: When I've done the time-consuming task of simmering a pot of beans to perfect tenderness, I start imagining all the different transformations I could lead it through. Instead of "using it up" on a single meal or freezing it to make that same meal again in the future, why not, I think, see how many totally different preparations that pot of perfection can yield? First, simmer the beans (a simple task made even simpler with the aid of a slow cooker). Next, come with me on an adventure. There are my twists on a classic bean-thickened tortilla soup with ancho chile from Michoacán (*sopa tarasca*); on the stick-to-your-ribs scrambled eggs and beans from Veracruz that I dress up with avocado and green onion; on the easy, bean-sauced enchilada relative called *enfrijoladas*, here with a filling of sweet plantain and bacon; and on a Gulf-style beans-and-greens dish turned into a great meal by the addition of clams and chorizo. I know some of you may be expecting a corn and bean salsa for a piece of grilled fish, but they don't eat beans that way in Mexico. I suspect that for the same reason I haven't seen many rice salads in Asia, I've never encountered many cooks serving cold bean preparations in Mexico. Beans are just too much a part of the cuisine's foundation to be relegated to a supporting role like that. Instead, I'm finishing with that classic Mexican snack/light meal, the *mollete*: an open-face sandwich of sorts smeared with mashed beans, broiled with oozy cheese and served with a bright salsa.

A GOOD-SIZE POT OF BEANS • *Una Olla Grande de Frijoles*

Makes about 8 cups

1 pound (about 2¼ cups) dried beans (any *Phaseolus* bean will work, from white navies to reds and blacks; I'm not talking about lentils, garbanzos or favas here), picked over for stones and debris

6 garlic cloves, peeled and cut in half
1 small white onion, cut into ¼-inch slices
Salt

In a 6-quart slow cooker, layer the beans, garlic and onion. Pour in 1½ quarts water and sprinkle in 1 teaspoon salt. Cover and turn the slow cooker on to high. Your beans will be done in 3 to 4 hours, though you can hold them for longer. (My slow cooker can be programmed to switch from high after 3½ hours to a "keep warm" temperature for another 6 hours. Some slow cookers click to "keep warm" automatically; others need to be switched manually.) Your beans are now ready to be used in any of the recipes below.

No Slow Cooker?

In a medium-large (4- to 6-quart) pot (preferably a Dutch oven), combine the beans, garlic, onion and 2½ quarts water. Bring to a rolling boil over medium-high heat, then reduce to medium-low and cook the beans at a gentle simmer, partially covered, until thoroughly tender, about 2 hours. (You'll find it necessary to add water from time to time to ensure that the level of liquid remains about the same.) Taste and season the beans with salt (usually 1 teaspoon) and simmer a few more minutes to allow the salt to dissolve.

SILKY TORTILLA SOUP • *Sopa de Tortilla Cremosa*

This soup is most attractive when made with brown or red beans. To make it heartier, feel free to add coarse shreds of rotisserie, grilled or roasted chicken.

Makes 5 cups, serving 4

2 dried ancho chiles, stemmed, seeded and torn into roughly 1-inch pieces

3 garlic cloves, peeled

1 cup cooked, seasoned beans with enough cooking liquid to cover

Half a 15-ounce can diced fire-roasted tomatoes, undrained

1 quart chicken or vegetable broth

Salt

About 20 tortilla chips (preferably sturdy, thicker ones from a local tortilla factory), roughly broken

¼ cup crumbled Mexican *queso fresco* or other fresh cheese such as feta or goat cheese

In a medium (8-inch) skillet set over medium heat, toast the chiles, stirring them nearly constantly until they change color noticeably, release their beautiful aroma and are starting to crisp a little on the edges, about 30 seconds (this is a little more toasting than you'd do for a sauce). Scoop half of the chiles into a blender jar; when cool, crumble the remaining half into a small bowl for serving.

Place the garlic in a small, microwave-safe bowl, cover with water and microwave at 100% for 1 minute. Drain and add to the blender, along with the beans, tomatoes and their liquids. Blend to a completely smooth puree and press through a medium-mesh sieve into a large (4-quart) saucepan. Stir in the broth, set over medium heat and bring to a simmer. Partially cover and simmer for 15 minutes or so to blend the flavors. Taste and season with salt, usually ½ teaspoon.

Serve the soup in warm bowls, topped with a handful of chips, a portion of the cheese and as much of the crumbled chile as you like.

SCRAMBLED EGGS WITH BEANS, GREEN ONIONS AND AVOCADO •
Huevos Tirados de Lujo

Serves 4

2 tablespoons olive oil, vegetable oil or butter

4 green onions, trimmed of roots and withered leaves, cut crosswise into ½-inch pieces

Hot fresh green chiles to taste (roughly 2 serranos or 1 jalapeño), stemmed, seeded if you wish and finely chopped

1½ cups cooked, seasoned beans, drained of all liquid

8 eggs, roughly beaten

Salt

1 ripe avocado, pitted, flesh scooped from the skin and cut into ½-inch pieces

A handful of cilantro leaves, if you have them

Your favorite salsa, for serving

In a large (10-inch) skillet (preferably nonstick or well-seasoned cast iron), heat the oil or butter over medium. When hot, add the green onions and chiles and stir until the onions have softened, about 5 minutes. Stir in the beans and cook until any liquid has reduced completely, about 2 minutes. Season the beaten eggs with ½ teaspoon salt, then add them to the pan and stir every few seconds, carefully scraping across the bottom to release everything, until the eggs are as done as you like. Divide between 4 warm plates. Top each portion with avocado and cilantro (if you have it) and serve right away with the salsa.

PLANTAIN-BACON *ENFRIJOLADAS* • *Enfrijoladas de Plátano con Tocino*

To achieve the perfect interplay between smoky, salty bacon and sweet, tangy plantain, you'll need plantains that are perfectly ripe. Look for ones that are soft, with a peel that's almost completely covered by black splotches.

Serves 4 to 6

6 thick slices (6 ounces) bacon, cut crosswise into ½-inch pieces

1 medium white onion, cut into ¼-inch pieces, plus a few slices for garnishing

2 large black-ripe plantains, peeled and cut into roughly ½-inch cubes

Salt

1½ cups cooked, seasoned beans with enough cooking liquid to cover

12 corn tortillas

A little vegetable oil

About ¼ cup crumbled Mexican *queso fresco* (or other fresh cheese such as feta or goat cheese) or grated Mexican *queso añejo* (or other garnishing cheese such as Romano or Parmesan)

A handful of flat-leaf parsley or cilantro leaves, if you have them

Scoop the bacon into a very large (12-inch) skillet and set over medium heat. When the bacon begins rendering its fat, add the onion and stir regularly until it's very tender and beginning to brown, about 7 minutes. Scoop *a quarter* of this mixture into a blender or food processor, leaving the remainder in the skillet. Return the skillet to medium heat and add the plantain. Cook, stirring regularly, until the plantain is golden and very sweet, about 6 minutes. Season with salt, usually ¼ teaspoon, depending on the saltiness of your bacon.

While the plantain is cooking, add the beans and cooking liquid to the onion and bacon in the blender or food processor and process until smooth. Scrape into a medium (3-quart) saucepan and stir in about 1 cup water, enough to give the mixture the consistency of a light cream soup. Bring to a simmer over medium heat and season with salt, usually a scant teaspoon. Reduce the heat to low while you get ready to serve.

Brush (or spray) both sides of each tortilla with a little oil, slide them into a plastic bag, fold over (don't seal) and microwave at 100% for 1 minute. Reheat the plantain mixture if it has cooled off and stir in ⅔ *cup* of the bean sauce. Two or three at a time, lay out the tortillas, spoon a portion of filling down the center of each one, roll up, arrange side-by-side on warm plates and ladle a generous amount of sauce over the top. When all are sauced, strew with the cheese, the sliced onion and the herb leaves if you have them.

Beans and Greens
with Clams and Chorizo
(page 289)

BEANS AND GREENS WITH CLAMS AND CHORIZO • *Frijoles y Quelites con Almejas y Chorizo*

I've also made this with bacon instead of chorizo but added a couple of chopped canned chipotle chiles *en adobo* for a lovely smoky spiciness.

Serves 4

8 ounces fresh Mexican chorizo sausage, casing removed (about 1 cup)

4 cups seasoned, cooked beans with enough cooking liquid to cover

Salt

4 ounces cooking greens such as spinach, chard, kale, mustard or lamb's quarters (*quelites*), stems or stalks removed,
leaves cut into 1½-inch pieces (about 4 loosely-packed cups)

1 to 1½ pounds clams (I like to soak them for several hours with a few tablespoons of cornmeal in the water, which encourages the clams to purge their sand)

In a large (4-quart) saucepan over medium heat, cook the chorizo, stirring to break up the clumps, until it is cooked through, about 10 minutes. Scoop out *half* the chorizo onto paper towels to drain. To what remains in the pot, add the beans with the cooking liquid and 2 cups water. Bring to a simmer, taste and season with salt, usually about 1 teaspoon, depending on the saltiness of your beans. Add the greens and simmer until they're barely done, anywhere from 30 seconds for spinach to 6 or 7 minutes for lamb's quarters. Immediately nestle the clams in the pot, cover and cook until the clams have opened, 5 to 8 minutes. Scoop portions of the beans and greens and clams into warm serving bowls, sprinkle with the reserved chorizo and serve right away.

CHEESY OPEN-FACE *MOLLETE* • *Mollete de Queso*

If you want a hearty meal, you'll need 2 *molletes* per person. Otherwise, a single *mollete* with a nice mound of salad greens makes a great lunch.

Makes 4 *molletes*

1 large fresh poblano chile

2 tablespoons olive oil, vegetable oil or bacon drippings
3 garlic cloves, peeled and finely chopped

1 cup seasoned, cooked beans with a little cooking liquid

Salt

2 *telera* rolls from a Mexican bakery
OR 2 submarine/hoagie/hero rolls

About 2 cups shredded, grated or crumbled cheese (a melting cheese like shredded jack or cheddar is essential as far as I'm concerned, but I like to combine the melting cheese with crumbled goat cheese and grated *queso añejo* or Parmesan for the perfect *mollete*)

About ½ cup of pretty much any salsa, though roasted tomatillo salsa is terrific here, for serving

Roast the chile over an open flame or close up under a preheated broiler, turning regularly, until evenly blackened and blistered, about 5 minutes for an open flame, 10 minutes for the broiler. Place in a bowl, cover with a kitchen towel and cool until handleable. Rub off the blackened skin, pull out the seedpod and scrape out the seeds. Rinse briefly to remove any stray seeds and bits of blackened skin. Cut into ¼-inch strips.

In a large (10-inch) skillet set over medium, heat the oil or bacon drippings. Add the garlic and stir for a minute until aromatic, then add the beans and cooking liquid. Mash them with an old-fashioned potato masher or the back of a large spoon until they are homogenous but still have a little texture. If necessary, add a little water to give the beans an easily spreadable consistency. Taste and season with a little salt if necessary.

Turn on the broiler and adjust the rack to its highest setting. Split the rolls as you would for making a sandwich. Spread the cut sides with a portion of the beans, lay them on a baking sheet (bean side up), scatter with the roasted poblano, sprinkle evenly with the cheese and run under the broiler.

When the cheese is beginning to brown (a minute or two), remove the *molletes* and serve them with salsa to spoon on *al gusto.*

Green Chile–Braised Beef with Potatoes and Caramelized Onions

Carne de Res Guisada con Chile Verde, Papas y Cebollas Caramelizadas

◇◇◇

Though practically anything from my slow cooker sings with a soulfulness that engages anyone within range of its arresting aroma, this green chile beef braise is all that with the volume turned up. It's meaty, spicy, sweet, herby, all fused through slow cooking into the flavor of a comforting embrace. Serve it in deep plates with warm tortillas and a salad. Or roll it into tacos or burritos. Scramble leftovers with eggs for a hearty brunch. Shred it and toss with pasta. It's welcome anywhere.

But all that flavor doesn't come for free. You need to caramelize the onions, roast the poblanos and brown the meat. After you've invested the 30 minutes or so that flavor creation takes—and you can even do that the night before, refrigerate, and start the cooking the next morning—the slow cooker takes over.

Serves 6

2 tablespoons vegetable oil, olive oil, freshly rendered pork lard or bacon drippings

2 pounds boneless beef short ribs or boneless beef chuck, cut into 3-inch pieces (when using chuck, I buy a beef chuck roast and cut it into roughly 2-inch chunks)

Salt

3 large fresh poblano chiles

2 medium white or red onions, sliced ¼-inch thick

1 pound small red- or white-skin boiling potatoes (I like ones that are about 1 inch across; if they're larger I cut them in halves or quarters)

Hot fresh green chiles to taste (roughly 2 serranos or 1 jalapeño), stemmed, seeded if you wish and roughly chopped

One 15-ounce can diced fire-roasted tomatoes, undrained

2 tablespoons Worcestershire sauce

1½ cups beef broth

Fresh hierbas de olor (aromatic herbs, such as a few bay leaves plus a few sprigs of thyme and marjoram, if you have them; otherwise a sprinkling of the same dried herbs will work)

In the stovetop-safe insert of your slow cooker or a very large (12-inch) skillet, heat the oil, lard or bacon drippings over medium-high. When hot, sprinkle the beef chunks generously all over with salt, then lay them in the pan in a single, uncrowded layer. Brown on all sides, about 10 minutes total.

While the beef is browning, roast the poblanos over an open flame or close up under a preheated broiler, turning them regularly, until evenly blackened and blistered, about 5 minutes for an open flame, 10 minutes for the broiler. Place in a bowl, cover with a kitchen towel and cool until handleable. Rub off the blackened skin, pull out the seedpods and scrape out the seeds. Rinse briefly to remove any stray seeds and bits of blackened skin. Chop the roasted chiles into ½-inch pieces.

When the beef is browned, remove it to a plate, leaving behind as much fat as possible. Reduce the heat under the insert or skillet to medium, then add the onions and cook, stirring regularly, until soft and richly golden, about 10 minutes. If you're using a skillet, transfer the onions to the slow cooker.

Distribute the potatoes, roasted poblanos and hot green chiles over the onions, smoothing everything evenly over the bottom. Sprinkle with 1 teaspoon salt. Lay the beef pieces in a single layer over the potatoes. Distribute the tomatoes on top. Sprinkle on the Worcestershire, then pour the beef broth over and around the meat. Nestle in (or sprinkle over) the herbs. Cover and turn the slow cooker on to high. Your Green Chile–Braised Beef will be done in about 6 hours, though you can hold it for longer. (My slow cooker can be programmed to switch from high after 6 hours to a "keep warm" temperature for up to another 6 hours. Some slow cookers click to "keep warm" automatically; others need to be switched manually.)

When you're ready to serve, remove the meat to a large, deep plate and coarsely shred it. Stir everything in the slow cooker, taste it and season with salt, usually about ½ teaspoon, depending on the saltiness of the broth. Mix in the beef, spoon into deep plates and dinner's ready.

Ideas for Garnishing:

I love topping this stew with something fresh—and if that something fresh is also crunchy, all the better. At the restaurant we make a quick salad out of thinly sliced (aka shaved) fennel and put it on top; you can achieve a similarly crunchy fresh effect with chopped onion (rinse it under cold water to rid it of sulfurous flavors). Chopped fresh chiles are great here, as are herbs like chopped fresh flat-leaf parsley. And, as is usually the case, these bowls benefit from a sprinkling of *queso fresco* or *queso añejo* and, for some, a squeeze of lime.

No Slow Cooker?

In a large (6- to 8-quart, at least 12 inches in diameter) heavy pot (preferably a Dutch oven), layer, from bottom to top, the browned beef, caramelized onions, and potatoes and chiles. Sprinkle generously with salt, add the tomatoes, broth mixture and herbs. Set the cover in place and braise in a 300-degree oven for about 3 hours, adding water occasionally if necessary to ensure that the liquid stays at about the same level. Finish as described.

Riffs on Green Chile–Braised Beef:

The beef can be replaced with lamb or goat shoulder for a truly special meal. Potatoes can be replaced with any number of cubed root vegetables, from the Mexican white (or other) sweet potatoes to small turnips, rutabaga and parsnips. And, of course, the poblanos can be replaced with any of the other meaty-fleshed chiles you find in your farmers' market or well-stocked grocery.

Lamb or Beef *Barbacoa*

Barbacoa de Borrego o Res

◇◇◇

Traditional *barbacoa*—the kind done with huge cuts of meat or whole animals in a hot pit in the ground—is the stuff dreams are made of. I mean, when you eat it, you're probably in Mexico, you're outside in some gloriously rustic place, and it's an occasion worthy of cooking a whole animal,which is all pretty dreamy. But when you strip away the rustic outdoor Mexico and that special occasion, the meat is fairly straightforward: beautifully seasoned and slow-cooked to that juicy, fall-apart tenderness that always makes my mouth water. That is a perfect description of what I'm offering here. Sure, it doesn't have the smokiness added by the pit's live embers (though I do brown the meat for depth of flavor before braising), but it can have the smoky herbiness of a charred agave leaf if you live near a Mexican grocery store that carries them (look or ask in the vegetable department for a *penca de maguey*). I see them more and more frequently these days. Even without the agave, a taco made from coarse shreds of this rich, red chile–flavored meat showered with salsa, onion and cilantro is super-satisfying: lamb for my more adventurous friends (lamb *barbacoa* is favored in central and southern Mexico), beef when it's a mixed group.

Serves 6

A 12-inch chunk of an agave leaf (penca de maguey, optional)

2 tablespoons vegetable or olive oil

3 pounds boneless lamb shoulder or boneless beef chuck

Salt

1 tablespoon brown sugar

½ cup Quick Red Chile *Adobo* (recipe follows)

Your favorite hot sauce or salsa, for serving (I like Tamazula or roasted tomatillo salsa here)

A little chopped white onion, for serving

A handful of cilantro leaves, for serving

If you're using the chunk of agave leaf, be sure not to touch the cut edges; the sap can cause skin irritation to those who aren't used to it. Roast the agave over an open flame or close up under a preheated broiler, turning every few minutes, until blackened on the outside and softening to almost pliable, 10 to 15 minutes depending on the thickness. Cut into 3 pieces.

In the stovetop-safe insert of your slow cooker or a very large (12-inch) skillet, heat the oil over medium-high. Pat the lamb or beef dry with paper towels, sprinkle generously on all sides with salt and lay it in the insert or skillet. Cook, turning occasionally, until richly brown on all sides, about 10 minutes. Fit the insert into the machine or transfer the meat to the slow cooker.

Stir together the sugar, *adobo* and 2 cups water, then pour around and over the lamb or beef. Nestle the pieces of agave leaf under and around the meat, if you're using them. Cover and turn on the slow cooker to high. Your *barbacoa* will be done in about 6 hours, though you can hold it for longer. (My slow cooker can be programmed to switch from high after 6 hours to a "keep warm" temperature for up to another 6 hours. Some slow cookers click to "keep warm" automatically; others need to be switched manually.)

When you're ready to serve, coarsely shred the lamb or beef and arrange it on a warm platter. Skim any fat from the sauce that remains in the slow cooker, then taste it. If you feel it would be better with more concentrated flavor, pour it into a medium saucepan or remove the insert and set it over high heat. Boil for a few minutes to reduce the quantity, then taste and season with salt, usually a generous ½ teaspoon. Spoon as much as you like over the lamb or beef. (I like to sprinkle coarse salt over the meat at this point.) Serve the *barbacoa* with the hot sauce or salsa, onion and cilantro. Grab a stack of warm tortillas, if you like, and you're ready to make some delicious tacos.

No Slow Cooker?

In a large (6- to 8-quart, at least 12 inches in diameter) heavy pot (preferably a Dutch oven), combine the ingredients as described. Set the cover in place and braise in a 300-degree oven for about 3 hours, adding water occasionally if necessary to ensure that the liquid stays at about the same level. Finish as described.

QUICK RED CHILE *ADOBO*

Scoop **a scant ½ cup powdered ancho chile** into a blender or small food processor. Bring 1¼ cups water to a boil, pour over the chile, *loosely cover* the blender or secure the top of the processor and pulse to blend thoroughly. In a small microwave-safe bowl, collect **8 peeled garlic cloves**, cover with water and microwave at 100% for 1 minute. Drain and add to the blender or processor, along with ½ **teaspoon ground cinnamon**, ¼ **teaspoon ground black pepper**, ⅛ **teaspoon ground cumin, 1 teaspoon dried oregano, 3 tablespoons apple cider vinegar** and **1½ teaspoons salt**. Process until smooth.

Roasted Garlic Chicken with Mushrooms, Potatoes and Spinach

Pollo al Mojo de Ajo con Hongos, Papas y Espinacas

◇◇

Y ou can tell I love slow-cooked dishes, because every time I write about them, I drift into reverie. I always put on groovy music and taste with my mind's palate all the goodness that comes from flavors mingling and deepening at that perfect temperature just below a simmer. And this dish is no different. Slow-cooked garlic is a personal favorite, as are chicken thighs and deliciously textured mushrooms like oysters and shiitakes. There's nothing like fresh-dug red-skin potatoes in June in Chicago, or the fingerlings that come on their heels. I could make this every month between May and November with ingredients from my local farmers' market, and it would taste thrillingly different each time, because one or another of the ingredients would be hitting a unique peak of flavor.

This recipe relies on Roasted Garlic *Mojo* for flavor. You can make it in a matter of minutes from ingredients you likely already have in your pantry. It's a long-lasting preparation that I always have in my refrigerator.

Serves 4

1 medium white onion, sliced ¼-inch thick

1 pound mushrooms (anything from the easily accessible oyster and shiitake to the over-the-top-flavorful wild varieties like morel, chanterelle, hedgehog and hen of the woods), well washed, tough stems removed and sliced (about 5 cups)

¾ pound small red- or white-skin boiling potatoes (I like ones that are about 1 inch across; if they're larger I cut them in halves or quarters)

Hot fresh green chiles to taste (roughly 3 serranos or 2 jalapeños), stemmed, seeded if you wish and finely chopped

⅔ cup Roasted Garlic *Mojo* (recipe follows; stir before measuring)

½ cup loosely packed, roughly chopped flat-leaf parsley leaves, plus a little more for serving

OR ¼ cup loosely packed, roughly chopped fresh epazote leaves, plus a little more for serving

Salt

1 tablespoon Worcestershire sauce

1½ cups chicken broth

8 small (about 2 ½ pounds) bone-in, skin-on chicken thighs

2 cups (about 2 ounces) loosely packed sliced spinach, stems removed

In a 6-quart slow cooker, combine the onion, mushrooms, potatoes, chiles, Roasted Garlic *Mojo*, herbs and 1 teaspoon salt. Mix well, spread into a flat layer and pour in the Worcestershire sauce and chicken broth. Lay the chicken thighs on top, skin side up, and sprinkle them with salt. Cover and turn the slow cooker on high. Your Roasted Garlic Chicken will be done in about 4 hours, though you can hold it for longer. (My slow cooker can be programmed to switch from high after 4 hours to a "keep warm" temperature for up to another 6 hours. Some slow cookers click to "keep warm" automatically; others need to be switched manually.)

When you're ready to serve, heat your broiler and adjust the rack to the upper third of the oven. Carefully transfer the chicken (still skin side up) to a rimmed baking sheet, pat the skin dry with paper towels, then slide under the hot broiler. In 1 or 2 minutes, the skin should be crispy and browning.

While the chicken is crisping, turn the slow cooker to high and stir in the spinach. When the spinach is wilted (it shouldn't take longer than 1 minute), taste and season with salt (usually ½ teaspoon, depending on the saltiness of your broth). Divide the mixture among 4 warm deep plates, top with 2 of the crispy chicken thighs and sprinkle with chopped herbs. Dinner's ready.

No Slow Cooker?

In a large (6- to 8-quart; at least 12 inches in diameter) heavy pot (preferably a Dutch oven), layer everything as described above. Set the cover in place and braise in a 300-degree oven for 2 to 3 hours, adding a little water if necessary to ensure that things don't dry out. Finish as described, setting the pot over medium heat to wilt the spinach.

Going Vegetarian:

This dish can be made without the chicken and by replacing the chicken stock with vegetable stock. I like to serve it with cubes of fresh Mexican cheese, goat cheese or not-too-salty feta. It's also delicious with grilled blocks of firm tofu.

ROASTED GARLIC *MOJO*

In a large (10-inch) dry skillet, roast **4 heads of garlic** (separated into cloves but not peeled) over medium heat, turning regularly until they're soft and blackened in spots, 10 to 15 minutes. Cool, peel, place in a food processor and pulse until roughly chopped. Turn the machine on and add **2 cups olive oil** in a steady stream. Stop the machine, add ¼ **cup lime juice** and **1 teaspoon salt** and pulse to incorporate. Store refrigerated in a sealed container.

Roasted Garlic Chicken with Mushrooms,
Potatoes and Spinach (page 296)

THE GRILL, STOVE AND OVEN

Weekend Dish: Slow-Grilled Pork Shoulder with Ancho Barbecue Sauce **302**

Green Chile Chicken Thighs **305**

Weekend Dish: Grilled Red Chile Ribs **308**

Grilled Lamb Chops with Charred Eggplant Salsa **311**

Weekend Dish: *Queso Fundido* Burger **314**

Grilled Salmon in Toasty Peanut Salsa **316**

Spicy, Garlicky Grilled Cauliflower Steaks with Browned Butter, Toasted Nuts and Tequila Raisins **319**

Grilled Fish with Creamy Cool Cucumber *Pipián* **322**

Chicken *Barbacoa* **324**

Beer-Glazed Beer-Can Chicken **327**

Cilantro-Poached Halibut **330**

Mussels (or Clams) with *Salsa Macha,* Mexican Beer and Ham **333**

Weekend Dish: Slow-Grilled Pork Shoulder with Ancho Barbecue Sauce

Espaldilla de Puerco con Salsa "Barbecue" de Chile Ancho

◇◇

In a book that's all about simplicity, why in the world would I include a recipe for pork shoulder that's marinated overnight, then slow-grilled for hours? The answer is clear: it's *really* good—the perfect combination of succulent meat, sweet and tangy red chile, and barbecue smokiness. And though the recipe takes a little planning ahead and regular basting, there's nothing difficult about making such a spectacular dish for a gathering of friends or family. Two small pieces of equipment will help you trade guesswork for confidence when slow-grilling any meat: an oven thermometer to set inside your grill and an instant-read thermometer to judge the temperature of the meat accurately.

Serves 4 to 6

1 bone-in pork shoulder roast (about 4 pounds)

1¼ cups Quick Red Chile *Adobo* (recipe follows; divided use)

1½ tablespoons vegetable oil, olive oil, bacon drippings or butter (each will add a different character to the sauce)

1 small red or white onion (red will make the sauce sweeter), thinly sliced

One 15-ounce can diced fire-roasted tomatoes in juice

1 tablespoon balsamic or sweet sherry vinegar

½ cup agave nectar or sugar

2 tablespoons Worcestershire sauce

Salt

Place the pork on a baking sheet, smear it all over with ¾ *cup* Quick Red Chile *Adobo*, cover with plastic wrap and refrigerate overnight.

Light a gas grill, setting the temperature at medium on the side burners (off in the center); or light a charcoal fire and let the coals burn until they're covered with gray ash and medium hot, then bank them to two sides. Lay the marinated pork in a V-shaped roasting rack set in a roasting pan. Pour 1 quart water into the roasting pan, set in the middle of the grill (the coolest part) and cover the grill. Cook at 275 to 300 degrees, basting every 30 minutes with the pan juices, until the shoulder reaches 190 degrees at the thickest part, 4 to 4½ hours depending on how diligent you are in keeping a consistent temperature in your grill. (Live-fire cooks will need to add a couple of pieces of charcoal every 20 or 30 minutes to maintain the temperature.)

While the pork is cooking, make the barbecue sauce. In a medium (3-quart) saucepan set over medium, heat the oil (or drippings or butter). When hot, add the onion and cook, stirring regularly, until it is soft and beginning to caramelize, about 7 minutes. Add the remaining ½ cup adobo and stir for a minute, then add the tomatoes and 1 cup water. Lower the heat and simmer until the mixture has the consistency of tomato paste, about 20 minutes. Scrape the sauce into a blender or food processor and process until smooth. Pour the sauce back into the pan and stir in the vinegar, agave nectar (or sugar), Worcestershire, a generous ¼ teaspoon salt and 1 cup water. Let the sauce simmer until it's the consistency of

Pork shoulder on the grill

thick barbecue sauce, 30 to 40 minutes.

During the pork's final 30 minutes of cooking, baste it several times with the barbecue sauce. When it's ready, transfer it to a cutting board, tent with foil and let it rest for about 30 minutes to re-absorb the juices. Reheat the barbecue sauce, thinning it out with some of the pork's pan juices or water if necessary. Cut the shoulder into ½-inch slices, arrange on a warm serving platter and set before your guests, passing the sauce for them to add to their liking.

Ancho Barbecue Sauce

QUICK RED CHILE *ADOBO*

Scoop **a scant ½ cup powdered ancho chile** into a blender or small food processor. Bring 1¼ cups water to a boil, pour over the chile, *loosely cover* the blender or secure the top of the processor and pulse to blend thoroughly. In a small microwave-safe bowl, collect **8 peeled garlic cloves**, cover with water and microwave at 100% for 1 minute. Drain and add to the blender or processor, along with ½ **teaspoon ground cinnamon**, ¼ **teaspoon ground black pepper**, ⅛ **teaspoon ground cumin**, **1 teaspoon dried oregano**, **3 tablespoons apple cider vinegar** and **1½ teaspoons salt**. Process until smooth.

Slow-Grilled Pork Shoulder with Ancho Barbecue Sauce (page 302)

Green Chile Chicken Thighs

Muslos de Pollo al Chile Verde

◇◇◇

This is a big mouthful of flavor: moist and meaty chicken thighs, roasted green chile and slow-cooked garlic, bright green cilantro and rousing lime. The magic all happens sealed up in a foil package—the old-fashioned "hobo pack" style. (Bring back any Scouts-era memories?) And to tell the truth, that rudimentary, make-do cooking method is an amazing way to cook, reminiscent of the French *en papillote*, where all the flavors are trapped together in a sealed packet, encouraging them to get to know each other in a very intimate way. Though the cooking time is short, the result tastes like it has cooked for hours.

Chicken thighs naturally have more fat than chicken breasts, which is why they work in a preparation like this (chicken breasts would probably turn out dry with this difficult-to-monitor, sealed-in cooking). Should they be boneless, skinless or bone-in, skin-on? Well, the bone and skin will definitely add more flavor, but the skin won't be all that attractive cooked in this steamy environment. Plus, the skin will render more fat into the packet—not bad, but maybe not to everyone's taste. Personally, I'd make the dish with bone-in, skin-on thighs, then pull off the skin just before serving (it usually sticks to the foil anyway). But that's just me.

Serves 4 to 8, depending on the size of the chicken thighs

4 (about 1 pound total) fresh poblano chiles

4 garlic cloves, peeled and finely chopped

2 tablespoons olive oil

Salt

1 pound small red- or white-skin boiling potatoes (I like ones that are about 1 inch across; if they're larger I cut them in halves or quarters), peeled if you wish

Two 10-inch pieces of banana leaf (optional; divided use)

8 chicken thighs—boneless, skinless (about 2 pounds total) or bone-in, skin-on (about 3½ pounds total) (see the headnote)

½ cup chopped cilantro

1 lime, cut into 8 wedges, for serving

Turn on a gas grill to medium-high or light a charcoal grill and let the coals burn until quite hot and covered with white ash. Roast the poblanos over the hottest part of the fire, turning them regularly until blackened and blistered all over, about 15 minutes. Place in a bowl, cover with a kitchen towel and cool until handleable. Rub off the blackened skin, pull out the seedpods and scrape out the seeds. Rinse briefly to remove any stray seeds and bits of blackened skin. Give the cleaned chiles a rough chop.

Scoop the garlic into a food processor or blender and pulse a few times until it's roughly chopped. Add the poblano and continue to pulse until finely chopped but not pureed. Pour in the oil and ½ teaspoon salt and pulse a few more times, just to combine.

Collect the potatoes in a microwave-safe bowl, sprinkle on a couple of tablespoons of water, cover with plastic wrap, poke a few holes in the top and microwave at 100% for 5 minutes, until nearly tender.

Cut 2 pieces of heavy-duty aluminum foil 2 feet long (lightweight foil tends to burn during the cooking process) and lay one on top of the other. If you're using the banana leaves, lay *one* over the left half of the foil. Arrange the chicken thighs (if there is skin, put that side down) over the banana leaf or left side of the foil in a single layer, leaving a 1-inch border around the edges. Sprinkle generously with salt. Distribute the potatoes over the chicken, then spoon on the poblano-garlic puree. Fold the uncovered side of the foil over the chicken, then seal the three open sides by folding them over several times.

Slide the packet directly over the hottest part of the grill, set the cover in place and let cook for 30 minutes. Remove the package from the heat, open up one side (carefully— there will be steam!) and check the chicken for doneness. If your grill temperature was right, the chicken thighs should be done; if not, re-seal the packet and grill for a few more minutes. Open up the package and transfer the chicken thighs to a platter lined with the remaining banana leaf (if you're using it), removing the skin from the thighs if you wish. Arrange the potatoes around the chicken and pour the juices that remain in the foil over the top. Taste a little of everything and sprinkle with salt if you think the dish needs it. Sprinkle generously with the cilantro and serve with the lime wedges for everyone to squeeze on *al gusto*.

Riffs on Green Chile Chicken:

Anything that has a precise cooking time won't fare well in this preparation, and it's not a long enough cooking time for cuts like pork or lamb shoulder and beef chuck. Duck thighs could work here, though they're not always that easily available. So for most of us it'll be chicken thighs. Potatoes, however, can be replaced with other vegetables (think winter squash, chayote, farmers' market onions, beets). And, of course, many different chiles can be substituted for the poblanos; think about other large ones that are not too hot. Any that have ripened to red or orange are particularly flavorful in the fall.

Weekend Dish: Grilled Red Chile Ribs

Costillas Adobadas y Asadas

◇◇

I grew up in a barbecue restaurant in Oklahoma City where small slabs of spareribs were dry-rubbed with a robust blend of chiles, herbs and spices, then rested overnight. Early the next morning, the hickory-fueled barbecue pit was heated to between 225 and 250 degrees, ready to cook the ribs slowly until the meat was tender—not fall-off-the-bone tender, which we considered fit only for the aged or infirm, but engagingly tender, giving each bite a sense of easy victory and satisfaction.

Today back ribs are more popular (hence more available) than spareribs. Most people consider them solidly meatier (back ribs are the part of the rib next to the lean pork loin) and quicker to prepare (spareribs include muscles that need longer, slower cooking). That said, when I have time, I enjoy cooking spareribs for their richness and their more robust flavor.

Since we're focusing here on quick and simple, I've written this recipe for back ribs that are baked just until tender, then given a smoky singe from the grill just before serving. (In the Riff, I describe how to cook the ribs in the more classic barbecue technique, slowly grill-roasting from start to finish over smoldering coals.) This quicker technique produces excellent results, satisfying American rib lovers while highlighting the classic Mexican red chile *adobo* that flavors the meaty morsels. And to keep the flavors continuing down that classic path, I suggest that you serve these ribs with a tangy roasted tomatillo salsa infused with the same red chile seasoning.

Serves 6

3 slabs (2 to 2½ pounds each; the smaller, the better) baby back ribs

1 cup Quick Red Chile *Adobo* (recipe follows; divided use)

12 ounces (4 to 6 medium) tomatillos, husked, rinsed and cut in half around the equator

4 tablespoons honey or agave nectar (divided use)

Lay the ribs on a rimmed baking sheet. Brush ½ *cup* of the *adobo* onto both sides of each slab. If time permits, cover and refrigerate for several hours or, best, overnight.

Heat the oven to 300 degrees. Place the ribs convex side up in a single layer and bake them until tender (you should be able to pull the meat away fairly easily with a fork inserted between the bones), about 2½ hours. You can let the ribs cool at room temperature for an hour or so, until you're ready to serve.

While the ribs are cooking, roast the tomatillos: Set a large (10-inch) skillet (nonstick or lined with foil) over medium-high heat and lay in the tomatillos cut side down. When the tomatillos are well browned, about 4 minutes, flip everything over and brown the other side. While still warm, scrape them (and any juices in the pan) into a blender jar. Measure in ¼ cup of the *adobo* and *2 tablespoons* of the honey (or agave nectar). Cover *loosely* and blend to a coarse puree. Scoop into a serving bowl, taste and season with salt, usually about ½ teaspoon. If needed, stir in a little water to give the mixture the consistency of an easily spoonable salsa. Refrigerate if not using within an hour or so.

When serving time arrives, heat a gas grill to medium-high or prepare a charcoal fire and let it burn until the coals are covered with white ash and quite hot. Scoop the remaining ¼ cup of the *adobo* into a small dish and stir in the remaining *2 tablespoons* honey (or agave nectar). Lay the ribs on the hot grill, convex side down. When they're richly browned, about 3 minutes, flip them over and brush them liberally with the sweetened *adobo*. Cover the grill and cook for several more minutes, until the *adobo* looks set and the ribs are heated through. Remove the ribs to a cutting board, cover with foil and let rest for a few minutes. Cut the ribs between the bones, pile on a warm platter and serve to your lucky guests with the salsa.

Riff: The Classic Barbecue Technique

Instead of baking the ribs first, prepare a small charcoal fire, letting the coals burn until medium hot. Bank the coals to opposite sides of your grill and nestle a rectangular disposable aluminum pan between the coals. Add 3 or 4 cups water to the pan. Set the grill grate in place and lay the ribs convex side up in a single layer in the center of the grill over the pan. (A rib rack that supports the ribs standing on their sides is an excellent piece of equipment to use here; it ensures even cooking and avoids burned edges close to the coals.) Cover the grill and cook at 225 to 250 degrees until the ribs are fork-tender, usually 3 hours. You'll need to add a couple of pieces of charcoal every 20 or 30 minutes to maintain the temperature. When the ribs are tender, brush them with the sweetened *adobo*, re-cover the grill and cook until the *adobo* looks set. Finish as described above.

QUICK RED CHILE *ADOBO*

Scoop **a scant ½ cup powdered ancho chile** into a blender or small food processor. Bring 1¼ cups water to a boil, pour over the chile, *loosely cover* the blender or secure the top of the processor and pulse to blend thoroughly. In a small microwave-safe bowl, collect **8 peeled garlic cloves**, cover with water and microwave at 100% for 1 minute. Drain and add to the blender or processor, along with ½ **teaspoon ground cinnamon**, ¼ **teaspoon ground black pepper**, ⅛ **teaspoon ground cumin**, **1 teaspoon dried oregano**, **3 tablespoons apple cider vinegar** and **1½ teaspoons salt**. Process until smooth.

Grilled Lamb Chops with Charred Eggplant Salsa

Chuletas de Borrego con Salsa de Berenjena Asada

◇◇

I admit it: I love spending time in the kitchen. I love the process of cooking—the chopping, searing, smelling, tasting and observing as beautiful dishes come to life before my eyes. But at times I need to get something festive on the table as quickly as possible (I'm sure you can relate), so I turn to quick-cooking, remarkable meats like lamb chops and dressing them up with something unexpected, such as a roasted eggplant salsa infused with smoky chipotles, lime and cilantro.

Serves 4

1 pound (2 medium-large round or 4 to 5 plum) ripe tomatoes

1 medium red onion, cut into ½-inch-thick slices

1 small (about 8 ounces) eggplant

8 unpeeled garlic cloves

3 canned chipotle chiles *en adobo*, stemmed

2 tablespoons chipotle canning sauce

About 3 tablespoons fresh lime juice

⅓ cup olive or vegetable oil

Salt

8 (about 1 pound total) lamb chops, about 1 inch thick

About 1 tablespoon chopped cilantro

Light a charcoal fire and let the coals burn until they are covered with white ash and medium hot, or heat a gas grill to medium. Lay the tomatoes, onion, eggplant and garlic on the grill grate (I lay down a perforated grill pan first to ensure that the garlic doesn't fall into the fire, and I poke a few holes in the eggplant with a knife to keep it from exploding as it chars). Grill the vegetables, turning occasionally, until they are softened and blotchy black all over. Timing will depend on the exact heat of your grill, but plan for 10 to 15 minutes for the garlic and onion, 15 to 20 minutes for the tomatoes and 20 to 30 minutes for the eggplant (which will probably have collapsed on itself by this point). Set the vegetables aside to cool.

Slip off the papery skins of the garlic and scoop into a blender or food processor. Add the chipotle chiles, the canning sauce and the lime juice. Blend until smooth, scrape *half* the mixture into a small bowl and stir in the oil and ½ teaspoon salt. Smear a light coating of this mixture on both sides of each lamb chop.

To the mixture remaining in the blender, add the soft eggplant flesh: cut the eggplant in half lengthwise, scrape out the flesh (leaving the charred skin behind) and scoop it into the blender. Blend until nearly smooth and scrape into a large bowl. Next, peel the tomatoes (if you wish), chop them into roughly ¼-inch pieces and scoop them into the bowl with the eggplant mixture. Chop the onion into ¼-inch pieces and add to the tomatoes. Stir in the cilantro. Taste and season with salt (about 1 teaspoon) and with extra lime juice if you feel the salsa needs a little more brightness.

Re-stoke the fire (it needs to be quite hot) or raise the heat on the gas grill to medium-high. When hot, lay the chops on the hottest part of the grill and let them sear undisturbed until there are dark grill marks underneath; flip the chops and grill to perfect doneness (about 3 minutes per side for medium-rare).

Lay 2 chops on each of 4 warm dinner plates, spoon on a portion of salsa and your beautiful dish is ready.

Riffs on Grilled Lamb Chops with Eggplant Salsa:

The salsa can be made with grilled tomatillos instead of tomatoes, and mint or basil can replace the cilantro. If lamb chops aren't right for your dinner table, make the dish with pork chops or pork tenderloin, with chicken breasts or a steak. The salsa goes with practically anything off the grill.

Queso Fundido Burger (page 314)

Weekend Dish: *Queso Fundido* Burger

Hamburguesa de Queso Fundido

◇◇

I probably shouldn't admit this, but I went years and years without ever eating a hamburger, that most American of American specialties. I'm not completely sure why, though it probably had something to do with being so completely infatuated with other flavors that eating a hamburger seemed like a step backward. Then my daughter came along, and somehow we bonded over hamburgers. Not just any hamburgers, but ones that were so well executed that we could argue about whether they were the *perfect* burger. It remained our private debate, never spilling into my life as a professional chef—until I was asked to participate in one of those culinary challenges that have become part of every chef's life nowadays, this one a hamburger challenge. I couldn't imagine not weaving in some classic Mexican touches, crowd-pleasing flavors I knew could win a competition. Flavors like the traditional Mexican *queso fundido*, melted cheese with chorizo sausage and roasted peppers. So, for those very special moments, I offer my mashup of the rich and delicious, gooey-melty *queso fundido* and a classic American burger. Cultural exchange never tasted better, unless, of course, it includes a big spoonful of roasted tomatillo salsa.

Serves 4

2 fresh poblano chiles

8 ounces fresh Mexican chorizo sausage, casing removed (about 1 cup)

1 tablespoon vegetable oil

1 medium white onion, sliced ¼-inch thick

2 garlic cloves, peeled and finely chopped

1½ pounds ground chuck (chuck offers a beefy flavor and richness I like for special occasions; you can choose a leaner cut if that makes sense for you)

1 to 2 canned chipotle chiles *en adobo*, seeded if you wish, finely chopped

8 thick slices Monterey jack cheese

4 hamburger buns, lightly toasted

Roast the chiles over an open flame or close up under a preheated broiler, turning them regularly, until evenly blackened and blistered, about 5 minutes for an open flame, 10 minutes for the broiler. Place in a bowl, cover with a kitchen towel and cool until handleable. Rub off the blackened skin, pull out the seedpods and scrape out the seeds. Rinse briefly to remove any stray seeds and bits of blackened skin. Cut into ¼-inch strips.

Set a large (10-inch) skillet over medium heat. Add the chorizo and cook, stirring to break up the clumps, until it is beginning to brown and is cooked through, about 10 minutes. Scrape onto a plate lined with paper towels and let cool. Return the skillet to medium heat, measure in the oil and add the onion. Cook, stirring regularly, until it is soft and beginning to caramelize, about 7 minutes. Stir in the garlic and poblano and cook for 2 minutes. Taste, season with salt, usually about ½ teaspoon, scrape the *rajas* into a bowl and cover to keep warm.

In a large bowl, combine the ground beef, the cooled chorizo and the chipotles. Mix thoroughly but lightly (to keep from turning out an overly compact texture). Divide into 4 portions, lightly pressing them into patties the size of your buns.

Heat a gas grill to medium-high on one side, medium on the other, or light a charcoal fire and let it burn until the charcoal is covered with white ash and quite hot, then bank the coals to one side.

Lay the hamburger patties on the hottest side of the grill and cook until the grill grate has seared beautiful marks on one side, about 2 minutes, then flip and cook until the hamburgers are a little less done than you like (usually a couple of minutes longer for rare to medium-rare). Move the burgers to the cooler side of the grill. Lay one piece of cheese on each burger, top with a portion of the warm *rajas* and then another piece of cheese. Close the lid and continue cooking until the cheese has melted, about 1 minute. Remove from the grill and place on the toasted buns. Serve immediately.

Grilled Salmon in Toasty Peanut Salsa

Salmón a la Parilla con Salsa de Cacahuate Tostado

◇◇

When the wild salmon start showing up in the late spring, this is the dish I dream of making. It's simplicity come to life in the best possible way, one that focuses on the stunning flavor and buttery texture of the salmon, the smoky and elemental draw of the grill and the perfect, rich gilding from a spoonful of red chile–peanut deliciousness.

If you don't have guajillo chiles, you can substitute New Mexicos or 2 anchos

Serves 4

3 unpeeled garlic cloves

3 dried guajillo chiles, stemmed, seeded and torn into large pieces

2 canned chipotle chiles *en adobo*, stemmed and roughly chopped

1 cup roasted, unsalted peanuts

Salt

Four 5- to 6-ounce boneless, skinless salmon fillets, preferably from wild-caught salmon

2 green or fresh spring "knob" onions, withered leaves removed, roots trimmed

OR 2 fresh ramps

A little olive or vegetable oil

On one side of a large (10-inch) dry skillet, roast the garlic over medium heat, turning regularly, until soft and blackened in spots, 10 to 15 minutes. On the other side, toast the guajillo chiles. Use a metal spatula to press the chile pieces flat against the hot surface of the pan. When they release their aroma and change color slightly (maybe even give off a faint wisp of smoke), about 10 seconds, flip them over and press down again to toast the other side. Scoop into a bowl and cover with ¾ cup very hot tap water to rehydrate, 10 to 15 minutes.

Cool the garlic until handleable, peel it and place it in a blender, along with the guajillo chiles (including their soaking liquid), the chipotles and the peanuts. Blend until nearly smooth, then scrape into a small bowl. Stir in a little more water if necessary to give the salsa an easily spoonable consistency. Taste and season with salt, usually about ½ teaspoon.

Heat a gas grill to medium-high or light a charcoal fire and let the coals burn until covered with white ash and very hot. Smear the salmon fillets and green onions (or ramps) with a little oil and sprinkle with salt. On the coolest part of your grill (usually toward an edge), grill the onions (or ramps), turning regularly, doing your best to keep the green parts farthest from the heat, until soft, about 15 minutes. Lay the salmon fillets on the hottest part of the grill, placing what had been their skin side down. When the grill grate has deeply seared marks into the salmon and the salmon has begun to release itself from the grate, about 3 minutes, depending on the heat of your fire, flip the fillets and cook to your desired degree of doneness, usually a couple of minutes longer for 1-inch-thick fillets to reach medium. Transfer to warm dinner plates.

Chop the green onions (or ramps) into small pieces. Spoon some salsa over each fillet, sprinkle with chopped onion (or ramps) and serve right away.

Grilled Salmon in
Toasty Peanut Salsa
(page 316)

Spicy, Garlicky Grilled Cauliflower Steaks with Browned Butter, Toasted Nuts and Tequila Raisins

Coliflor Picante a la Parilla con Mantequilla Dorada, Ajo,

Cacahuates Tostadas y Pasitas Borrachas

◇◇

This is a wacky but irresistible dish. First, it's cauliflower cut into slabs or chunks, seared on the grill and basted with spicy garlic butter. Second, it's not really saucy like most of my food. Instead, the spicy garlic butter is spooned over, after being studded with a playful mix of toasted nuts, boozy raisins and fresh herbs. This is the kind of meal I like to serve in the backyard after a trip to the farmers' market, accompanied, perhaps, by some herbed rice and a salad of interesting greens dressed with something creamy. While cauliflower steaks make for a gorgeous presentation, carving them from a head of cauliflower means sacrificing a lot of valuable end pieces, so sometimes I grill cauliflower chunks and call it a day.

Serves 4

1 to 2 small heads (2 pounds total) cauliflower (if you're cutting the cauliflower into steaks, you'll need 2 heads)

Salt

⅔ cup raisins

¼ cup tequila or fruit juice

1 cup toasted peanuts or hulled, toasted pumpkin seeds

12 tablespoons (6 ounces) butter, or half butter and half olive oil

4 garlic cloves, peeled and finely chopped

1 to 2 tablespoons Mexican hot sauce (like Tamazula, Valentina or Búfalo)

½ teaspoon ground black pepper

About 1/3 cup chopped cilantro or flat-leaf parsley

Several tablespoons grated Mexican *queso añejo* or other garnishing cheese such as Romano or Parmesan

Trim away any of the cauliflower's stem that protrudes beyond the head, then set the cauliflower head stem side down on your cutting board and cut it into "steaks" or chunks. For steaks, use a large knife to trim off an inch or so from both the right and left sides of the head (this gives you two flat sides; save the trimmings to sprinkle on a salad). Then cut what remains into 1-inch-thick slabs. For chunks, simply cut the cauliflower into roughly 2-inch pieces, avoiding as much of the hard core as possible. Arrange the cauliflower on a large plate in a single layer, cover with plastic and micro-wave at 100% until crisp-tender, about 5 minutes. Uncover, season with a little salt and let cool.

Heat a gas grill to medium-high or light a charcoal fire and let it burn until the coals are covered with white ash and the fire is quite hot.

While the grill is heating, in a small, microwave-safe bowl combine the raisins and tequila (or juice). Cover, microwave at 100% for 30 seconds and let cool to room tem-perature without uncovering. Scoop the raisins into a food processor (liquid and all) and pulse a few times to roughly chop. Add the peanuts (or pumpkin seeds) and pulse 6 or 8 times more, to roughly chop them, too. Transfer the mixture to a bowl.

Melt the butter (or butter and oil) in a small (1- to 2-quart) saucepan over medium heat. Cook, swirling the pan regularly for a couple of minutes, until the butter is golden brown. Add the garlic and stir for a minute, then pour into the bowl with the raisin-nut mixture. Stir in the hot sauce, black pepper, 3 tablespoons water and, if you're not using salted butter, a little salt.

Liberally brush the cauliflower on both sides with the buttery part of the mixture (leave the solids in the bowl), sprinkle with salt and grill until richly marked by the grill grate, 4 to 5 minutes per side. Remove to warm dinner plates. Re-warm the buttery mixture for 30 seconds in the microwave, stir in the chopped cilantro (or parsley) and spoon over the cauliflower steaks. Sprinkle with the cheese and your cauliflower steaks are ready.

Riffs on Grilled Cauliflower Steaks:

Truthfully, any vegetable you want to grill can be dressed with the buttery mixture. Also, that mixture makes a good pasta sauce, with or without grilled vegetables.

Spicy, Garlicky Grilled
Cauliflower Steaks with
Browned Butter, Toasted
Nuts and Tequila Raisins
(page 319)

Grilled Fish with Creamy Cool Cucumber *Pipián*

Pescado Asado en Pipián de Pepino

◇◇

Okay, before some of you say, "This is *not* a *pipián*!" I'll admit you're right. Sort of. Typically a *pipián* is a simple, warm, *mole*-like sauce with a greater focus on the nuts or seeds used for thickening than on the chiles. And you know what? If you replaced the cucumber in this sauce with tomatillos, eliminated the cream and served it warm, you'd have a classic green *pipián*. So if this sauce isn't exactly a *pipián*, what is it? "Delicious" would be my first response, quickly followed by "a creamy cucumber–pumpkin seed salsa," which isn't all that much easier to fit into a well-known category. Just know that during the summer, when you're thinking about grilling fish, this is a recipe you'll want to turn to.

Serves 4

4 garlic cloves, peeled

1 medium-large (14-ounce) cucumber (this is a great place to use the equivalent weight of cucumbers from the farmers' market—cucumbers like lemon, Persian or pickling), peeled and chopped into ½-inch pieces

1 large fresh serrano chile or small jalapeño, stemmed, seeded if you wish and roughly chopped

⅓ cup hulled, toasted pumpkin seeds, plus a few extra for serving

½ cup roughly chopped cilantro (1 small roughly chopped *hoja santa* leaf if you have it would be a great substitute here), plus more for serving

2 tablespoons Mexican *crema*, sour cream, *crème fraîche* or Greek-style yogurt

Salt

Four 5-ounce fish fillets (I like this with halibut, striped bass, snapper, or salmon; pretty much any fish, or shellfish, works), preferably ¾- to 1-inch thick

A little olive oil for coating the fish

Place the garlic in a small, microwave-safe bowl, cover with water and microwave at 100% for 1 minute. Remove from the water and cool. In a blender jar, combine the cooled garlic, cucumber, chile, pumpkin seeds and cilantro (or *hoja santa*). Blend until smooth, adding a little water if necessary to keep the mixture moving through the blades. (Thicker mixtures come out more uniformly smooth than liquid ones when blended.) Add the *crema* (or one of its stand-ins), blend to combine, scrape into a small dish, taste and season with salt (usually 1 teaspoon). If not serving within an hour or so, cover and refrigerate.

Turn on a gas grill to medium-high or light a charcoal grill and let the coals burn until quite hot and covered with white ash. Brush or spray both sides of the fish with olive oil, then sprinkle both sides with salt. Lay the fish what had been skin side down on the hottest part of the grill and let it cook until the grate has seared in beautiful grill marks, and the fish releases itself from the grates, about 3 minutes, depending on the heat of your grill. Flip the fish and cook until as done as you like, 1 or 2 minutes longer for fish that's medium to medium-rare at the center.

Lay a piece of grilled fish on each of 4 warm dinner plates. Spoon on some of the cool *pipián*, sprinkle with pumpkin seeds (I like to crush them roughly between my fingers first), and, if you have any, some herb leaves—cilantro, torn *hoja santa*, mint, basil are all welcome. Your beautiful creation is ready.

Chicken *Barbacoa*

Barbacoa de Pollo

◇◇

When I lived in Guerrero years ago, in the hills high above Chilpancingo, a lot of the marketplace cooks made what they called *barbacoa de pollo*. It was typically whole chickens, richly marinated in red chile *adobo*, slowly steamed over broth that filled the air with the aroma of sweet onions and anisey avocado leaves. When you ordered it, they'd pull portions off the tender chicken and douse them with the steaming juice—juice that by then had been seasoned with red chile that dripped down from the birds. It's a simple dish, best made with the full-flavored free-range chickens of small-town Mexican markets. My version of *barbacoa de pollo*, which is more of a braised dish than a steamed one, tastes best with a good chicken, too.

The avocado leaves (which are available dry in many Mexican grocery stores) add a unique flavor; banana leaves, which are much easier to find, are tasty, too, though not as distinctive. Even without any leaves to provide that special touch, the dish is wonderful, especially when it's served up with avocado, cilantro, lime and a good roasted tomatillo salsa. And, of course, warm tortillas for making tasty tacos.

Serves 4

3 tablespoons vegetable or olive oil

1 large (4-pound) whole chicken

Salt

1 medium white onion, sliced ¼-inch thick

¼ cup Quick Red Chile *Adobo* (recipe follows), plus more if desired

A handful of dried or fresh avocado leaves (optional)

OR a 12-inch piece of banana leaf torn into several smaller pieces (optional)

1 ripe avocado, pitted, flesh scooped from the skin and diced

A handful of cilantro leaves

1 lime, cut into 8 wedges, for serving

About 1 cup store-bought or homemade salsa, preferably green salsa made from roasted tomatillos, for serving

Turn on the oven to 250 degrees. In a large (7- or 8-quart) heavy pot (preferably a Dutch oven) set over medium, heat the oil. Sprinkle the chicken generously all over with salt, and when the oil is hot, lay it in the pot breast side down. Scatter the onion around the chicken and let both brown, reaching into the pot occasionally and stirring the onion. When the chicken's breast is richly browned, 3 to 4 minutes, flip the bird with tongs and brown the other side. Stir the *adobo* into 2 cups water and pour it over and around the chicken. Nestle in the avocado leaves (or banana leaves), if you're using them. Cover the pot, slide it into the oven and cook until the chicken meat can be pulled from the bone, about 1½ hours.

Carefully transfer the chicken to a cutting board (if it falls apart, simply transfer the pieces). Taste the broth and season with salt; it usually needs a generous teaspoon. If you want a spicier, more robust flavor, stir in another tablespoon or two of *adobo* and bring the sauce to a simmer for a minute to let the flavor settle in. (If you used either of the leaves, now is the time to fish them out and discard.) Pull the chicken meat from the bones and add it back to the pot to warm for a minute or two. Serve the *barbacoa* in warm shallow bowls with a few generous spoonfuls of broth and some diced avocado and cilantro leaves. Pass the lime wedges and salsa separately (for everyone to squeeze or spoon on *al gusto*), along with warm tortillas.

QUICK RED CHILE *ADOBO*

Scoop **a scant ½ cup powdered ancho chile** into a blender or small food processor. Bring 1¼ cups water to a boil, pour over the chile, *loosely cover* the blender or secure the top of the processor and pulse to blend thoroughly. In a small microwave-safe bowl, collect **8 peeled garlic cloves**, cover with water and microwave at 100% for 1 minute. Drain and add to the blender or processor, along with ½ **teaspoon ground cinnamon**, ¼ **teaspoon ground black pepper**, ⅛ **teaspoon ground cumin**, **1 teaspoon dried oregano**, **3 tablespoons apple cider vinegar** and **1½ teaspoons salt**. Process until smooth.

Beer-Glazed Beer-Can Chicken (page 327)

Beer-Glazed Beer-Can Chicken

Pollo Cocido Sobre Lata de Cerveza, Glaceado con Cerveza

You've seen this before, I'm sure, but never with these flavors. And since this is really just a novel way to turn out a roast chicken, adding wonderful flavors is what sets this preparation apart. If you've never done a beer-can chicken before, the can becomes the support over which you slide the cavity of the chicken so that it can roast sitting upright. Chicken roasts well that way.

A couple of production notes: Get a kosher chicken, because they come salted (meaning they're slightly brined, meaning the meat will be juicier when roasted). If you don't have a kosher chicken, dissolve 1 cup table salt and 2 tablespoons sugar in 2 quarts of cold water in a large pot, slide in the chicken and brine for 1 hour. Remove and pat dry.

I've called for a dark Mexican beer, but none of the common ones come in cans. I've made this recipe using the malty-flavored (glass-bottled) Negra Modelo and really loved it. So I solve my problem by buying a can of Modelo Especial and pouring the contents into a glass (I assure you, I can always think of something to do with it). Then I cut the top off the can, pour half (¾ cup) of the dark beer into the can and use that as the support for the chicken.

Serves 4

1 teaspoon ground black pepper

1 tablespoon dried oregano, preferably Mexican

½ teaspoon ground cumin

Salt

1 large (4-pound) whole chicken, preferably kosher

One 12-ounce can dark Mexican beer (divided use; see the headnote)

1 head of garlic, sliced in half around the equator (divided use)

4 to 6 cups chopped root vegetables; (potatoes, carrots, onions and the like; ¾-inch pieces are good; optional)

2 to 3 tablespoons vegetable or olive oil (optional)

½ teaspoon chile flakes

3 tablespoons (¾-ounce) chopped *piloncillo* (Mexican raw sugar) or brown sugar

Turn on the oven to 375 degrees and set a rack on the lowest level; if there's a second rack, remove it. Mix together the pepper, oregano, cumin and ½ teaspoon salt (1 teaspoon if your chicken is neither kosher nor brined). (For the freshest taste, I like to start with whole spices and grind them in an electric spice grinder or mortar and pestle just before using.) Pat the chicken dry with paper towels and rub *a generous couple of teaspoons* of the spice mixture all over it.

A proper beer-can chicken, nestled firmly over the can and standing upright on the baking sheet

Pour *half of the can (¾ cup)* of beer into a measuring cup. Use a can opener to cut the top off the can. Drop *1* of the garlic head halves and ½ teaspoon of the spice mixture into the can with the remaining beer. Stand the can in the center of a 13×9-inch baking dish and fit the chicken over it, nestling the can firmly into the chicken's cavity. (The bird will be standing upright over the can.) If you're using the vegetables, toss them with the oil, sprinkle them with salt and scatter them evenly around the chicken. Slide the chicken into the oven to roast for 1 hour, occasionally stirring the vegetables, if using.

Meanwhile, make the beer glaze: In a small (2-quart) saucepan, combine the remaining *¾ cup* of beer with the remaining spice mixture, the other garlic half, the chile flakes and the *piloncillo* (or brown sugar). Set over medium heat and simmer, stirring frequently, until the sauce is reduced and syrupy, about 30 minutes.

When the chicken's hour is up, check its temperature; a thermometer inserted into the thigh should read about 145 degrees. Brush the beer glaze all over the chicken and slide it back into the oven to roast until it's golden and an instant-read thermometer inserted into the same spot reads 155 to 160 degrees, about 15 minutes more.

Remove the chicken to a cutting board and carefully lift it off the beer can (the chicken and can will be hot, so use tongs). Tent the bird loosely with foil and let it rest for 5 to 10 minutes. Meanwhile, if you've roasted vegetables, pour the contents of the can (minus the garlic) into the roasting pan, toss with the vegetables and slide into the oven to cook until they're fully tender and most of the liquid has evaporated, about 10 minutes.

Cut the chicken into quarters and transfer a portion to each of 4 warm dinner plates, along with the vegetables if you have them. Dinner's ready.

Beer-roasted
vegetables

Cilantro-Poached Halibut

Pescado al Cilantro

◇◇

As you read through this preparation, it will seem so simple that you hardly need a recipe to make it: prepare a flavorful poaching liquid, gently cook some fish in it, enrich the liquid with dairy. True, it's simple, but the outcome is greater than the sum of such straightforward parts. First, when you cook cilantro, it takes on a different flavor—less in-your-face herbal, more mellow and sweet. In fact, some of you will hardly recognize cilantro's cooked flavor as cilantro at all. But not to worry, the broth is bolstered by lime zest and serrano chile. And, as you might expect, a second handful of cilantro gets added just before the sauce is blended, to add beautiful color and freshness. And the dairy? You can choose among several options. There's always Greek-style yogurt in my refrigerator, so that's what I use most often. It's not as rich and creamy as real Mexican *crema* or *crème fraîche,* but it's thoroughly satisfying. The milky whiteness of halibut is beautiful against the pale green sauce, but so is the succulent ivory of black cod or the rosiness of salmon. Any of those will elicit praise from anyone who tries a mouthful.

Serves 4 for dinner

2 tablespoons butter or olive oil

1 small white onion, sliced ¼-inch thick

½ to 1 fresh serrano chile, stemmed, seeded if you wish and roughly chopped

1 cup chicken broth

1 cup roughly chopped cilantro, plus a few more tablespoons for serving (divided use)

Zest (colored part only) of ½ lime, removed in strips with a vegetable peeler

Salt

Four 5-ounce fillets skinless halibut, salmon or other meaty fish OR four 4-ounce fillets flounder or other delicate fish

¼ cup Mexican *crema*, *crème fraîche*, heavy cream or Greek-style yogurt

Heat the butter (or oil) in a large (10-inch) skillet set over medium. Add the onion and chile and cook, stirring, until richly golden, 9 to 10 minutes. Add the broth, ½ *cup* of the cilantro and the lime zest and bring it all to a simmer. Taste and season with salt, usually a scant teaspoon (it should taste slightly salty). Slide the fish into the liquid in a single layer. Reduce the heat to medium-low, cover and cook for 5 or 6 minutes, until the fillets are medium-rare (they'll almost flake under firm pressure—thick fillets will need more time than thinner ones). Remove from the heat and let the fish sit in the broth, still covered, for 1 to 2 more minutes to finish cooking. (I like it when the fish is just barely cooked through; if you prefer yours more well done, let it sit a little longer.) Transfer the fish to a rimmed baking sheet and slide into a low oven to keep warm.

Pour the sauce in the pan into a *loosely covered* blender and add the *crema* (or one of its stand-ins) and the remaining ½ *cup* cilantro. Blend until smooth, taste and season with additional salt if you think it needs some. Divide the fish among 4 warm dinner plates, spoon a portion of sauce over each one and sprinkle with a little more cilantro. Beautiful, simple, delicious.

Cilantro-Poached Halibut (page 330)

Mussels (or Clams) with *Salsa Macha*, Mexican Beer and Ham

Mejillones (o Almejas) con Salsa Macha, Cerveza Mexicana y Jamón

◆◇

Salsa macha is one those flavors that folks all over the world love. I've found versions all over East Asia, something similar in North Africa, a milder version in Argentina. In a nutshell, it's chopped-up dried red chile, oil, garlic, sometimes nuts or seeds, perhaps a few local flavors. There's something compelling about the mix, and it can be stored for months, making it an easy-to-grab seasoning for adding to omelets or roasted potatoes, for smearing on steaks or chicken thighs just before they come off the grill, for slathering on corn on the cob or mixing with goat cheese for a dip. If I were choosing a fifth secret weapon (see pages 33–40), this would be it. A jar of *salsa macha* is almost always in my refrigerator. (For you lovers of spice, adding a few arbol or other small spicy dried chiles will add greater pizzazz.)

Here *salsa macha* seasons the broth for steaming mussels or clams: straightforward, robust flavors that are scrumptious sopped up with crusty bread.

Serves 4

For making 2 cups salsa macha
   (considerably more than you need, but
   it keeps for months in the refrigerator):

1½ ounces (⅓ cup) nuts (almonds, peanuts, or pecan pieces, or a mixture)

1 tablespoon sesame seeds

2 ounces dried ancho or guajillo chiles, stemmed, seeded and cut into small (roughly ¼-inch) pieces (a generous ½ cup)

1 tablespoon vinegar (cider vinegar works well here)

Salt

A generous ½ teaspoon dried herb such as Mexican oregano, marjoram or thyme

1½ to 2 cups olive oil

4 garlic cloves, peeled and finely chopped

About 1 cup (5 ounces) chopped ham (¼-inch pieces are good)

1 cup Mexican beer (a malty one like Negra Modelo works well here)

2 cups chicken broth (in a pinch you can use water, though the cooking juices won't be quite as delicious)

4 pounds mussels or clams, well
   scrubbed, any beards pulled off (when
   I have time, I soak them in water for a
   couple of hours with a few tablespoons

of cornmeal to ensure that they spit out
   any sand they're harboring)
½ cup chopped cilantro or flat-leaf parsley
Crusty bread, for serving

Make the *salsa macha*: Combine the nuts and sesame seeds in a large (10-inch) skillet and set over medium heat. Cook, stirring frequently, until the nuts are golden and fragrant, about 5 minutes. Add the chile pieces and cook, stirring, until they have just started to change color and add their aroma to the kitchen, about 1 minute more. Transfer everything to a blender or small food processor, add the vinegar, 1 teaspoon salt and the herb and pulse until finely chopped but not pulverized (the nuts and chiles should be slightly bigger than the sesame seeds). Scrape the mixture into a medium bowl.

In a medium (3-quart) saucepan, heat the oil over medium. Add the chopped garlic and cook until the garlic floats to the surface and starts to sizzle, a minute or 2. Pour the oil over the chile mixture and stir to combine. Let the salsa cool and settle a little before proceeding with the recipe.

Set a large (5- to 6-quart) soup pot over medium-high heat and spoon in 2 tablespoons of the oil from the *salsa macha*. When hot, add the ham and cook, stirring regularly, until beginning to crisp and brown. Scoop out *half* of the ham and drain it on paper towels. To the pot, add the beer, broth, mussels (or clams) and *3 tablespoons* of the solids from the *salsa macha*. (Store the remaining *salsa macha* in a closed container in the refrigerator for up to 3 months.) Cover and bring to a boil. Boil about 5 minutes, until the mussels (or clams) have all opened. Remove from the heat, scoop out the bivalves with a slotted spoon or tongs and divide them among 4 warm bowls. Taste the broth and season with salt, usually ½ teaspoon, plus a little more *salsa macha* if you think the broth needs it. Stir in *half* the cilantro, then ladle the broth into each bowl and sprinkle with the reserved ham and the remaining *half* of the cilantro. Serve with lots of crusty bread.

Riffs on Mussels with _Salsa Macha_:

You can simplify the recipe by sautéing the ham with a little chopped garlic and chopped, stemmed arbol (or other small dried) chile in place of the _salsa macha._ Also, this recipe works well as a cold appetizer: Cool the mussels, break off the empty shells, arrange the mussels in shallow bowls, then splash them with the broth (sometimes I reduce the broth by half, to make it punchier and cool it). Serve sprinkled with a shower of cilantro and the crispy bits of ham.

A DOZEN DESSERTS: MEXICAN CHOCOLATE AND FARMERS' MARKET FRUIT

Mexican Chocolate–Pumpkin Seed Cake **338**

Unbaked Mexican Chocolate Flan **341**

Nutty Triple-Chocolate Pudding **344**

Warm Rice Pudding with Mexican Chocolate and Toasted Almonds **346**

Mexican Chocolate Truffles **348**

Mexican Chocolate Sorbet **350**

Coconut Bread Pudding **351**

Farmers' Market Fruit with Warm Tequila-Lime *Espuma* **354**

Mango Ricotta Cheesecake **356**

Plantains (or Fresh Fruit) with 24-Hour *Cajeta* and Bitter Chocolate **358**

Raspberry Soft-Serve Ice Cream **361**

Coconut-Lime Ice Pops **363**

Mexican Chocolate–Pumpkin Seed Cake

Pastel de Chocolate y Pepitas

◇◇

This is one of my favorite cakes. For me, the flecks of Mexican chocolate and the unique, toasty flavor of pumpkin seeds make it altogether seductive. It goes together in a flash using a food processor. It's moist and sturdy (it'll remind you of a cake that almost wants to be a moist bar cookie). And it keeps well in the refrigerator for days. You can pack it up and carry it across town or on a plane across the country. I've even packed it tightly and mailed it. The pumpkin-seed crust is an unexpected pleasure. If the splash of tequila isn't your thing, simply replace it with water.

Serves 8

8 tablespoons (4 ounces, 1 stick) unsalted butter, slightly softened and cut into ½-inch pieces, plus another tablespoon or two for greasing the pan

1¾ cups hulled, toasted, salted pumpkin seeds (divided use)

1 cup plus 2 tablespoons granulated sugar (divided use)

3 eggs at room temperature

⅓ cup all-purpose flour

¼ teaspoon baking powder

1 tablespoon tequila

3 ounces Mexican chocolate, chopped into pea-size pieces

Confectioners' sugar, for serving (optional)

Turn the oven on to 350 degrees and position the rack in the lower third. Butter the bottom and sides of a 9-inch cake pan, then lay in a round of parchment paper cut to fit the pan and slather it generously with more butter (about a tablespoon). Sprinkle ½ cup of the pumpkin seeds in an even layer over the parchment, then sprinkle the seeds evenly with *2 tablespoons* of the granulated sugar.

Measure the remaining *1¼ cups* pumpkin seeds and *1 cup* granulated sugar into a food processor. Pulse the machine until the seeds are pulverized and resemble damp sand. Add the eggs and butter and pulse until incorporated. Add the flour, baking powder and tequila and continue to pulse, just until you have a smooth batter. Add the chocolate to the batter and pulse until it's mixed in—two or three times should do it. Scrape the batter into the prepared pan and bake until a toothpick inserted in the center comes out clean, 35 to 40 minutes. Let the cake cool for 10 minutes in the pan on a cooling rack, then upend it onto a serving platter and remove the parchment paper. The cake will have a crunchy layer of candied *pepitas* on top, which looks even more beautiful with a sprinkling of confectioners' sugar.

MEXICAN CHOCOLATE

Mexican chocolate is different from other chocolates. It's more coarsely ground than our typical chocolate so it doesn't melt to an oozy mass (it was originally developed to dissolve into liquid to serve as a beverage). And its flavor is generally more rustic, less subtle than, say, a fine Belgian offering. When you taste one of the artisan chocolates in Oaxaca or Michoacán or Chiapas, the experience is uniquely bold, showing off a side of chocolate that the Europeans thought needed to be tamed. Those are the chocolate flavors I find most beguiling— perhaps a little bit wild, but in a good way. Unfortunately, the mass-produced brands from Mexico have little of that uniqueness—actually little chocolate flavor in comparison with the artisan varieties. Occasionally some of the regional and artisan varieties from Mexico make their way across the border and into specialty and Mexican groceries. Taza chocolate, made in the United States, currently offers a Mexican-style chocolate that reminds me much more of the artisan chocolates I enjoy in Mexico.

Mexican Chocolate–Pumpkin Seed Cake (page 338)

Unbaked Mexican Chocolate Flan

Flan de Chocolate Mexicano Sin Hornear

◇◇◇

I'm including this recipe here for two reasons. First, because it's as easy-breezy as making the Italian classic panna cotta (which essentially it is), though you have to be up for caramelizing sugar and for making the flans a day ahead to allow the caramel in each mold to dissolve. And second, because the preparation contains no eggs and you can swap out the half-and-half for almond milk, making the dessert vegan (if you use a vegan gelling agent). Half-and-half gives the dessert a beautifully creamy texture; almond milk turns out a flan that's lighter. Both deliver the satisfaction of a really good caramel custard.

Serves 4 to 6

¾ cup plus 2 tablespoons sugar (divided use)

2 cups half-and-half or almond milk

4 ounces Mexican chocolate, chopped into small pieces

One 3-inch piece of cinnamon stick, preferably Mexican *canela*

1 packet (2¼ teaspoons) powdered gelatin (2 packets—4½ teaspoons—if using almond milk)

2 teaspoons pure vanilla extract, preferably Mexican

Choose six 6-ounce or four 8-ounce molds—custard cups, coffee cups or individual soufflé dishes—and set them on a baking sheet.

Into a small (1- to 1½-quart) saucepan, measure ¾ *cup* of sugar. Dribble ⅓ cup water around and over the sugar, evenly moistening it, then set the pan over medium-high heat. When the mixture comes to a full boil, wash down the sides of the pan with a brush dipped in water (this dissolves any clinging sugar crystals). Reduce the heat to medium and boil without stirring until the syrup begins to turn golden, 3 to 5 minutes. Now carefully start gently swirling the pan over the heat until the syrup is a deep straw color. Remove from the heat and continue swirling until the color is a rich amber. Quickly pour a portion of caramel into each of the molds. Immediately tilt the molds to cover the bottoms evenly. Let the caramel set while you make the custard.

In a medium (3-quart) saucepan, heat the half-and-half (or almond milk), the remaining *2 tablespoons* sugar, the chopped Mexican chocolate and the cinnamon stick over medium, stirring regularly until the chocolate has dissolved and the liquid is steaming. Turn off the heat, cover the pan and let stand 20 minutes. While the mixture is steeping, pour ⅓ cup water into a large bowl, sprinkle on the powdered gelatin and let soften; it'll take about 10 minutes. When the chocolate mixture is ready, remove and discard the cinnamon stick, reheat to steaming over medium, pour over the softened gelatin and add the vanilla. Stir until the gelatin has dissolved; it should take only a minute or so. (Little bits of Mexican chocolate will settle to the bottom of your flans, so they have a dark speckled top when unmolded. If that's not the look you're going for, pour the mixture through a fine strainer.)

Immediately ladle the warm mixture into the caramelized molds, dividing it evenly. Let cool to room temperature, about 20 minutes, then refrigerate overnight. (For best results, let the custards sit for about 24 hours so the hard caramelized sugar dissolves into caramel sauce.)

When you're ready to serve, run a small knife around the edge of each flan, penetrating to the bottom. Quickly turn each mold over onto a serving plate. One by one, grasp the plate and mold firmly and shake up and down, back and forth, side to side, until you hear the flan drop onto the plate. Remove the mold and scrape out any sticky dissolving caramel from the inside, letting it drizzle down on the flan. Dessert's ready.

Riffs on Unbaked Mexican Chocolate Flan:

You can simply omit the Mexican chocolate (plus the cinnamon stick if you wish) for a classic vanilla flan. I like to steep a few strips of lime zest with the half-and-half when I'm taking that approach. If using the almond milk and no chocolate, you can emphasize the almondiness by adding a few drops of almond extract to the custard.

Nutty Triple-Chocolate
Pudding (page 344)

Nutty Triple-Chocolate Pudding
Natilla de Tres Chocolates y Pepitas

◇◇◇

Anywhere in the world that chocolate has won over hearts and palates—which is just about everywhere—it has brought nuts along as part of the perfect flavor package. Gianduja/Nutella (hazelnuts and chocolate) and Reese's Cups (peanuts and chocolate) are two of the most famous duos. All you have to do is mention either one of these simple preparations and people get rapturous. Though this pudding recipe can be made with hazelnuts or peanuts, I created it to showcase the delightful richness and gentle earthiness of toasted pumpkin seeds. And in spite of the fact that it's a simple preparation, layering it with tangy *crema* or Greek-style yogurt dresses it up a lot.

Serves 6

¾ cup hulled toasted pumpkin seeds, roasted peanuts, or toasted hazelnuts

4 ounces Mexican chocolate, coarsely chopped

⅓ cup sugar

¼ cup cocoa powder (choose a really good one, preferably one labeled "natural," which is stronger, rather than "Dutched"), plus a little extra for serving

2 tablespoons cornstarch

¼ teaspoon salt

2 cups whole milk or almond milk

1½ ounces dark chocolate (I like 55% to 70%), finely chopped

1 to 2 teaspoons pure vanilla extract, preferably Mexican (depending on how vanilla-tasting you want the pudding)

About 1 cup thick Mexican *crema*, *crème fraîche* or Greek-style yogurt (if yours is really tangy, you may want to stir in a couple teaspoons sugar)

In a food processor, combine the toasted pumpkin seeds (or peanuts or hazelnuts), Mexican chocolate and sugar. Pulse (1-second pulses) until finely chopped, then run the processor until everything forms a paste, 3 or 4 minutes. (The finer, the better here.) Measure in the cocoa, cornstarch and salt, then pulse to combine.

Pour the milk (or almond milk) into a microwave-safe measuring cup and microwave at 100% until steaming hot. That takes 2 minutes in my microwave; be careful that it doesn't boil over. With the processor running, pour the hot milk into the chocolate mixture in a steady stream. (If you have a processor that is smaller than 14 cups, add only half the milk.)

Set a strainer over a large (4-quart) saucepan and pour the chocolate mixture through it, catching anything (chocolate, nutty material) that's not very finely chopped. (Add any remaining milk that didn't make it into the processor.) Set the pot over medium heat and whisk constantly until the mixture comes to a boil. Boil, whisking constantly, for 2 minutes. Remove from the heat and add the chopped dark chocolate and vanilla. (When I only have fat-free milk or I choose almond milk, I like to add 2 tablespoons butter along with the chocolate.) Stir until the chocolate is completely dissolved, then scrape the mixture into a bowl, set over a bowl of ice and stir every few minutes until cool (this will ensure that the pudding cools quickly without forming a thick skin on top).

Scoop ¼ cup of the chocolate pudding into each of 6 small coffee cups. Top each with 1½ tablespoons *crema* (or one of its stand-ins), then spread on another ¼ cup of pudding. Top each with a 1-tablespoon dollop of *crema* and sprinkle with a little cocoa to give it a finished look. Refrigerate until you're ready to serve.

Warm Rice Pudding with Mexican Chocolate and Toasted Almonds

Arroz con Leche Tibio con Chocolate Mexicano y Almendras Tostadas

◇◆◇

R ice pudding is a Mexican staple, but usually just scented with a little cinnamon—plus, for some cooks, a dash of vanilla—and studded with raisins. I've written recipes for a version that's infused with lime zest and almonds, another that's shot through with coconut and a very rich version with egg yolks. Who knows why I waited this long to employ the obvious gilding of Mexican chocolate? And since everyone loves *warm* rice pudding, I say why not make this very creamy version in the rice cooker while you're eating dinner, then spoon up the just-made, soulful goodness for everyone to ooh and ah about? It couldn't be easier. Or tastier.

Serves 6

3 tablespoons butter

1 cup medium-grain rice (you can use Arborio or any other risotto rice)

4 cups milk (whole milk provides the greatest creaminess; divided use)

⅔ cup sugar

One 3-inch piece of cinnamon stick, preferably Mexican *canela* (optional)

Salt

¾ cup dried fruit (raisins, currants, cherries, chopped mango or apricots; optional)

4 ounces Mexican chocolate, roughly chopped

About ½ cup (2 ounces) slivered almonds, toasted in a 325-degree oven until lightly browned

Measure the butter into a rice cooker and turn the appliance to "cook." When the butter is melted, add the rice and stir for a minute, then add *3½ cups* of the milk, the sugar, the cinnamon stick if you're using it and ¼ teaspoon salt. Cover the rice cooker and let the rice cook, stirring every 10 minutes, until the appliance switches to the "keep warm" mode, 35 to 40 minutes. If you're using dried fruit, stir it in at the 30-minute mark. Taste a grain of rice: It should be very close to done at the core. If not, sprinkle in a little milk, re-cover and cook 5 minutes more. Uncover the rice cooker, add the chocolate and remaining ½ *cup* milk and stir until the chocolate is melted and the rice is enticingly creamy-looking. Spoon the warm pudding into small, shallow serving bowls, sprinkle with the toasted almonds and serve without hesitation.

Riffs on Warm Rice Pudding:

If someone you are cooking for is lactose intolerant, make this rice pudding with soy milk, almond milk or coconut milk. In fact, my favorite way to make it is with coconut milk, but I am crazy passionate about the flavor of coconut milk. You can, of course, make this rice pudding with the more traditional flavors by simply omitting the chocolate (and the almonds, for that matter).

REHEATING MADE-AHEAD RICE PUDDING

This version will set up into a solid mass as it cools. If you're planning on making it ahead, I suggest that once it's done you quickly scoop it into a microwave-safe baking dish, let it cool to room temperature and refrigerate until you're ready to serve. When that time comes, stir enough milk or cream into the pudding to make it creamy again, then cover with plastic wrap and microwave on 50% power, stirring regularly, until warm (usually a couple of minutes).

MEXICAN CINNAMON (*CANELA*)

What we call cinnamon in the United States is really a variety of cassia bark, and it has a more aggressive flavor than true cinnamon. Mexican cinnamon (*canela*) is often called "Ceylon cinnamon" or "true cinnamon," and its flavor is more delicate and flowery. It is easy to tell the two apart when you have the sticks in front of you: American cinnamon is thick and so hard it's difficult to grind in an electric spice grinder; Mexican cinnamon is thin, flaky and so soft you can easily break it up with your fingers and grind it in an electric spice grinder or mortar. When ground, American cinnamon will have a more pronounced cinnamon oil aroma (think Red Hots or other cinnamon candy).

Mexican Chocolate Truffles

Trufas de Chocolate Mexicano

◇◇◇

Maybe you feel the need to offer your guests something sweet at the end of a nice dinner, but you're not very comfortable making desserts. Maybe you're thinking that for an upcoming potluck, little chocolate bites would be more welcome than a big dessert. Maybe you're looking for an interesting food gift you can make for a friend. For any of those occasions, these truffles might be just what you're looing for.

To tell the truth, they're based on a recipe my dear late friend, master chocolatier Elaine Gonzalez, gave me when I told her I was looking for something sweet and simple to make with my then five-year-old daughter. I've modified the recipe to incorporate Mexican chocolate (the original called for all bittersweet), and I suggest rolling the truffles in a mixture of cocoa powder and granulated sugar (the coarseness of the sugar balances the rustic texture of the Mexican chocolate). These easy, explosively chocolatey truffles were a hit with my daughter, as they are with anyone I offer them to. Though they're best at a cool room temperature (I don't choose to serve them when it's really warm), they need to be stored in the refrigerator.

Makes 18 chocolate candies

4 ounces Mexican chocolate, chopped into small pieces

4 ounces bittersweet chocolate, chopped into small pieces

½ cup whipping cream

½ cup unsweetened cocoa powder (choose a really good one, preferably one labeled "natural," which is stronger, rather than "Dutched")

½ cup sugar

In a food processor, combine the chocolates and pulse until completely pulverized (they should look dusty, a little like cocoa powder.) Measure the cream into a glass measuring cup and microwave at 100% until steaming, about 1 minute. Turn on the food processor and slowly pour in the cream. Process until the chocolate is completely smooth, about 1 minute, then scrape the mixture into a pie pan or similar dish and smooth it level. Cover with plastic wrap and refrigerate until barely firm, 30 to 45 minutes.

While the chocolate mixture is chilling, clean the food processor and measure in the cocoa powder and sugar. Pulse until the two are combined but you can still feel the grain of the sugar, and transfer to a large, flat plate.

Line a baking sheet with parchment paper. Use a pair of small spoons (or a very small ice cream–type scoop) to scoop out roughly shaped balls of chocolate about ¾ inch in diameter (about 1½ teaspoons of chocolate mixture) and drop them onto the baking sheet. (Don't let the balls touch—they'll stick together.) Continue until all the chocolate is used. Then use your hands to quickly roll each candy, one by one, into a ball. Finally, roll the chocolate balls in the cocoa-sugar mixture to coat evenly. Store the truffles in a single layer in a sealed container in the refrigerator. Let warm to cool room temperature before serving.

Mexican Chocolate Sorbet

Nieve de Chocolate Mexicano

◇◇

L ittle is simpler than this very chocolatey, creamy Mexican chocolate sorbet. That is, it's simple if you have an ice cream maker, you can start it several hours before you want to serve it, and you have access to good Mexican chocolate. Though it's tasty with the inexpensive grocery-store brands of Mexican chocolate, this sorbet has so few ingredients that the quality of the chocolate is what really shines through.

Serves 4 to 6

1⅓ cups sugar

6 ounces Mexican chocolate, roughly chopped

3 tablespoons cocoa powder (choose a really good one, preferably one labeled "natural," which is stronger, rather than "Dutched")

Salt

1½ teaspoons pure vanilla extract, preferably Mexican

In a blender, combine the sugar and chocolate. In a medium (3-quart) saucepan, bring 2¼ cups water to a boil. Pour the hot water into the blender, let the mixture sit for a few minutes, then blend, *loosely covered*, for 2 minutes—the mixture should be very smooth. Scoop in the cocoa powder and a big pinch of salt and blend for another 2 minutes. Let cool to room temperature, then stir in the vanilla. Pour the sorbet base into the canister of your ice cream maker and freeze according to the manufacturer's instructions, stopping when the sorbet is nearly the consistency of soft-serve ice cream. Scrape the sorbet into a freezer container, cover and freeze for 3 to 4 hours before serving.

Coconut Bread Pudding

Budín de Pan y Coco

◇◇

A simple bread pudding is one of the most comforting desserts I know, but only if the texture is tender, not leaden. That's not hard to achieve, as long as you think of bread pudding as more than a way to use up leftovers that otherwise would go on the compost pile. What I mean is that good bread pudding takes good bread. And a little richness, here offered by butter and the natural fattiness of tropical coconut milk. Toast the bread, as I've described below, and the result is utterly seductive.

Serves 6 to 8

6 tablespoons (3 ounces) butter, cut into pieces, plus more for greasing the pan

14 ounces bread (I like brioche or challah, but cakey white sandwich bread works well, too), crusts trimmed off if you wish, cut into ½-inch cubes (about 8 cups)

3 eggs

1 teaspoon pure vanilla extract, preferably Mexican

¼ teaspoon salt

One 14-ounce can coconut milk (regular, not "light")

½ cup granulated sugar

Confectioners' sugar, for serving

Turn on the oven to 400 degrees. Scoop the butter into a large, microwave-safe bowl and melt in the microwave at 50% power for 1 minute. Scoop the bread into the bowl and stir slowly until it is evenly coated. Spread the bread on a rimmed baking sheet, slide it into the oven and toast, stirring every 5 minutes, until it is richly browned, about 15 minutes. Remove the bread and turn the oven down to 300 degrees. Butter an 8-inch-square baking dish and scoop the bread into it.

In a medium bowl, whisk together the eggs, vanilla and salt. In a small (1- to 2-quart) saucepan, heat the coconut milk and granulated sugar over medium-low, stirring until the mixture is just warm (not close to boiling) and the sugar is dissolved. Pour the warm coconut milk into the eggs in a slow stream, whisking constantly, until well combined. Pour the custard over the bread. Let the bread soak up the custard for 15 minutes, gently stirring the mixture every few minutes. Slide the baking dish into the oven and bake until the bread pudding is barely set at the center, about 30 minutes. Sprinkle with confectioners' sugar, cut into pieces, place them on small plates and you're ready to delight a few friends.

Riffs on Coconut Bread Pudding:

I love pecans and almonds with coconut, so occasionally I like to toast some chopped pieces of my chosen nut along with the bread. Grated lime zest added to the coconut mixture is a plus. Chopped-up dried mango is enticing, and so are raisins and dried currants. And, of course, chopped Mexican (or other) chocolate is always welcome here.

Farmers' Market Fruit with Warm
Tequila-Lime *Espuma* (page 354)

Farmers' Market Fruit with Warm Tequila-Lime *Espuma*

Fruta de la Temporada con Espuma de Limón y Tequila

◇◇

Besides simply being one of the best-tasting concoctions on the planet, this *espuma* owes its origins to Italian zabaglione (or French sabayon), with tequila and lime replacing wine as you whisk egg yolks and sugar to a luscious froth over simmering water. You can make it in a matter of minutes, and when you serve it warm from the stove, as the Italians do, it's an ethereal experience. Especially if you've taken time to get farmers' market peaches or apricots or nectarines. It's magic over berries, too. And in the fall I love it over roasted pears or apples. It's pretty much the easiest way to make a big impression. My note to you: to get the best consistency, whisk the mixture continuously—don't stop!—and make sure to scrape the sides of the bowl.

Serves 4

About 1 pound perfectly ripe, in-season
    fruit (berries and stone fruits all work),
    pitted if necessary and cut into ½-inch
    slices (berries can remain whole)
4 egg yolks
¼ cup sugar
2 tablespoons fresh orange juice

2 tablespoons fresh lime juice
¼ cup tequila
Grated zest (colored part only) of ½ lime
Shortbread cookies, candied almonds
    or anything else crisp and sweet, for
    serving

Divide the fruit among 4 shallow serving bowls. Fill a large (4-quart) saucepan with 1 inch water and set it over medium-high heat. In a stainless steel bowl big enough to rest at least halfway into the saucepan, whisk together the egg yolks, sugar, juices, tequila and lime zest.

When the water reaches a boil, lower the heat so it is at a low simmer. Nestle the bowl into the saucepan. Whisk the yolk mixture continuously until it becomes thick and fluffy, about 3 minutes. Remove the bowl from the saucepan. Drape a few spoonfuls of the warm *espuma* over the fruit in each bowl and serve immediately, with the cookies or nuts either on the side or crumbled on top.

Riff: Cool *Espuma*

The warm *espuma* from this recipe needs to be served right away or it deflates into an unappetizing consistency. The French, however, make a cool version, sabayon, by allowing the beaten cooked mixture to cool just to room temperature and folding in whipped cream. Beat ½ cup heavy cream to soft peaks and fold it into the room-temperature *espuma*. Cover it, stick it in the fridge and spoon it over fruit when you're ready (it will keep for a day or so).

Mango Ricotta Cheesecake

Pastel de Requesón con Mango

It may come as a surprise to you that cheesecake is one of Mexico's favorite desserts. Come to think of it, cheesecake is one of the whole world's favorite desserts (I think I've eaten it on nearly every continent), but each culture gives it a unique touch. When you make it with ricotta (Mexico loves ricotta, which in Spanish is called *requesón*), the texture is light. And when you perfume it with Mexico's unique vanilla and top it with a delicious tropical fruit like mango (infused with lime and mint), the result is stellar.

Since in *More Mexican Everyday* we're exploring the simplest ways to achieve wonderful made-from-scratch flavor, I'm offering you a very simple but unconventional way to make cheesecake. Instead of cheesecake's typical long, slow and careful baking followed by a requisite long chilling, my approach is really streamlined. Whip together the ingredients in a food processor or blender, microwave at 50% power just until hot, pour into individual vessels (crusts, cups), chill for an hour and serve with fresh mango. (Of course, other fruit is welcome here, too, from berries to peaches to caramelized apples.) For me, the result is a hundred times better than no-bake cheesecakes but just about as easy.

This beautiful creation is based on a recipe from Topolobampo's brilliant pastry chef, Jennifer Jones.

Makes one 9-inch tart or 12 individual tarts

1 cup (8 ounces) fresh ricotta, preferably the dryer kind called "hand-dipped"

One 8-ounce package cream cheese, cut into 6 pieces

⅓ cup sugar

1 egg plus 2 egg yolks

¼ cup heavy cream

1 teaspoon pure vanilla extract, preferably Mexican

12 store-bought mini graham cracker pie crusts, baked, cooled and, if you wish, removed from foil molds (optional) OR one 9-inch Maria Cookie (or Graham Cracker) Crust (recipe follows), made in a 1-inch-deep tart pan, with a removable bottom, baked and cooled (optional)

1½ cups chopped mango (from 2 of the large round mangos or 3 to 4 of the flatter—and I think more flavorful—yellow ones called honey, Manila or champagne mangos)

Finely chopped or grated zest (colored part only) of 1 lime
About 2 tablespoons chopped mint leaves, plus extra leaves for garnish

In a food processor or blender, combine the cheeses, sugar, eggs, egg yolks, cream and vanilla. Blend until very smooth, about 1 minute. Pour into a microwave-safe bowl, cover with plastic wrap, poke a few holes in the top and microwave at 50% power for 2 minutes. Uncover and stir and re-cover. Now, microwave 7 more times at 50% power for 1 minute each, uncovering after each visit to the microwave, stirring gently and re-covering. After the final heating, the mixture should be very hot to the touch (about 160 degrees) and thick.

Immediately divide the mixture among the prepared crusts, place in the single crust or simply divide it among small cups (I have little juice glasses and small cappuccino cups that are perfect for this). Refrigerate until completely cool, about 1 hour.

Mix the mango with the lime zest and mint, spoon onto the cooled cheesecake, decorate each portion with a piece of mint and you've got a dessert that's guaranteed to please.

MARIA COOKIE (OR GRAHAM CRACKER) CRUST

6 tablespoons (3 ounces) butter
4 ounces (about 18) Mexican Maria cookies or (about 16) graham crackers
3 tablespoons sugar

Heat the oven to 325 degrees. Place the butter in a small microwave-safe bowl and melt in the microwave at 50% power for 1 minute. Break the cookies (or crackers) into a food processor and pulse until the consistency of sand. Add the sugar and melted butter and continue to pulse until the mixture begins to clump together in places. Press the mixture evenly over the bottom and sides of a 9-inch tart pan with a removable bottom. Bake until lightly browned, about 15 minutes.

Plantains (or Fresh Fruit) with 24-Hour Cajeta and Bitter Chocolate

Plátano Macho (o Otra Fruta) con Cajeta de 24 Horas y Chocolate Amargo

◇◇◇

If you've never tasted the satiny richness and caramely complexity of homemade *cajeta* (known as *dulce de leche* in other Latin American countries), here's an easy way to do it. Instead of standing anxiously over a pot of milk, sugar and cinnamon as it slowly reduces to a glossy amber, stirring frequently to ensure that it isn't scorching on the bottom, just measure everything into a slow cooker and let it cook overnight. You'll be amazed at how simple it is to make something so remarkably good.

Because *cajeta* derives its caramel color from slowly reducing *milk* sugars, not from caramelized granulated sugar, the flavor is completely different from that of a traditional caramel sauce. Slowly simmering milk concentrates natural sweetness, sugar gives a glossy texture and cinnamon provides sparkle. The result is elementally delicious, especially when all or part of the milk is the naturally more complex and tangy goat's milk.

While this is classic on sautéed, sweet-ripe plantains, it's equally tasty on cut-up raw bananas or practically any fruit you bring home from the farmers' market. Add shaved chocolate and crumbled cookies and you have a beautiful dessert, even if you don't fancy yourself a dessert maker.

Serves 4 (with nearly 2 cups extra *cajeta* for other uses)

2 quarts milk (cow's milk or half cow's milk, half goat's milk)

2 cups sugar

One 3-inch piece of cinnamon stick, preferably Mexican *canela*

½ teaspoon baking soda dissolved in 1 tablespoon water

2 large black-ripe plantains (or an equivalent amount of bananas, apples or pears, peaches or nectarines, raspberries or strawberries)

4 tablespoons (2 ounces) butter (if using plantains)

About 1 ounce bittersweet chocolate, coarsely grated

About ½ cup crumbled cookies (Mexican Maria cookies, vanilla wafers, Famous Chocolate Wafers, graham crackers, Mexican polvorones)

OR about ½ cup chopped, toasted nuts (pretty much any nut is welcome here)

Pour the milk into a slow cooker. Whisk in the sugar. Add the cinnamon and dissolved baking soda (the soda neutralizes acid and helps promote browning). Stir well. Turn the slow cooker on to high and cook *uncovered* for about 24 hours. After 18 hours or so, the *cajeta* will have darkened to light golden-brown. That's when to begin keeping an eye on it. Stir it from time to time to make sure it's cooking evenly. When it is noticeably thick and richly golden, test a couple of drops on a cold plate. The cooled *cajeta* should be the consistency of a light caramel sauce. If yours is still a little runny, let it cook longer. When your *cajeta* is ready, pour it through a fine-mesh strainer set over a bowl or wide-mouth storage jar. (It will keep a month or more covered in the refrigerator.)

If you are using plantains, peel them and cut them on a diagonal into ¼-inch (or slightly bigger) slices. Melt the butter in a very large (12-inch) skillet over medium heat. When it begins to brown, lay in the plantains in a single layer. (If they don't all fit, fry the plantains in 2 batches.) When they are browned underneath, about 3 minutes, turn them over and brown the other side. If you are using fresh fruit, cut it into bite-size pieces (after peeling and pitting, if that's appropriate). Divide the fruit among 4 dessert plates.

Top each plate of fruit with a portion of grated chocolate, several tablespoons of warm *cajeta* (reheat it in a microwave if it has cooled off) and a sprinkling of crumbled cookies (or nuts). A beautifully enjoyable dessert awaits.

Raspberry Soft-Serve Ice Cream (page 361)

Raspberry Soft-Serve Ice Cream

Helado de Frambuesa, Tipo Soft Serve

◇◇

There's something about the texture (and brain-freezing experience) of soft-serve that makes me happy. Maybe it's because I was weaned on the stuff, a Dairy Queen being three doors from my grandma Fanny's house. Still, nostalgia aside, soft-serve is really good, with a near-melting texture that begs you to consume it fast, a lightness that begs you to consume a lot, a simplicity that begs you just to enjoy the uncomplicated pleasure. To provide creaminess in such a light (read "low in fat") ice cream, you need to add more concentrated milk solids in the form of powdered milk, thicken the mixture with xanthan gum (available in the bulk aisle of well-stocked grocery stores or from Bob's Red Mill) and enrich it with agave nectar. That may sound unusual, but it's not at all difficult. Blend, freeze, eat.

Raspberries are my favorite fruit here, because they're not watery. Blueberries work well too. Strawberries will produce a soft-serve that's a little icier.

Makes about 1 quart, serving 6 to 8

1 cup (about 5 ounces) fresh raspberries

2 cups whole milk

⅔ cup buttermilk (low-fat is fine)

½ cup powdered milk

¾ cup agave nectar

¾ teaspoon (3 grams) xanthan gum

In a blender, combine all the ingredients and blend until smooth. Strain to remove the raspberry seeds if you like (I don't mind them). Refrigerate, covered, until thoroughly cold (if you started with cold milk, this should take about an hour). Pour into the canister of your ice cream maker and freeze according to the manufacturer's instructions, stopping when the ice cream is nearly the consistency of soft-serve. Scrape the ice cream into a freezer container, cover and slide into your freezer for an hour or 2 to let the ice cream firm up a little more. This ice cream loses some of its vibrancy, not to mention its soft-serve texture, after twenty-four hours, so try to eat it the day it's made (it won't be difficult).

Coconut-Lime Ice Pops (page 363)

Coconut-Lime Ice Pops

Paletas de Coco con Limón

◇◇

There's little more satisfying on a summer day than an ice pop, a satisfaction that's even better if it conjures memories of icy bites and sweet drips during summer's school break or family vacations. Or if that first taste takes you to the summer lushness of a Chicago park, as it does for my daughter, where the Mexican *paleta* vendors jingle the bells on their pushcarts and offer flavors like cucumber-lime and spicy mango to go with the more predictable strawberry and watermelon. One of my favorites is coconut—simple to make if you have ice pop molds, which are easy to find these days online or wherever a wide variety of cookware is sold. The easiest coconut milk to use for making these pops is one that has a little natural stabilizer (often guar gum) to keep the coconut fat evenly distributed through the milk (look at the ingredient list on the label). You can use light coconut milk, too, which has much of the coconut fat removed, but it'll give your ice pops a skim-milk feel.

Makes 10 to 12 pops

Two 13- to 14-ounce cans coconut milk (the commonly available Thai Kitchen brand works well)

½ cup sugar

½ cup fresh lime juice (from 2 or 3 limes)

Finely grated zest (colored part only) of 1 large lime

In a blender, combine the coconut milk, sugar, lime juice and zest. Blend for a minute or two, until the sugar has dissolved. Pour the mixture through a fine-mesh strainer into a large measuring cup or pitcher, then divide it evenly among 10 to 12 ice pop molds, leaving about ¼-inch headroom for expansion. Secure the lids and insert the sticks through the holes, making sure that they're straight and that 1½ to 2 inches of each stick remains exposed. Slide the molds into the freezer.

When the ice pops are firmly set—this will take about 2 hours in most freezers—they're ready to serve. Remove the lids from the molds, then either squeeze the sides of each mold to pop out the pop or invert the mold and run it briefly under warm water to release your icy treats.

Riffs on Coconut-Lime Ice Pops:

You can replace the lime zest with a little fresh mint (or even basil) to give the pops a very fresh and interesting flavor. A few drops of vanilla extract will focus the rich sweetness of the coconut. And a splash of rum (not too much, or the pops won't freeze solid) will make them taste like a tiki drink. Replace a quarter of the coconut milk with pureed pineapple and you'll have a piña colada on a stick.

INDEX ◇◇◇

Note: Page numbers in *italics* refer to photographs.

A

Adobo de Chile Verde, 32, 33–34, 35

Adobo Rápido de Chiles Secos, 32, 36, 37–38

agave leaf: Lamb or Beef *Barbacoa*, 294–95

agave nectar:

    Cinnamon Agave Syrup, 238

    Raspberry Soft-Serve Ice Cream, *360*, 361

    Slow-Grilled Pork Shoulder with Ancho
        Barbecue Sauce, 302–3, *304*

    Spring Green *Licuado*, 224, *225*

    "Sturdy Greens" Salad with Mango and
        Habanero, *137*, 138–39

Albondigas al Chipotle, 116, 117–18, *119*,
    120–21

*Alcachofas Guisadas con Jitomates, Jalapeños,
    Aceitunas y Alcaparras*, 218–19

almonds:

    Horchata French Toast, *242*, 243–45

    Mustard Greens Soup with Poblanos and
        Almonds, 129–30

    Ribbon Salad with Creamy Two-Chile
        Vinagreta, 192–93

    "Sturdy Greens" Salad with Mango and
        Habanero, *137*, 138–39

    Warm Rice Pudding with Mexican Chocolate
        and Toasted Almonds, 346–47

    Xoco's Granola, 228

amaranth: Xoco's Granola, 228

ancho chile powder, 37

    Eggs Poached with Ancho Chile, Kale, Potatoes
        and Fresh Cheese, 134–36

    Quick Red Chile *Adobo*, 32, *36*, 37–38

ancho chiles, 28–29, *28*

    Kuri (or Butternut or Pumpkin) Soup with
        Ancho and Apple, 180–81

    Mussels (or Clams) with *Salsa Macha*, Mexican
        Beer and Ham, 333–35

    Open-Face Red Chile–Chard Omelet, *229*,
        230–31

    Red Peanut *Mole* with Chicken, *104*, 105–10, *109*

    Silky Tortilla Soup, 285–86

apples: Kuri (or Butternut or Pumpkin) Soup with
    Ancho and Apple, 180–81

arbol chiles: Charred Cucumber Salad with Red
    Chile and Lime, *187*, 188–89

Arroz a la Tumbada, *66*, 67–68

Arroz al Chipotle con Camarones, 260, *261*

Arroz con Chile Poblano y Espinacas, 264–65

Arroz con Chorizo y Lentejas, 256–57

*Arroz con Leche Tibio con Chocolate Mexicano y
    Almendras Tostadas*, 346–47

*Arroz Cremoso y Frijoles en Tres Sabores
    Clásicos*, 250–52

*Arroz de Frijol Negro con Plátanos y Puerco
    Ahumado*, *253*, 254–55

*Arroz Frito Picante con Huevo, Tocino, Jalapeños
    en Escabeche y Cilantro*, 266–67

Arroz Rojo Mexicano, 262–64

*Arroz Rojo Mexicano y Tres Comidas que Lo
    Utiliza*, 262–64

Arroz Verde con Pollo, 258–59

artichokes:

    Braised Artichokes with Tomatoes, Jalapeños,
        Olives and Capers, 218–19

    how to trim, 201

    Shell Beans and Artichokes with Roasted
        Tomatillos, Cilantro and Añejo Cheese, 201–3

asparagus:

    Four Seasons Grilled Salad with Smoky Knob
        (or Green) Onions and Sesame, 156–58

asparagus (*continued*)
  Grilled Asparagus with Creamy Pasilla Chile,
    198–99, *200*
avocados:
  Chicken *Barbacoa,* 324–25
  Grilled Tostadas with Bacon, Avocado Mayo
    and Heirloom Tomatoes, *149,* 150–51
  Guacamole, 88, *88*
  Mexican Chicken Soup, 270–71
  Pork and Black Bean Dinner, *99,* 100–103, *101*
  Pork Carnitas Dinner, 280–82, *283*
  Scrambled Eggs with Beans, Green Onions and
    Avocado, 286
  Spaghetti Squash *Fideos* with Chipotle,
    Chorizo, *Crema* and Avocado, *184,* 185–86

B
bacon, 32
  Black Bean Rice with Plantains and Smoky
    Pork, *253,* 254–55
  Butternut with Bacon, Tomatillo and Chipotle,
    173, 174–75
  Carne Asada Dinner, *85,* 86–91
  Eggs Poached with Ancho Chile, Kale, Potatoes
    and Fresh Cheese, 134–36
  Grilled Tostadas with Bacon, Avocado Mayo
    and Heirloom Tomatoes, *149,* 150–51
  Plantain-Bacon *Enfrijoladas,* 287
  Roasted Chayote with Herbs and Tofu (riff),
    143
  Spicy Bacon-and-Egg Fried Rice with Pickled
    Jalapeños and Cilantro, 266–67
balance, 26–28
banana leaves, 31
  Green Chile Chicken Thighs, 305–7
Banana Pepper–Leek Soup with White Beans and
    Crispy Chorizo, 212–13
Barbacoa de Borrego o Res, 294–95
Barbacoa de Pollo, 324–25
barbecue technique, classic, 309
basil: Coconut-Lime Ice Pops (riff), 364
beans:
  A Good-Size Pot of Beans, 284–85

Banana Pepper–Leek Soup with White Beans
    and Crispy Chorizo, 212–13
Beans and Greens with Clams and Chorizo,
    288, 289
Black Bean Rice with Plantains and Smoky
    Pork, *253,* 254–55
Carne Asada Dinner, *85,* 86–91
Cheesy Open-Face Mollette, 289–90
Creamy Rice and Beans in Three Classic
    Flavors, 250–52
Crispy Rice Cakes with White Beans, Roasted
    Garlic, Aged Cheese and Smoky Chile,
    265–66
Five Simple Meals from a Pot of Beans, 284
Fresh Fava Bean *Enfrijoladas,* *165,* 166-68; riffs
    on, 168
Garlicky Tomato Rice, 251–52
Greens and Beans with Red Chile and Fresh
    Cheese, 126–27, *128*
Grilled Asparagus with Creamy Pasilla Chile
    (riff), 199
Herby Green Chile Rice, *249,* 251–52
Open-Face Egg-Chorizo Tortas, 234–35, *236*
Plantain-Bacon *Enfrijoladas,* 287
Pork and Black Bean Dinner, *99,* 100–103, *101*
Pork Carnitas Dinner, 280–82, *283*
Red Chile Short Rib Soup, 272–74, *275*
Scrambled Eggs with Beans, Green Onions and
    Avocado, 286
Shell Beans and Artichokes with Roasted
    Tomatillos, Cilantro and Añejo Cheese, 201–3;
    riffs on, 203
Silky Tortilla Soup, 285–86
Smoky Red Chile Rice, 251–52
Spicy Chipotle Eggplant with Black Beans, *214,*
    215–16, *217*
beef:
  Carne Asada Dinner, *85,* 86–91
  Chipotle Meatballs, *116,* 117–18, *119,* 120–21
  Green Chile–Braised Beef with Potatoes and
    Caramelized Onions, 291–93
  Grilled Skirt Steaks, 89–90, *90*
  Lamb or Beef *Barbacoa,* 294–95

Queso Fundido Burger, *313*, 314–15

Red Chile Short Rib Soup, 272–74, *275*

Roasted Tomatillo Enchiladas, *72*, 73–75

beer: Mussels (or Clams) with *Salsa Macha*,
   Mexican Beer and Ham, 333–35

Beer-Glazed Beer-Can Chicken, *326*, 327–28, *328*

beets:

   Carrot, Beet and Orange *Licuado*, *225*, 227

   Four Seasons Grilled Salad with Smoky Knob
      (or Green) Onions and Sesame, 156–58

   Jícama-Beet Salad with Radicchio, Peanuts and
      Lime, *159*, 160–61

Berengena al Chipotle con Frijoles Negros, *214*,
   215–16, *217*

Black Bean Rice with Plantains and Smoky Pork,
   253, 254–55

blenders, 24

Bread Pudding, Coconut, 351–52

breakfast anytime, 222

   Butternut-Pecan Muffins with Brown Sugar
      Crumble, *239*, 240–41

   Carrot, Beet and Orange *Licuado*, *225*, 227

   Cornmeal Pancakes, 237–38

   Horchata French Toast, *242*, 243–45

   Open-Face Egg-Chorizo Tortas, 234–35, *236*

   Open-Face Red Chile–Chard Omelet, *229*, 230–31

   Open-Face Squash Blossom Omelet with
      Charred Tomato, Chile and Goat Cheese,
      232–33

   Spring Green *Licuado*, *224*, *225*

   Stone Fruit (or Mango) *Licuado*, *225*, 226

   Xoco's Granola, 228

brining, chicken, 112–13

Budín de Pan y Coco, 351–52

butternut squash:

   Butternut-Pecan Muffins with Brown Sugar
      Crumble, *239*, 240–41

   Butternut with Bacon, Tomatillo and Chipotle,
      173, 174-75; riffs on, 175

   Fettuccine with Butternut Squash and Red
      Poblano *Crema*, *176*, 177–79

   Kuri (or Butternut or Pumpkin) Soup with
      Ancho and Apple, 180–81

C

cabbage: Red Chile Pozole with Pork, 276–78, *279*

cactus fruits: Red Chile Short Rib Soup, 272–74, *275*

cactus paddles:

   cleaning, 164

   Nopal Cactus and Poached Egg in Roasted
      Tomato–Chipotle Broth, *162*, 163–64

cakes:

   Mango Ricotta Cheesecake, 356–57

   Mexican Chocolate–Pumpkin Seed Cake, 338–
      39, *340*

*Calabacitas Rostizadas al Mojo de Ajo con Chile
   Güero*, 182–83

Calabacitas y Elote con Rajas y Crema, 52–53, *52*

Calabaza Enchipotlada, *173*, 174–75

Caldo de Pollo, 270–71

*Camotes de Diferentes Variedades con Chile
   Poblano y Tomate Verde*, 147–48

capers: Braised Artichokes with Tomatoes,
   Jalapeños, Olives and Capers, 218–19

Carne Asada Dinner, *85*, 86–91

   Grilled Skirt Steaks, 89–90, *90*

   Guacamole, 88, *88*

   Salsa, 88

*Carne de Res Guisada con Chile Verde, Papas y
   Cebollas Caramelizadas*, 291–93

carrot juice: Carrot, Beet and Orange *Licuado*,
   225, 227

carrots:

   Mexican Chicken Soup, 270–71

   Mexican Red Rice, 262–64

   Roasted Sunchoke Salad (riff), 197

cashews: Xoco's Granola, 228

cauliflower: Spicy, Garlicky Grilled Cauliflower
      Steaks with Browned Butter, Toasted Nuts
      and Tequila Raisins, 319–20, *321*

Cebollitas Rostizadas con Crema y Queso Añejo,
   154–55

Celery Root Pancakes with Chipotle *Crema* and
   Cilantro, 208-9; riffs on, 209

Cena Completa de Carne Asada, *85*, 86–91

Cena Completa de Carnitas de Puerco, 280–82,
   283

chard: Open-Face Red Chile–Chard Omelet, *229*, 230–31

Charred Cucumber Salad with Red Chile and Lime, *187*, 188-89; riffs on, 189

chayote:
Four Seasons Grilled Salad with Smoky Knob (or Green) Onions and Sesame, 156–58
Red Chile Short Rib Soup, 272–74, *275*
Roasted Chayote with Herbs and Tofu (or Goat Cheese), 142–43

Chayote Asado con Hierbas y Tofu (o Queso de Cabra), 142–43

cheese, 30
Banana Pepper–Leek Soup with White Beans and Crispy Chorizo, 212–13
Braised Artichokes with Tomatoes, Jalapeños, Olives and Capers, 218–19
Butternut with Bacon, Tomatillo and Chipotle, *173*, 174–75
Celery Root Pancakes with Chipotle *Crema* and Cilantro, 208–9
Cheesy Open-Face Mollette, 289–90
Creamy Rice Soup with Poblano and Spinach, 264–65
Crispy Cakes of Greens, Potato and Green Chile, *131*, 132–33
Crispy Rice Cakes with White Beans, Roasted Garlic, Aged Cheese and Smoky Chile, 265–66
Eggs Poached with Ancho Chile, Kale, Potatoes and Fresh Cheese, 134–36
Fettuccine with Butternut Squash and Red Poblano *Crema,* *176*, 177–79
Four Seasons Grilled Salad (riff), 158
Fresh Corn in Spicy-Herby Broth, 144–45
Fresh Fava Bean *Enfrijoladas,* *165*, 166–68
Greens and Beans with Red Chile and Fresh Cheese, 126–27, *128*
Herby, Spicy Fried Corn, 146
Herby Green Chile Rice, *249*, 251–52
Huevos Rancheros, 60, *61*, 62–63, *63*
Mango Ricotta Cheesecake, 356–57
Open-Face Egg-Chorizo Tortas, 234–35, *236*

Open-Face Red Chile–Chard Omelet, *229*, 230–31
Open-Face Squash Blossom Omelet with Charred Tomato, Chile and Goat Cheese, 232–33
Pan-Roasted Summer Squash with Garlic *Mojo* and Güero Chile, 182–83
Pickled Tomatillo Salad with Little Gem Lettuce and Pumpkin Seeds, 152–53
Plantain-Bacon *Enfrijoladas,* 287
Queso Fundido Burger, *313*, 314–15
Roasted Chayote with Herbs and Tofu (or Goat Cheese), 142–43
Roasted Knob Onions with *Crema* and Aged Mexican Cheese, 154–55
Roasted Tomatillo Enchiladas, *72*, 73–75
Shell Beans and Artichokes with Roasted Tomatillos, Cilantro and Añejo Cheese, 201–3
Silky Tortilla Soup, 285–86
Skillet Tacos, 93–98
Spaghetti Squash *Fideos* with Chipotle, Chorizo, *Crema* and Avocado, *184*, 185–86
Spicy, Garlicky Grilled Cauliflower Steaks with Browned Butter, Toasted Nuts and Tequila Raisins, 319–20, *321*
Spicy Chipotle Eggplant with Black Beans, *214*, 215–16, *217*
"Sturdy Greens" Salad with Mango and Habanero, *137*, 138–39
Tomatillo-Sauced *Chilaquiles,* 75, *76*, 77–78

chicken:
Beer-Glazed Beer-Can Chicken, *326*, 327–28, *328*
brining, 112–13
Chicken *Barbacoa,* 324–25
Creamy Roasted Poblano Rajas over chicken breasts, 55
Fresh Fava Bean *Enfrijoladas,* *165*, 166–68
Green Chile Chicken Thighs, 305–7
Herb Green Chicken and Rice, 258–59
Mexican Chicken Soup, 270–71
Pork (or Chicken) with Roasted Tomatillos, Poblanos and Potatoes, 79, *80*, 81–84

Red Chile Roast Chicken, *111*, 112–15

Red Peanut *Mole* with Chicken, *104*, 105–10, *109*

Roasted Garlic Chicken with Mushrooms, Potatoes and Spinach, 296–98, *299*

Roasted Tomatillo Enchiladas, *72*, 73–75

Skillet Tacos, 93–98

Sorrel *Salsa Verde* with Shrimp (riff), 211

Yellow *Mole* with Grilled Fennel and Portobello Mushrooms (riff), 206

Chilaquiles Verdes, 75, 76, 77–78

chile flakes, homemade, 188

chiles, 28–29. *See also specific chiles*

Open-Face Squash Blossom Omelet with Charred Tomato, Chile and Goat Cheese, 232–33

Pork and Black Bean Dinner, *99*, 100–103, *101*

Red Chile Short Rib Soup, 272–74, *275*

Ribbon Salad with Creamy Two-Chile *Vinagreta,* 192–93

whole dried chiles, 38

chipotle chiles *en adobo,* 29

Butternut with Bacon, Tomatillo and Chipotle, *173*, 174–75

Celery Root Pancakes with Chipotle *Crema* and Cilantro, 208–9

Chipotle Meatballs, *116*, 117–18, *119*, 120–21

Chipotle Rice with Shrimp, 260, *261*

Four Seasons Grilled Salad with Smoky Knob (or Green) Onions and Sesame, 156–58

Grilled Lamb Chops with Charred Eggplant Salsa, 311–12

Grilled Salmon in Toasty Peanut Salsa, 316–17, *318*

Nopal Cactus and Poached Egg in Roasted Tomato–Chipotle Broth, *162*, 163–64

Queso Fundido Burger, *313*, 314–15

Red Peanut *Mole* with Chicken, *104*, 105–10, *109*

Ribbon Salad with Creamy Two-Chile *Vinagreta,* 192–93

Smoky Red Chile Rice, 251–52

Spaghetti Squash *Fideos* with Chipotle, Chorizo, *Crema* and Avocado, *184*, 185–86

Spicy Chipotle Eggplant with Black Beans, *214*, 215–16, *217*

Sweet-Sour Dark Chipotle Seasoning, *32*, 40, 42, 43

chocolate:

Mexican Chocolate–Pumpkin Seed Cake, 338–39, *340*

Mexican Chocolate Sorbet, 350

Mexican Chocolate Truffles, 348–49

Nutty Triple-Chocolate Pudding, *343*, 344–45

Plantains (or Fresh Fruit) with 24-Hour *Cajeta* and Bitter Chocolate, 358–59

for sweeter *mole,* 108

Unbaked Mexican Chocolate Flan, 341–42

Warm Rice Pudding with Mexican Chocolate and Toasted Almonds, 346–47

chorizo:

Banana Pepper–Leek Soup with White Beans and Crispy Chorizo, 212–13

Beans and Greens with Clams and Chorizo, *288*, 289

Carne Asada dinner, *85*, 86–91

Chorizo Rice with Lentils, 256–57

Open-Face Egg-Chorizo Tortas, 234–35, *236*

Queso Fundido Burger, *313*, 314–15

Spaghetti Squash *Fideos* with Chipotle, Chorizo, *Crema* and Avocado, *184*, 185–86

chuck: Queso Fundido Burger, *313*, 314–15

Chuletas de Borrego con Salsa de Berenjena Asada, 311–12

cilantro, 31

Carne Asada dinner, *85*, 86–91

Celery Root Pancakes with Chipotle *Crema* and Cilantro, 208–9

Chipotle Rice with Shrimp, 260, *261*

Cilantro-Poached Halibut, 330–31, *332*

Crispy Rice Cakes with White Beans, Roasted Garlic, Aged Cheese and Smoky Chile, 265–66

Green Chile *Adobo, 32*, 33–34, *35*

Green Chile Chicken Thighs, 305–7

Grilled Fish with Creamy Cool Cucumber *Pipián,* 322–23

Grilled Tostadas with Bacon, Avocado Mayo and Heirloom Tomatoes, *149*, 150–51

cilantro (*continued*)
Herb Green Chicken and Rice, 258–59
Mexican Red Rice, 262–64
Pork Carnitas Dinner, 280–82, *283*
Shell Beans and Artichokes with Roasted
Tomatillos, Cilantro and Añejo Cheese,
201–3
Spicy Bacon-and-Egg Fried Rice with Pickled
Jalapeños and Cilantro, 266–67
Tomato–Green Chile Seafood Rice, *66,* 67–68
Cinco Comidas de Una Sola Olla de Frijoles, 284
cinnamon, Mexican (*canela*), note, 347
Cinnamon Agave Syrup, 238
clams:
Beans and Greens with Clams and Chorizo,
288, 289
Mussels (or Clams) with *Salsa Macha,* Mexican
Beer and Ham, 333–35
Tomato–Green Chile Seafood Rice, *66,* 67–68
Coconut Bread Pudding, 351-52; riffs on, 352
Coconut-Lime Ice Pops, *362,* 363-64; riffs on, 364
*Coliflor Picante a la Parilla con Mantequilla
Dorada, Ajo, Cacahuates Tostadas y Pasitas
Borrachas,* 319–20, *321*
corn:
Creamy Zucchini, Corn and Roasted Poblanos,
52–53, *52*
Fresh Corn in Spicy-Herby Broth, 144–45
Herby, Spicy Fried Corn, 146
removing kernels from, 145
Cornmeal Pancakes, 237-38; savory riff on, 238
corn tortillas:
Grilled Tostadas with Bacon, Avocado Mayo
and Heirloom Tomatoes, *149,* 150–51
Huevos Rancheros, 60, 61, 62–63, *63*
reheating, 98
Roasted Tomatillo Enchiladas, *72,* 73–75
Skillet Tacos, 93–98
Costillas Adobadas y Asadas, 308–10
cream:
Banana Pepper–Leek Soup with White Beans
and Crispy Chorizo, 212–13
Celery Root Pancakes with Chipotle *Crema* and
Cilantro, 208–9

Cilantro-Poached Halibut, 330–31, *332*
Creamy Rice Soup with Poblano and Spinach,
264–65
Fettuccine with Butternut Squash and Red
Poblano *Crema, 176,* 177–79
Grilled Asparagus with Creamy Pasilla Chile,
198–99, *200*
Grilled Fish with Creamy Cool Cucumber
Pipián, 322–23
Mango Ricotta Cheesecake, 356–57
Nutty Triple-Chocolate Pudding, *343,* 344–45
Poblano Cream Sauce, 55
Ribbon Salad with Creamy Two-Chile
Vinagreta, 192–93
Roasted Knob Onions with *Crema* and Aged
Mexican Cheese, 154–55
Roasted Poblano Cream Soup, 53–55, *54*
Roasted Sunchoke Salad with Creamy Garlic
Mojo and Herbs, 196–97
Roasted Tomatillo Enchiladas, *72,* 73–75
Sabayon (riff), 355
Spaghetti Squash *Fideos* with Chipotle,
Chorizo, *Crema* and Avocado, *184,* 185–86
Spicy Chipotle Eggplant with Black Beans, *214,*
215–16, *217*
Squash Blossom Soup, 190–91
Tomatillo-Sauced *Chilaquiles, 75, 76,* 77–78
Creamy Rice and Beans in Three Classic Flavors,
250–52
Creamy Roasted Poblano *Rajas* and Two
Delicious Dishes to Make from Them, 47–51
Creamy Zucchini, Corn and Roasted Poblanos,
46, 52–53, *52*
preparation, *47, 48, 49, 51*
Roasted Poblano Cream Soup, 53–55, *54*
Creamy Zucchini, Corn and Roasted Poblanos, *46,*
52–53, *52*
crema, 31
Crema de Arroz con Chile Poblano y Espinacas,
264–65
Crema de Calabaza con Chile Anchos y Manzana,
180–81
*Crema de Chile Güero y Poros con Alubias y
Chorizo,* 212–13

Crema de Flores de Calabaza, 190–91

Crema de Quelites de Mostaza, Chile Poblano y Almendra, 129–30

Crema Poblana, 53–55, *54*

crème fraîche, 31

Crispy Cakes of Greens, Potato and Green Chile, *131*, 132–33

Crispy Rice Cakes with White Beans, Roasted Garlic, Aged Cheese and Smoky Chile, 265–66

cucumbers:

    Charred Cucumber Salad with Red Chile and Lime, *187*, 188–89

    Grilled Fish with Creamy Cool Cucumber *Pipián*, 322–23

D

desserts, 336–64

    Coconut Bread Pudding, 351–52

    Coconut-Lime Ice Pops, *362*, 363–64

    Farmers' Market Fruit with Warm Tequila-Lime *Espuma*, *353*, 354–55

    Mango Ricotta Cheesecake, 356–57

    Maria Cookie (or Graham Cracker), Crust, 357

    Mexican Chocolate–Pumpkin Seed Cake, 338–39, *340*

    Mexican Chocolate Sorbet, 350

    Mexican Chocolate Truffles, 348–49

    Nutty Triple-Chocolate Pudding, *343*, 344–45

    Plantains (or Fresh Fruit) with 24-Hour *Cajeta* and Bitter Chocolate, 358–59

    Raspberry Soft-Serve Ice Cream, *360*, 361

    Unbaked Mexican Chocolate Flan, 341–42

    Warm Rice Pudding with Mexican Chocolate and Toasted Almonds, 346–47

E

eggplant:

    Grilled Lamb Chops with Charred Eggplant Salsa, 311–12

    Salsa-Braised Fish (or Tofu or Eggplant), 64, *65*, 67

    Spicy Chipotle Eggplant with Black Beans, *214*, 215–16, *217*

eggs:

    Coconut Bread Pudding, 351–52

    Cornmeal Pancakes, 237–38

    Eggs Poached with Ancho Chile, Kale, Potatoes and Fresh Cheese, 134–36; riffs on, 135

    Farmers' Market Fruit with Warm Tequila-Lime *Espuma*, *353*, 354–55

    Fresh Fava Bean *Enfrijoladas*, *165*, 166–68

    Horchata French Toast, *242*, 243–45

    Huevos Rancheros, 60, *61*, 62–63, *63*

    Mango Ricotta Cheesecake, 356–57

    Nopal Cactus and Poached Egg in Roasted Tomato–Chipotle Broth, *162*, 163–64

    Open-Face Egg-Chorizo Tortas, 234–35, *236*

    Open-Face Red Chile–Chard Omelet, *229*, 230–31

    Open-Face Squash Blossom Omelet with Charred Tomato, Chile and Goat Cheese, 232–33

    Scrambled Eggs with Beans, Green Onions and Avocado, 286

    Spicy Bacon-and-Egg Fried Rice with Pickled Jalapeños and Cilantro, 266–67

Enchiladas Verdes, 72, 73–75

Enfrijoladas de Haba Fresca, *165*, 166–68; riffs on, 168

Enfrijoladas de Plátano con Tocino, 287

Ensalada a la Parilla "Cuatro Estaciones" con Cebollitas Ahumaditas y Ajonjolí, 156–58

Ensalada de Aguaturma con Ajo Cremoso y Hierbas, 196–97

Ensalada de Jícama, Betabel, Radicchio, Cacahuates y Limón, *159*, 160–61

Ensalada de Listones con Vinagreta de Dos Chiles, 192–93

Ensalada de Pepino Carbonizado con Chile Seco y Limón, *187*, 188–89

Ensalada de Quelites con Mango y Habanero, *137*, 138–39

epazote, 31

    Fresh Corn in Spicy-Herby Broth, 144–45

    Herby, Spicy Fried Corn, 146

    Roasted Garlic Chicken with Mushrooms, Potatoes and Spinach, 296–98, *299*

    Tomato–Green Chile Seafood Rice, *66*, 67–68

equipment, 23–26

Espaldilla de Puerco con Salsa "Barbecue" de Chile Ancho, 302–3, *304*

Esparragos a la Parilla, Chile Pasilla Cremoso, 198–99, *200*

Esquites Caldosos, 144–45

Esquites Fritos, 146

F

Farmers' Market Fruit with Warm Tequila-Lime *Espuma*, *353*, 354–55

fennel:
  Grilled Asparagus with Creamy Pasilla Chile (riff), 199
  without fronds, 206
  Yellow *Mole* with Grilled Fennel and Portobello Mushrooms, 204–6, *207*

Fettuccine with Butternut Squash and Red Poblano *Crema*, *176*, 177–79; riffs on, 178–79

Fideos de Calabaza Espaguieti al Chipotle con Chorizo, Crema y Aguacate, *184*, 185–86

fish:
  Cilantro-Poached Halibut, 330–31, *332*
  Grilled Fish with Creamy Cool Cucumber *Pipián*, 322–23
  Grilled Salmon in Toasty Peanut Salsa, 316–17, *318*
  Salsa-Braised Fish (or Tofu or Eggplant), 64, *65*, 67
  Tomato–Green Chile Seafood Rice, *66*, 67–68
  Yellow *Mole* with Grilled Fennel and Portobello Mushrooms (riff), 206

Five Simple Meals from a Pot of Beans, 284
  A Good-Size Pot of Beans, 284–85
  Beans and Greens with Clams and Chorizo, *288*, 289
  Cheesy Open-Face Mollette, 289–90
  Plantain-Bacon *Enfrijoladas*, 287
  Scrambled Eggs with Beans, Green Onions and Avocado, 286
  Silky Tortilla Soup, 285–86

flan:
  classic vanilla (riff), 342
  Unbaked Mexican Chocolate Flan, 341–42

Flan de Chocolate Mexicano Sin Hornear, 341–42

food processor, 25

Four Seasons Grilled Salad with Smoky Knob (or Green) Onions and Sesame, 156-58; riffs on, 158

French toast: *Horchata* French Toast, *242*, 243–45

Frijol con Puerco, 99, 100–103, *101*

Frijoles Frescos y Alcachofas con Tomate Verde Asado, Cilantro y Queso Añejo, 201–3

Frijoles y Quelites con Almejas y Chorizo, *288*, 289

Frijoles y Quelites en Chile Guajillo con Queso Fresco, 126–27, *128*

frisée leaves:
  Ribbon Salad with Creamy Two-Chile *Vinagreta*, 192–93
  "Sturdy Greens" Salad with Mango and Habanero, *137*, 138–39

fruit:
  Farmers' Market Fruit with Warm Tequila-Lime *Espuma*, *353*, 354–55
  Plantains (or Fresh Fruit) with 24-Hour *Cajeta* and Bitter Chocolate, 358–59
  Stone Fruit (or Mango) *Licuado*, *225*, 226
  Warm Rice Pudding with Mexican Chocolate and Toasted Almonds, 346–47

Fruta de la Temporada con Espuma de Limón y Tequila, *353*, 354–55

G

garlic, 31
  Crispy Rice Cakes with White Beans, Roasted Garlic, Aged Cheese and Smoky Chile, 265–66
  Garlicky Tomato Rice, 251–52
  Pan-Roasted Summer Squash with Garlic *Mojo* and Güero Chile, 182–83
  Roasted Garlic Chicken with Mushrooms, Potatoes and Spinach, 296–98, *299*
  Roasted Garlic *Mojo*, *32*, 39–40, *41*
  Roasted Sunchoke Salad with Creamy Garlic *Mojo* and Herbs, 196–97
  Spicy, Garlicky Grilled Cauliflower Steaks with Browned Butter, Toasted Nuts and Tequila Raisins, 319–20, *321*

gelatin: Unbaked Mexican Chocolate Flan, 341–42

goat: Green Chile–Braised Beef with Potatoes and Caramelized Onions (riff), 291–93

Graham Cracker (or Maria Cookie) Crust, 357

granola: Xoco's Granola, 228

Granola Estilo Xoco, 228

green chiles, 29

    Carne Asada Dinner, *85*, 86–91

    Creamy Rice and Beans in Three Classic Flavors, 250–52

    Crispy Cakes of Greens, Potato and Green Chile, *131*, 132–33

    Green Chile *Adobo, 32*, 33–34, *35*

    Green Chile–Braised Beef with Potatoes and Caramelized Onions, 291-93; riffs on, 293

    Green Chile Chicken Thighs, 305-7; riffs on, 307

    Green Chile Riff on Red Chile–Chard Omelet, 231

    Grilled Tostadas with Bacon, Avocado Mayo and Heirloom Tomatoes, *149*, 150–51

    Herby Green Chile Rice, *249*, 251–52

    Mexican Red Rice, 262–64

    Pork Carnitas Dinner, 280–82, *283*

    Roasted Chayote with Herbs and Tofu (or Goat Cheese), 142–43

    Roasted Garlic Chicken with Mushrooms, Potatoes and Spinach, 296–98, *299*

    Scrambled Eggs with Beans, Green Onions and Avocado, 286

    Shrimp Skillet Tacos with Green Chile *Adobo* and caramelized onions, *92*, 93–98, *95*, *96*

    Tangy Sorrel *Salsa Verde* with Stir-Fried Shrimp, 210–11

    Tomato–Green Chile Seafood Rice, *66*, 67–68

greens:

    Beans and Greens with Clams and Chorizo, *288*, 289

    Crispy Cakes of Greens, Potato and Green Chile, *131*, 132–33

    Eggs Poached with Ancho Chile, Kale, Potatoes and Fresh Cheese, 134–36

    Four Seasons Grilled Salad (riff), 158

    Fresh Fava Bean *Enfrijoladas, 165*, 166–68

    Greens and Beans with Red Chile and Fresh Cheese, 126–27, *128*

    Mustard Greens Soup with Poblanos and Almonds, 129–30

    Open-Face Red Chile–Chard Omelet, *229*, 230–31

    Pickled Tomatillo Salad with Little Gem Lettuce and Pumpkin Seeds, 152–53

    Spring Green *Licuado*, *224*, *225*

    "Sturdy Greens" Salad with Mango and Habanero, *137*, 138–39

    Tangy Sorrel *Salsa Verde* with Stir-Fried Shrimp, 210–11

grill; grill pan, 24–25

grilled foods:

    classic barbecue technique, 309

    Four Seasons Grilled Salad with Smoky Knob (or Green) Onions and Sesame, 156–58

    Green Chile Chicken Thighs, 305–7

    Grilled Asparagus with Creamy Pasilla Chile, 198–99, *200*; riffs on, 199

    Grilled Fish with Creamy Cool Cucumber *Pipián*, 322–23

    Grilled Lamb Chops with Charred Eggplant Salsa, 311-12; riffs on, 312

    Grilled Red Chile Ribs, 308–10

    Grilled Salmon in Toasty Peanut Salsa, 316–17, *318*

    Grilled Skirt Steaks, 89–90, *90*

    Grilled Tostadas with Bacon, Avocado Mayo and Heirloom Tomatoes, *149*, 150–51; riffs on, 151

    Queso Fundido Burger, *313*, 314–15

    Slow-Grilled Pork Shoulder with Ancho Barbecue Sauce, 302–3, *304*

    Spicy, Garlicky Grilled Cauliflower Steaks with Browned Butter, Toasted Nuts and Tequila Raisins, 319–20, *321*

    Yellow *Mole* with Grilled Fennel and Portobello Mushrooms, 204–6, *207*

Guacamole, 88, *88*

guajillo chiles:

    dried, 29, *29*

    Greens and Beans with Red Chile and Fresh Cheese, 126–27, *128*

    Mussels (or Clams) with *Salsa Macha*, Mexican Beer and Ham, 333–35

guajillo chiles (*continued*)
  Yellow *Mole* with Grilled Fennel and Portobello
    Mushrooms, 204–6, *207*
güero chiles: Pan-Roasted Summer Squash with
    Garlic *Mojo* and Güero Chile, 182–83

H

habanero chile: "Sturdy Greens" Salad with
    Mango and Habanero, *137*, 138–39
halibut: Cilantro-Poached Halibut, 330–31, *332*
ham:
  Black Bean Rice with Plantains and Smoky
    Pork, *253*, 254–55
  Mussels (or Clams) with *Salsa Macha*, Mexican
    Beer and Ham, 333–35
Hamburguesa de Queso Fundido, *313*, 314–15
hazelnuts: Nutty Triple-Chocolate Pudding, *343*,
    344–45
Helado de Frambuesa, Tipo Soft Serve, *360*, 361
herbs, 31
  Fresh Corn in Spicy-Herby Broth, 144–45
  Green Chile–Braised Beef with Potatoes and
    Caramelized Onions, 291–93
  Herb Green Chicken and Rice, 258–59
  Herby, Spicy Fried Corn, 146
  Herby Green Chile Rice, *249*, 251–52
  Mexican Chicken Soup, 270–71
  Roasted Chayote with Herbs and Tofu (or Goat
    Cheese), 142–43
  Roasted Sunchoke Salad with Creamy Garlic
    Mojo and Herbs, 196–97
  Spring Green *Licuado*, 224, *225*
  Yellow *Mole* with Grilled Fennel and Portobello
    Mushrooms, 204–6, *207*
hoja santa, 31, *31*, 206
  Grilled Fish with Creamy Cool Cucumber
    Pipián, 322–23
hominy (note), 276
Horchata French Toast, *242*, 243–45
Hotcakes de Harina de Maiz, 237–38
*Huevos Pochados con Chile Ancho, Berza, Papas y
    Queso Fresco*, 134–36
Huevos Rancheros, 60, *61*, 62–63, *63*

Huevos Tirados de Lujo, 286

I

ice cream: Raspberry Soft-Serve Ice Cream, *360*,
    361
ice pops: Coconut-Lime Ice Pops, *362*, 363–64
ingredients, 28–32

J

jalapeño chiles:
  Braised Artichokes with Tomatoes, Jalapeños,
    Olives and Capers, 218–19
  Fresh Corn in Spicy-Herby Broth, 144–45
  Grilled Fish with Creamy Cool Cucumber
    Pipián, 322–23
  Mexican Chicken Soup, 270–71
  Roasted Tomato Salsa, *56*, 57–58, *59*, 60
  Spicy Bacon-and-Egg Fried Rice with Pickled
    Jalapeños and Cilantro, 266–67
Jícama-Beet Salad with Radicchio, Peanuts and
    Lime, *159*, 160–61
Jones, Jennifer, 356

K

kale:
  Eggs Poached with Ancho Chile, Kale, Potatoes
    and Fresh Cheese, 134–36
  Greens and Beans with Red Chile and Fresh
    Cheese, 126–27, *128*
knives, 23–24
Kuri (or Butternut or Pumpkin) Soup with Ancho
    and Apple, 180–81; riffs on, 181

L

lactose intolerance, 347
lamb:
  Green Chile–Braised Beef with Potatoes and
    Caramelized Onions (riff), 291–93
  Grilled Lamb Chops with Charred Eggplant
    Salsa, 311–12
  Lamb or Beef *Barbacoa*, 294–95
leeks: Banana Pepper–Leek Soup with White
    Beans and Crispy Chorizo, 212–13

lentils: Chorizo Rice with Lentils, 256–57

lettuce:

Pickled Tomatillo Salad with Little Gem
Lettuce and Pumpkin Seeds, 152–53

Red Chile Pozole with Pork, 276–78, *279*

Licuado de Drupas, *225*, 226

Licuado Verde, *224*, *225*

lime juice:

Carrot, Beet and Orange *Licuado*, *225*, 227

Charred Cucumber Salad with Red Chile and
Lime, *187*, 188–89

Coconut-Lime Ice Pops, *362*, 363–64

Grilled Lamb Chops with Charred Eggplant
Salsa, 311–12

Jícama-Beet Salad with Radicchio, Peanuts and
Lime, *159*, 160–61

Pickled Tomatillo Salad with Little Gem
Lettuce and Pumpkin Seeds, 152–53

Spring Green *Licuado*, *224*, *225*

Stone Fruit (or Mango) *Licuado*, *225*, 226

"Sturdy Greens" Salad with Mango and
Habanero, *137*, 138–39

limes:

Farmers' Market Fruit with Warm Tequila-Lime
Espuma, *353*, 354–55

Mexican Chicken Soup, 270–71

Pork Carnitas Dinner, 280–82, *283*

Red Chile Pozole with Pork, 276–78, *279*

*Lomo de Puerco (o Pollo) en Salsa Verde con
Papas*, 79, *80*, 81–84

M

mango:

Mango Ricotta Cheesecake, 356–57

Stone Fruit (or Mango) *Licuado*, *225*, 226

"Sturdy Greens" Salad with Mango and
Habanero, *137*, 138–39

Maria Cookie (or Graham Cracker) Crust, 357

masa harina, 30–31

mayonnaise: Fresh Corn in Spicy-Herby Broth,
144–45

*Mejillones (o Almejas) con Salsa Macha, Cerveza
Mexicana y Jamón*, 333–35

Mexican Chicken Soup, 270-71; riffs on, 271

Mexican Chocolate–Pumpkin Seed Cake, 338–39,
340

Mexican Chocolate Sorbet, 350

Mexican Chocolate Truffles, 348–49

Mexican Red Rice and Three Delicious Dishes to
Make from It, 262–64

Creamy Rice Soup with Poblano and Spinach,
264–65

Crispy Rice Cakes with White Beans, Roasted
Garlic, Aged Cheese and Smoky Chile,
265–66

half batch for 6-cup rice cooker, 264

Mexican Red Rice, 262–64

Spicy Bacon-and-Egg Fried Rice with Pickled
Jalapeños and Cilantro, 266–67

microwave, 25

Miel de Agave y Canela, 238

Miel de Piloncillo, 244–45

milk:

Plantains (or Fresh Fruit) with 24-Hour *Cajeta*
and Bitter Chocolate, 358–59

Raspberry Soft-Serve Ice Cream, *360*, 361

Stone Fruit *Licuado* (riff), 226

Warm Rice Pudding with Mexican Chocolate
and Toasted Almonds, 346–47

mint: Coconut-Lime Ice Pops (riff), 364

Mojo de Ajo Asado, *32*, 39–40, *41*

molasses: Sweet-Sour Dark Chipotle Seasoning,
216

*Mole Amarillo con Hinojo Asado y Hongo
Portobello*, 204–6, *207*

Mole de Cacahuate con Pollo, *104*, 105–10, *109*

Mole de Olla, 272–74, *275*

Mollete de Queso, 289–90

Molletes de Chorizo y Huevo, 234-35, *236*; riffs on,
235

morita chiles: Ribbon Salad with Creamy Two-
Chile *Vinagreta*, 192–93

mortar, 25, *59*

muffins: Butternut-Pecan Muffins with Brown
Sugar Crumble, *239*, 240–41

Muffins de Calabaza y Nuez, *239*, 240–41

mushrooms, 30
Roasted Garlic Chicken with Mushrooms, Potatoes and Spinach, 296–98, *299*
Yellow *Mole* with Grilled Fennel and Portobello Mushrooms, 204–6, *207*
Muslos de Pollo al Chile Verde, 305–7
mussels:
cold appetizer (riff), 335
Mussels (or Clams) with *Salsa Macha*, Mexican Beer and Ham, 333-35; riffs on, 335
Tomato–Green Chile Seafood Rice, *66*, 67–68
Mustard Greens Soup with Poblanos and Almonds, 129-30; riffs on, 130

N

Natilla de Tres Chocolates y Pepitas, *343*, 344–45
Nieve de Chocolate Mexicano, 350
nixtamal (pozole) corn:
note, 276
Red Chile Pozole with Pork, 276–78, *279*
Nopal Cactus and Poached Egg in Roasted Tomato–Chipotle Broth, *162*, 163–64
Nopales Navegantes, *162*, 163–64
nuts. *See also specific nuts*
Coconut Bread Pudding (riff), 352
Mussels (or Clams) with *Salsa Macha*, Mexican Beer and Ham, 333–35
Plantains (or Fresh Fruit) with 24-Hour *Cajeta* and Bitter Chocolate, 358–59
Spicy, Garlicky Grilled Cauliflower Steaks with Browned Butter, Toasted Nuts and Tequila Raisins, 319–20, *321*
Nutty Triple-Chocolate Pudding, *343*, 344–45

O

oats: Xoco's Granola, 228
olives: Braised Artichokes with Tomatoes, Jalapeños, Olives and Capers, 218–19
Omelet Abierto de Chile Rojo y Acelgas, *229*, 230–31
Omelet Abierto de Flores, Jitomate Tatemado, Chile y Queso de Cabra, 232–33

omelets:
Open-Face Red Chile–Chard Omelet, *229*, 230–31
Open-Face Squash Blossom Omelet with Charred Tomato, Chile and Goat Cheese, 232–33
onions, 31
A Good-Size Pot of Beans, 284–85
Charred Cucumber Salad with Red Chile and Lime, *187*, 188–89
Chicken *Barbacoa*, 324–25
Chorizo Rice with Lentils, 256–57
Cilantro-Poached Halibut, 330–31, *332*
Creamy Roasted Poblano *Rajas*, 47–51, *50*
Four Seasons Grilled Salad with Smoky Knob (or Green) Onions and Sesame, 156–58
Fresh Fava Bean *Enfrijoladas*, *165*, 166–68
Green Chile–Braised Beef with Potatoes and Caramelized Onions, 291–93
Grilled Asparagus with Creamy Pasilla Chile, 198–99, *200*
Grilled Lamb Chops with Charred Eggplant Salsa, 311–12
Grilled Salmon in Toasty Peanut Salsa, 316–17, *318*
Kuri (or Butternut or Pumpkin) Soup with Ancho and Apple, 180–81
Mexican Chicken Soup, 270–71
Nopal Cactus and Poached Egg in Roasted Tomato–Chipotle Broth, *162*, 163–64
Open-Face Egg-Chorizo Tortas, 234–35, *236*
Open-Face Squash Blossom Omelet with Charred Tomato, Chile and Goat Cheese, 232–33
Plantain-Bacon *Enfrijoladas*, 287
Pork and Black Bean Dinner, *99*, 100–103, *101*
Queso Fundido Burger, *313*, 314–15
Red Chile Pozole with Pork, 276–78, *279*
Red Peanut *Mole* with Chicken, *104*, 105–10, *109*
Ribbon Salad with Creamy Two-Chile *Vinagreta*, 192–93
Roasted Garlic Chicken with Mushrooms, Potatoes and Spinach, 296–98, *299*

Roasted Knob Onions with *Crema* and Aged
  Mexican Cheese, 154–55
Roasted Sunchoke Salad with Creamy Garlic
  Mojo and Herbs, 196–97
Salsa Verde with Young Turnip and Red Onion,
  211
Scrambled Eggs with Beans, Green Onions and
  Avocado, 286
Skillet Tacos, *92*, 93–98, *95*
Slow-Grilled Pork Shoulder with Ancho
  Barbecue Sauce, 302–3, *304*
Squash Blossom Soup, 190–91
Steamed Roots with Roasted Poblano and
  Tomatillo, 147–48
"Sturdy Greens" Salad with Mango and
  Habanero, *137*, 138–39
Tangy Sorrel *Salsa Verde* with Stir-Fried
  Shrimp, 210–11
Open-Face Egg-Chorizo Tortas, 234–35, *236*
Open-Face Red Chile–Chard Omelet, *229*, 230–
  31
Open-Face Squash Blossom Omelet with Charred
  Tomato, Chile and Goat Cheese, 232–33
orange juice:
  Carrot, Beet and Orange *Licuado*, *225*, 227
  "Sturdy Greens" Salad with Mango and
    Habanero, *137*, 138–39

P
Paletas de Coco con Limón, *362*, 363–64
pancakes:
  Celery Root Pancakes with Chipotle *Crema* and
    Cilantro, 208–9
  Cornmeal Pancakes, 237–38
Pan-Roasted Summer Squash with Garlic *Mojo*
  and Güero Chile, 182–83
parsley:
  Braised Artichokes with Tomatoes, Jalapeños,
    Olives and Capers, 218–19
  Crispy Rice Cakes with White Beans, Roasted
    Garlic, Aged Cheese and Smoky Chile,
    265–66
  Fresh Corn in Spicy-Herby Broth, 144–45

Green Chile *Adobo*, *32*, 33–34, *35*, 94, 143
Mexican Red Rice, 262–64
Roasted Garlic Chicken with Mushrooms,
  Potatoes and Spinach, 296–98, *299*
Tomato–Green Chile Seafood Rice, *66*, 67–68
parsnips:
  Celery Root Pancakes (riff), 209
  Roasted Sunchoke Salad (riff), 197
  Steamed Roots with Roasted Poblano and
    Tomatillo, 147–48
pasilla (negro) chiles, Grilled Asparagus with
  Creamy Pasilla Chile, 198–99, *200*
Pasta con Calabaza, Chile Poblano Rojo y Crema,
  176, 177–79
Pastel de Chocolate y Pepitas, 338–39, *340*
Pastel de Requesón con Mango, 356–57
peanuts:
  Grilled Salmon in Toasty Peanut Salsa, 316–17,
    318
  Jícama-Beet Salad with Radicchio, Peanuts and
    Lime, *159*, 160–61
  Nutty Triple-Chocolate Pudding, *343*, 344–45
  Red Peanut *Mole* with Chicken, *104*, 105–10,
    109
  Spicy, Garlicky Grilled Cauliflower Steaks with
    Browned Butter, Toasted Nuts and Tequila
    Raisins, 319–20, *321*
  Xoco's Granola, 228
peas:
  Herb Green Chicken and Rice, 258–59
  Mexican Red Rice, 262–64
pecans: Butternut-Pecan Muffins with Brown
  Sugar Crumble, *239*, 240–41
peppers: Ribbon Salad with Creamy Two-Chile
  Vinagreta, 192–93
Pescado al Cilantro, 330–31, *332*
Pescado Asado en Pipián de Pepino, 322–23
Pescado Horneado con Salsa de Molcajete, 64, *65*,
  67
Pickled Tomatillo Salad with Little Gem Lettuce
  and Pumpkin Seeds, 152–53
Piloncillo Syrup, 244–45
pineapple: Spring Green *Licuado*, 224, *225*

plantains:

Black Bean Rice with Plantains and Smoky Pork, *253*, 254–55

Plantain-Bacon *Enfrijoladas,* 287

Plantains (or Fresh Fruit) with 24-Hour *Cajeta* and Bitter Chocolate, 358–59

Plátano Macho (o Otra Fruta) con Cajeta de 24 Horas y Chocolate Amargo, 358–59

plates, warming, 84

poblano chiles, 29, *29*

Cheesy Open-Face Mollette, 289–90

Creamy Rice and Beans in Three Classic Flavors, 250–52

Creamy Rice Soup with Poblano and Spinach, 264–65

Creamy Roasted Poblano *Rajas* and Two Delicious Dishes to Make from Them, 47–51

Creamy Zucchini, Corn and Roasted Poblanos, 52–53, *52*

Fettuccine with Butternut Squash and Red Poblano *Crema, 176,* 177–79

Green Chile–Braised Beef with Potatoes and Caramelized Onions, 291–93

Green Chile Chicken Thighs, 305–7

Green Chile Riff on Red Chile–Chard Omelet, 231

Herb Green Chicken and Rice, 258–59

Mustard Greens Soup with Poblanos and Almonds, 129–30

Poblano Cream Sauce, 55

Pork (or Chicken) with Roasted Tomatillos, Poblanos and Potatoes, 79, *80*, 81–84

preparing, *47, 48, 49, 51*

Queso Fundido Burger, *313,* 314–15

red (note), 177

Roasted Poblano Cream Soup, 53–55, *54*

Roasted Sunchoke Salad with Creamy Garlic *Mojo* and Herbs, 196–97

Squash Blossom Soup, 190–91

Steamed Roots with Roasted Poblano and Tomatillo, 147–48

Pollo Adobado y Rostizado, 111, 112–15

Pollo al Mojo con Hongos, Papas y Espinacas, 296–98, *299*

Pollo Cocido Sobre Lata de Cerveza, Glaceado con Cerveza, 326, 327–28, *328*

pork:

Black Bean Rice with Plantains and Smoky Pork, *253*, 254–55

Chipotle Meatballs, *116,* 117–18, *119,* 120–21

Grilled Red Chile Ribs, 308–10

Pork (or Chicken) with Roasted Tomatillos, Poblanos and Potatoes, 79, *80*, 81–84

Pork and Black Bean Dinner, *99,* 100–103, *101*

Pork Carnitas Dinner, 280–82, *283*

Red Chile Pozole with Pork, 276–78, *279*

Roasted Chayote with Herbs and Tofu (riff), 143

Roasted Tomatillo Enchiladas, *72,* 73–75

Skillet Tacos, 93–98

Slow-Grilled Pork Shoulder with Ancho Barbecue Sauce, 302–3, *304*

potatoes:

Celery Root Pancakes with Chipotle *Crema* and Cilantro, 208–9

Crispy Cakes of Greens, Potato and Green Chile, *131,* 132–33

Eggs Poached with Ancho Chile, Kale, Potatoes and Fresh Cheese, 134–36

Green Chile–Braised Beef with Potatoes and Caramelized Onions, 291–93

Green Chile Chicken Thighs, 305–7

Mustard Greens Soup with Poblanos and Almonds, 129–30

Pork (or Chicken) with Roasted Tomatillos, Poblanos and Potatoes, 79, *80*, 81–84

Red Chile Roast Chicken, *111,* 112–15

Red Chile Short Rib Soup, 272–74, *275*

Roasted Garlic Chicken with Mushrooms, Potatoes and Spinach, 296–98, *299*

Roasted Poblano Cream Soup, 53–55, *54*

Roasted Sunchoke Salad (riff), 197

Steamed Roots with Roasted Poblano and Tomatillo, 147–48

Yellow *Mole* with Grilled Fennel and Portobello Mushrooms, 204–6, *207*

Pozole Rojo de Puerco, 276–78, *279*

pressure cooker, 26

puddings:
    Coconut Bread Pudding, 351–52
    Nutty Triple-Chocolate Pudding, *343*, 344–45
    Warm Rice Pudding with Mexican Chocolate
       and Toasted Almonds, 346–47
pumpkin: Kuri (or Butternut or Pumpkin) Soup
    with Ancho and Apple, 180–81
pumpkin seeds:
    Grilled Fish with Creamy Cool Cucumber
       Pipián, 322–23
    Mexican Chocolate–Pumpkin Seed Cake, 338–
       39, *340*
    Nutty Triple-Chocolate Pudding, *343*, 344–45
    Pickled Tomatillo Salad with Little Gem
       Lettuce and Pumpkin Seeds, 152–53
    Spicy, Garlicky Grilled Cauliflower Steaks with
       Browned Butter, Toasted Nuts and Tequila
       Raisins, 319–20, *321*
    Xoco's Granola, 228

Q

quajillo chiles: Grilled Salmon in Toasty Peanut
    Salsa, 316–17, *318*
Queso Fundido Burger, *313*, 314–15
Quick Red Chile *Adobo*:
    32, *36*, 37-38; riffs on, 135
    Chicken *Barbacoa,* 324–25
    Chipotle Rice with Shrimp, 260, *261*
    Eggs Poached with Ancho Chile, Kale, Potatoes
       and Fresh Cheese, 134–36
    Grilled Red Chile Ribs, 308–10
    Lamb or Beef *Barbacoa,* 294–95
    Red Chile Pozole with Pork, 276–78, *279*
    Red Chile Riff on Green Chile Skillet Tacos, 97
    Red Chile Roast Chicken, *111*, 112–15, *113*
    simplest uses for, 38
    Skillet Tacos (riff), 97
    Slow-Grilled Pork Shoulder with Ancho
       Barbecue Sauce, 302–3, *304*

R

radicchio: Jícama-Beet Salad with Radicchio,
    Peanuts and Lime, *159*, 160–61

radishes: Red Chile Pozole with Pork, 276–78, *279*
raisins: Spicy, Garlicky Grilled Cauliflower Steaks
    with Browned Butter, Toasted Nuts and
    Tequila Raisins, 319–20, *321*
Rajas Poblanos con Crema, 47–51
ramps: Grilled Salmon in Toasty Peanut Salsa,
    316–17, *318*
Raspberry Soft-Serve Ice Cream, *360*, 361
Red Chile Pozole with Pork, 276–78, *279*; riffs on,
    278
Red Chile Riff on Green Chile Skillet Tacos, 97
Red Chile Roast Chicken, *111*, 112–15
Red Chile Short Rib Soup, 272–74, *275*; riffs on, 274
Red Peanut *Mole* with Chicken, *104*, 105–10, *109*
Ribbon Salad with Creamy Two-Chile *Vinagreta,*
    192–93
ribs: Grilled Red Chile Ribs, 308–10
rice. *See also* rice cookers
Chipotle Meatballs, *116*, 117–18, *119*, 120–21
    Four Seasons Grilled Salad (riff), 158
    Horchata French Toast, *242*, 243–45
    Mexican Chicken Soup, 270–71
    reheating rice pudding, 347
    Tomato–Green Chile Seafood Rice, *66*, 67–68
    Warm Rice Pudding with Mexican Chocolate
       and Toasted Almonds, 346-47; riffs on, 347
rice cookers, 26, 246–67
    Black Bean Rice with Plantains and Smoky
       Pork, *253*, 254–55
    Chipotle Rice with Shrimp, 260, *261*
    Chorizo Rice with Lentils, 256–57
    Creamy Rice and Beans in Three Classic
       Flavors, 250–52
    Creamy Rice Soup with Poblano and Spinach,
       264–65
    Crispy Rice Cakes with White Beans, Roasted
       Garlic, Aged Cheese and Smoky Chile, 265–66
    Garlicky Tomato Rice, 251–52
    half batch, 264
    Herb Green Chicken and Rice, 258–59
    Herby Green Chile Rice, *249*, 251–52
    Mexican Red Rice and Three Delicious Dishes
       to Make from It, 262–64

rice cookers (*continued*)
  note, 248
  Smoky Red Chile Rice, 251–52
  Spicy Bacon-and-Egg Fried Rice with Pickled
    Jalapeños and Cilantro, 266–67
ricotta: Mango Ricotta Cheesecake, 356–57
Roasted Chayote with Herbs and Tofu (or Goat
    Cheese), 142-43; riffs on, 143
Roasted Garlic *Mojo,* 32, 39–40, *41*
  Pan-Roasted Summer Squash with Garlic *Mojo*
    and Güero Chile, 182–83
  Roasted Garlic Chicken with Mushrooms,
    Potatoes and Spinach, 296–98, *299*
  Roasted Sunchoke Salad with Creamy Garlic
    Mojo and Herbs, 196–97
  simplest uses for, 39–40
Roasted Knob Onions with *Crema* and Aged
    Mexican Cheese, 154–55
Roasted Poblano Cream Soup, 53–55, *54*
Roasted Sunchoke Salad with Creamy Garlic
    Mojo, 196–97
Roasted Tomatillo Enchiladas, *72,* 73–75
Roasted Tomatillo Sauce Base and Three
    Delicious Dishes to Make from It, 69, *70,* 71,
    71
  Pork (or Chicken) with Roasted Tomatillos,
    Poblanos and Potatoes, 79, *80,* 81–84
  Roasted Tomatillo Enchiladas, *72,* 73–75
  Tomatillo-Sauced *Chilaquiles,* 75, *76,* 77–78
Roasted Tomato Salsa and Three Delicious Dishes
    to Make from It, *56,* 57–58, *58, 59,* 60
  Huevos Rancheros, 60, *61,* 62–63, *63*
  Salsa-Braised Fish (or Tofu or Eggplant), 64, *65,*
    67
  Tomato–Green Chile Seafood Rice, *66,* 67–68
rutabaga: Steamed Roots with Roasted Poblano
    and Tomatillo, 147–48

S
Sabayon (riff), 355
salads:
  Charred Cucumber Salad with Red Chile and
    Lime, *187,* 188–89

Four Seasons Grilled Salad with Smoky Knob
    (or Green) Onions and Sesame, 156–58
Jícama-Beet Salad with Radicchio, Peanuts and
    Lime, *159,* 160–61
Pickled Tomatillo Salad with Little Gem
    Lettuce and Pumpkin Seeds, 152–53
Ribbon Salad with Creamy Two-Chile
    Vinagreta, 192–93
Roasted Sunchoke Salad with Creamy Garlic
    Mojo and Herbs, 196–97
"Sturdy Greens" Salad with Mango and
    Habanero, *137,* 138–39
salmon: Grilled Salmon in Toasty Peanut Salsa,
    316–17, *318*
*Salmón a la Parilla con Salsa de Cacahuate
    Tostado,* 316–17, *318*
salsa:
  for *Carne Asada* Dinner, 88
  Cheesy Open-Face Mollette, 289–90
  Chicken *Barbacoa,* 324–25
  Crispy Rice Cakes with White Beans, Roasted
    Garlic, Aged Cheese and Smoky Chile,
    265–66
  Grilled Lamb Chops with Charred Eggplant
    Salsa, 311–12
  Grilled Salmon in Toasty Peanut Salsa, 316–17,
    318
  Huevos Rancheros, 60, *61,* 62–63, *63*
  Mussels (or Clams) with *Salsa Macha,* Mexican
    Beer and Ham, 333–35
  Roasted Tomato Salsa, *56,* 57–58, *59, 60*
  Salsa-Braised Fish (or Tofu or Eggplant), 64, *65,*
    67
  Tangy Sorrel *Salsa Verde* with Stir-Fried
    Shrimp, 210–11
  Tomato–Green Chile Seafood Rice, *66,* 67–68
*Salsa de Molcajete y Tres Platillos Deliciosos que
    la Utiliza,* 57–58, *58, 59,* 60
*Salsa de Tomate Verde Asado con Tres Platillos
    Deliciosos que la Utiliza,* 69, 71, *71*
Salsa Negra, 32, 40, *42,* 43
*Salsa Verde de Vinagrera con Camarones
    Salteados,* 210–11

Salsa Verde with Young Turnip and Red Onion, 211
sausage:
    Banana Pepper–Leek Soup with White Beans
       and Crispy Chorizo, 212–13
    Beans and Greens with Clams and Chorizo,
       288, 289
    Carne Asada dinner, *85*, 86–91
    Chorizo Rice with Lentils, 256–57
    Open-Face Egg-Chorizo Tortas, 234–35, *236*
    Queso Fundido Burger, *313*, 314–15
    Spaghetti Squash *Fideos* with Chipotle,
       Chorizo, *Crema* and Avocado, *184*, 185–86
Scrambled Eggs with Beans, Green Onions and
    Avocado, 286
serrano chiles:
    Cilantro-Poached Halibut, 330–31, *332*
    Fresh Corn in Spicy-Herby Broth, 144–45
    Green Chile *Adobo, 32*, 33–34, *35*
    Grilled Fish with Creamy Cool Cucumber
       Pipián, 322–23
    Herby, Spicy Fried Corn, 146
    Mexican Chicken Soup, 270–71
    Pickled Tomatillo Salad with Little Gem
       Lettuce and Pumpkin Seeds, 152–53
    Roasted Tomatillo Sauce Base and Three
       Delicious Dishes to Make from It, 69, *70*, 71, *71*
sesame seeds: Four Seasons Grilled Salad with
    Smoky Knob (or Green) Onions and Sesame,
    156–58
Shell Beans and Artichokes with Roasted
    Tomatillos, Cilantro and Añejo Cheese, 201–3
short ribs: Red Chile Short Rib Soup, 272–74, *275*
shrimp:
    Chipotle Rice with Shrimp, 260, *261*
    Fettuccine with Butternut Squash and Red
       Poblano *Crema* (riff), 178–79
    Shrimp Skillet Tacos with Green Chile *Adobo*
       and caramelized onions, *92*, 93–98, *95*, *96*
    Tangy Sorrel *Salsa Verde* with Stir-Fried
       Shrimp, 210–11
    Tomato–Green Chile Seafood Rice, *66*, 67–68
Silky Tortilla Soup, 285–86
skillets, 24

Skillet Tacos, 93–98
    Shrimp Skillet Tacos with Green Chile *Adobo*
       and caramelized onions, *92*
skirt steaks:
    Carne Asada Dinner, *85*, 86–91, *87*
    Grilled Steaks, 89–90, *90*
    note, 91
    Skillet Tacos, 93–98
slow cooker, 25–26, 268–99
    A Good-Size Pot of Beans, 284–85
    Beans and Greens with Clams and Chorizo,
       288, 289
    Cheesy Open-Face Mollette, 289–90
    Five Simple Meals from a Pot of Beans, 284
    Green Chile–Braised Beef with Potatoes and
       Caramelized Onions, 291–93
    Lamb or Beef *Barbacoa,* 294–95
    Mexican Chicken Soup, 270–71
    Plantain-Bacon *Enfrijoladas,* 287
    Pork Carnitas Dinner, 280–82, *283*
    Red Chile Pozole with Pork, 276–78, *279*
    Red Chile Short Rib Soup, 272–74, *275*
    Roasted Garlic Chicken with Mushrooms,
       Potatoes and Spinach, 296–98, *299*
    Scrambled Eggs with Beans, Green Onions and
       Avocado, 286
    Silky Tortilla Soup, 285–86
Slow-Grilled Pork Shoulder with Ancho Barbecue
    Sauce, 302–3, *304*
Smoky Red Chile Rice, 251–52
Sopa de Tortilla Cremosa, 285–86
sorbet: Mexican Chocolate Sorbet, 350
sorrel: Tangy Sorrel *Salsa Verde* with Stir-Fried
    Shrimp, 210-11; riffs on, 211
soups:
    Banana Pepper–Leek Soup with White Beans
       and Crispy Chorizo, 212–13
    Creamy Rice Soup with Poblano and Spinach,
       264–65
    Fresh Corn in Spicy-Herby Broth, 144–45
    Kuri (or Butternut or Pumpkin) Soup with
       Ancho and Apple, 180–81
    Mexican Chicken Soup, 270–71

soups (*continued*)

    Mustard Greens Soup with Poblanos and Almonds, 129–30

    Red Chile Short Rib Soup, 272–74, *275*

    Roasted Poblano Cream Soup, 53–55, *54*

    Silky Tortilla Soup, 285–86

    Squash Blossom Soup, 190–91

sour cream, 31–32

Spaghetti Squash *Fideos* with Chipotle, Chorizo, *Crema* and Avocado, *184*, 185–86

Spicy, Garlicky Grilled Cauliflower Steaks with Browned Butter, Toasted Nuts and Tequila Raisins, 319–20, *321*

Spicy Bacon-and-Egg Fried Rice with Pickled Jalapeños and Cilantro, 266–67

Spicy Chipotle Eggplant with Black Beans, *214*, 215–16, *217*

spinach:

    Creamy Rice Soup with Poblano and Spinach, 264–65

    Fresh Fava Bean *Enfrijoladas,* *165*, 166–68

    Roasted Garlic Chicken with Mushrooms, Potatoes and Spinach, 296–98, *299*

Spring Green *Licuado*, 224, *225*

squash:

    Butternut-Pecan Muffins with Brown Sugar Crumble, *239*, 240–41

    Butternut with Bacon, Tomatillo and Chipotle, *173*, 174–75

    Creamy Zucchini, Corn and Roasted Poblanos, 52–53, *52*

    Fettuccine with Butternut Squash and Red Poblano *Crema,* *176*, 177–79

    Kuri (or Butternut or Pumpkin) Soup with Ancho and Apple, 180–81

    Pan-Roasted Summer Squash with Garlic *Mojo* and Güero Chile, 182–83

    Ribbon Salad with Creamy Two-Chile *Vinagreta,* 192–93

    Spaghetti Squash *Fideos* with Chipotle, Chorizo, *Crema* and Avocado, *184*, 185–86

squash blossoms:

    Open-Face Squash Blossom Omelet with Charred Tomato, Chile and Goat Cheese, 232–33

    Squash Blossom Soup, 190-91; riffs on, 191

Steamed Roots with Roasted Poblano and Tomatillo, 147–48

Stone Fruit (or Mango) *Licuado, 225,* 226; riff on, 226

"Sturdy Greens" Salad with Mango and Habanero, *137*, 138–39

sunchokes: Roasted Sunchoke Salad with Creamy Garlic *Mojo* and Herbs, 196–97

sweet potatoes:

    Celery Root Pancakes (riff), 209

    Roasted Sunchoke Salad (riff), 197

    Steamed Roots with Roasted Poblano and Tomatillo, 147–48

Sweet-Sour Dark Chipotle Seasoning, 32, 40, *42*, 43

    simplest uses for, 43

    Spicy Chipotle Eggplant with Black Beans, *214*, 215–16, *217*

T

tacos, 93, 172

    Skillet Tacos, *92*, 93–98

Tacos al Sartén, 92, 93–98

Tangy Sorrel *Salsa Verde* with Stir-Fried Shrimp, 210–11

taro: Celery Root Pancakes (riff), 209

tequila:

    Farmers' Market Fruit with Warm Tequila-Lime *Espuma, 353,* 354–55

    Spicy, Garlicky Grilled Cauliflower Steaks with Browned Butter, Toasted Nuts and Tequila Raisins, 319–20, *321*

tofu:

    Roasted Chayote with Herbs and Tofu (or Goat Cheese), 142–43

    Salsa-Braised Fish (or Tofu or Eggplant), 64, *65*, 67

Tomates Verdes Encurtidos con Lechuguita Orejona y Pepitas, 152–53

tomatillos, 30, *30*

    Butternut with Bacon, Tomatillo and Chipotle, *173*, 174–75

Carne Asada Dinner, *85*, 86–91

Grilled Red Chile Ribs, 308–10

Pickled Tomatillo Salad with Little Gem
Lettuce and Pumpkin Seeds, 152–53

Pork (or Chicken) with Roasted Tomatillos,
Poblanos and Potatoes, 79, *80*, 81–84

Roasted Tomatillo Enchiladas, *72*, 73–75

Roasted Tomatillo Sauce Base and Three
Delicious Dishes to Make from It, 69, *70*, 71,
71

Shell Beans and Artichokes with Roasted
Tomatillos, Cilantro and Añejo Cheese, 201–3

Steamed Roots with Roasted Poblano and
Tomatillo, 147–48

Tangy Sorrel *Salsa Verde* with Stir-Fried
Shrimp, 210–11

Tomatillo-Sauced *Chilaquiles*, 75, *76*, 77-78; riffs
on, 78

tomatoes, canned fire-roasted, 30

Braised Artichokes with Tomatoes, Jalapeños,
Olives and Capers, 218–19

Chipotle Meatballs, *116*, 117–18, *119*, 120–21

Green Chile–Braised Beef with Potatoes and
Caramelized Onions, 291–93

Mexican Red Rice, 262–64

Nopal Cactus and Poached Egg in Roasted
Tomato–Chipotle Broth, *162*, 163–64

Pork and Black Bean Dinner, *99*, 100–103, *101*

Pork Carnitas Dinner, 280–82, *283*

Red Peanut *Mole* with Chicken, *104*, 105–10,
109

Silky Tortilla Soup, 285–86

Slow-Grilled Pork Shoulder with Ancho
Barbecue Sauce, 302–3, *304*

Spaghetti Squash *Fideos* with Chipotle,
Chorizo, *Crema* and Avocado, *184*, 185–86

Yellow *Mole* with Grilled Fennel and Portobello
Mushrooms, 204–6, *207*

tomatoes, fresh:

Four Seasons Grilled Salad with Smoky Knob
(or Green) Onions and Sesame, 156–58

Grilled Lamb Chops with Charred Eggplant
Salsa, 311–12

Grilled Tostadas with Bacon, Avocado Mayo
and Heirloom Tomatoes, *149*, 150–51

Open-Face Squash Blossom Omelet with
Charred Tomato, Chile and Goat Cheese,
232–33

preparing, *58*, *59*

Tomato–Green Chile Seafood Rice, *66*, 67–68

tomatoes, sundried: Garlicky Tomato Rice, 251–52

Torrejas Sabor a Horchata, *242*, 243–45

tortas: Open-Face Egg-Chorizo Tortas, 234–35,
236

tortilla chips:

homemade, 79

Silky Tortilla Soup, 285–86

tortillas:

Plantain-Bacon *Enfrijoladas*, 287

Pork Carnitas Dinner, 280–82, *283*

reheading (note), 98

rolling, *74*

*Tortitas de Apionabo con Crema Enchipotlada y
Cilantro,* 208–9

Tortitas de Quelites, Papa y Chile Verde, 131,
132–33

*Tortitas Doradas de Arroz con Alubias, Ajo
Asado, Queso Añejo y Chile Ahumado,*
265–66

tostadas, grilled, riffs on, 151

*Tostadas Asadas a la Parilla con Tocino,
Mayonesa de Aguacate y Tomates
"Heirloom", 149*, 150–51

Trufas de Chocolate Mexicano, 348–49

truffles: Mexican Chocolate Truffles, 348–49

turnips:

Roasted Sunchoke Salad (riff), 197

Salsa Verde with Young Turnip and Red Onion,
211

Steamed Roots with Roasted Poblano and
Tomatillo, 147–48

U

umami, 22, 27

Una Olla Grande de Frijoles, 284–85

Unbaked Mexican Chocolate Flan, 341–42

V

Vampiro, 225, 227

W

Warm Rice Pudding with Mexican Chocolate and
Toasted Almonds, 346–47
weekend dishes:
Fettuccine with Butternut Squash and Red
Poblano *Crema, 176*, 177–79
Grilled Red Chile Ribs, 308–10
Pork Carnitas Dinner, 280–82, *283*
Queso Fundido Burger, *313*, 314–15
Red Chile Pozole with Pork, 276–78, *279*
Red Peanut *Mole* with Chicken, *104*, 105–10, *109*
Shell Beans and Artichokes with Roasted
Tomatillos, Cilantro and Añejo Cheese, 201–3
Slow-Grilled Pork Shoulder with Ancho
Barbecue Sauce, 302–3, *304*
Worcestershire sauce, 32

X

xantham gum: Raspberry Soft-Serve Ice Cream,
360, 361

xoconostles: Red Chile Short Rib Soup, 272–74,
275
Xoco's Granola, 228

Y

Yellow *Mole* with Grilled Fennel and Portobello
Mushrooms, 204–6, *207*
yogurt:
Cornmeal Pancakes (riff), 238
Greek-style, 31–32
Roasted Sunchoke Salad with Creamy Garlic
Mojo and Herbs, 196–97
Steamed Roots with Roasted Poblano and
Tomatillo, 147–48
yuca: Celery Root Pancakes (riff), 209

Z

Zabaglione [Sabayon] (riff), 354, he355
zucchini:
Creamy Zucchini, Corn and Roasted Poblanos,
52–53, *52*
Squash Blossom Soup, 190–91